SAMUEL TUNDE AB

WORKBOOK PRESS
RECOMMENDED
LITERARY BOOK COMPETITION 2021

NIGERIAN NEO-PENTECOSTALISM:

A GLIMPSE INTO AFRICAN MODERN CHRISTIANITY

WORKBOOK PRESS LLC
187 E Warm Springs Rd,
Suite B285, Las Vegas, NV 89119, USA

Website: https://workbookpress.com/
Hotline: 1-888-818-4856
Email: admin@workbookpress.com

Ordering Information:
Quantity sales. Special discounts are available on quantity purchases by corporations, associations, and others.
For details, contact the publisher at the address above.

Library of Congress Control Number:
ISBN-13: 978-1-956017-11-3 (Paperback Version)
978-1-956017-12-0 (Digital Version)

REV. DATE: 20/07/2021

Author's email: samuelabednego301@yahoo.com

Nigerian Neo-Pentecostalism:

A Glimpse into African Modern Christianity

TABLE OF CONTENTS

Endorsement

This book is not only "A Glimpse into African Modern Christianity" but an invitation to see the downward trend of Christian spirituality in the world today, particularly in Nigeria. Dr. A. Tunde Samuel invites us to re-examine the kind of Christianity that is spreading worldwide today, particularly in Africa. It is pointed out that this is not the kind of life designed for Christians to live. You cannot read this book without being overwhelmed by some thoughts-provoking questions or ideas.

The book reminds us, indirectly, the question asked by Jesus: "When the Son of Man comes, will he find faith on the earth" (Luke 18:8)? In addressing the ungodliness of the Last Days, the Scripture says that we should have nothing to do with those who are "having a form of godliness but denying its power (2 Tim. 3:5). Therefore, a book like this is written to prepare all Christians to know more about the "godlessness" coming in the last days. As you read this book, you will indeed find a wealth of ideas that will likely give you a better sense of direction in your spiritual growth. I am very much pleased to recommend this new book, Nigerian Neo-Pentecostals to all Christians who have the desire to follow the Word of truth. The Lord bless you and keep you.

Rev. Dr. Daniel A. Iselaiye
Ohio, United States

I must commend the author for the time, grace and courage to write this book. Pertinent issues affecting the lives of many Christians in Nigeria are clearly presented. Readers will find the book very interesting to read. It elucidates major issues relating to practice of Christianity in Nigeria, Africa, and beyond. It will go a long way in getting the ignorant out of their dungeon.

Prof. Tanimola M. Akande FMCPH
Professor of Public Health
Dept. of Epid. & Community Health,
University of Ilorin, Ilorin, Nigeria.

Dedication

To the glory and honor of Christ Jesus, the Son of the living God, and to the body of Christ worldwide.

Acknowledgement

My profound gratitude goes to God Almighty for His love, faithfulness, mercy, and the generous grace He bestowed on me. He has forgiven me in Christ Jesus His Dear Son, who shed His blood on the cross for the forgiveness of my sins, and from the ash heap He lifted me, making me a co-heir and a beneficiary of His agape love and mercy with those He has redeemed. He has made me worthy to be called His dear son. To Him be all glory forever.

The Southern Baptist Theological Seminary (SBTS) remains a great citadel of knowledge and a quarry ground of remaking and remolding for me. My journey through my doctoral studies at SBTS has been a tremendous blessing. This book is one of the products of my dissertation. Dr. John Klaassen (my main supervisor) not only mentored me through my doctoral work but also imprinted on me the virtue of hard and diligent work. Tough professors are not enemies. God uses them as tools to sharpen students in order to bring out the best in them. Both Dr. Klaassen and Dr. George Martin have acted in this capacity as I journeyed through SBTS. I also extend a hearty "thank you" to everyone that participated in the questionnaire I sent out when I was writing my dissertation.

Space does not allow for me to talk about all of the fathers in faith who took their precious time to read through the draft of this book. Such fathers include Rev. Dr. R. S. Babatunde, Rev. Dr. Daniel Iselaye, Rev. Joseph Ezeigbo, and Prof. T. M. Akande. Further, space does not allow for me to speak elaborately on the impact of Rev. Dr. S. O. Y. Baba, Rev. Dr. Tunde Aremu, Rev. Dr. S. O. Asonibare, Rev. Joseph O. Kolawole, Rev. Dr Michael Olajide, Rev. Joseph Ali, Rev. Mike Oye, Rev. Onofuhro

Emmanuel, Rev. Dr. J. S. Owoye, Rev. Dr. E. O. Malolmo, Rev. Dr. Sam Adedayo, Rev Matthew Tsado, Rev. Dr Sam Love Adebiyi, Dr J. A. Adewumi, Ambassador Lola Charles (the president of International Alliance to Restore Biblical Truths), and many others. They all granted me audience to have interview sessions with them. In addition, Gary Maxey and Peter Ozodo's The Seduction of the Nigerian Church has served as great tool and amazing template that enhanced my bearings while I writing this book. I am thankful to these two noble men of God. My profound gratitude also goes to dear brothers in Christ, Rev. Dr. B. M. Owojaiye and Rev. Dr. James O. Adeyanju, who both allowed me to quote again and again from the depth of their knowledge. Kudos also to my brothers Torey J. S. Teer, Akin Ibimidu, Shedrach Adamu, and David Olawoyin for their good job of editing. Bravo to the entire community of Nigerian Students Fellowship (NSF) here at SBTS Campus under the leadership of Rev. Amos Y. Luka.

God is always making use of my darling wife, Peace, as an encourager and divine resource to tap from. Her God-given wisdom, Spirit-filled life, and immense contributions fueled the completion of this book. I could not have come this far if not for Peace's support. Finally, our children—Temple, Gospel, and Miracle—are instruments whom God used, along with my wife, as my prayer partners.

Foreword

Abednego Tunde (A. T.) Samuel's orthodox evangelical background features prominently in this work. His hermeneutic (i.e., rule of biblical interpretation) employing grammatico-historical interpretation and application is what evangelical scholars and preachers promote. This approach is what prevents the misinterpretation and misapplication of biblical texts that lead to abuse and all kinds of manipulations.

Yet, Samuel is not averse to Pentecostalism, or even Neo-Pentecostalism. While he is committed to seeking understanding through objective inquiry and analysis, he would also commend aspects of Pentecostalism found to be true to the Word of God in interpretation and application. So, it is not a matter of throwing out the baby with the bath water. He is therefore painstaking and objective in his study and—at the same time—critical of issues and practices in Neo-Pentecostalism that constitute abuse and misinterpretation of the mind of the ultimate biblical author—the Holy Spirit. In this book, you will see the ***ten major gospel's emphases*** of the Neo-Pentecostalism, and the urgent need to rediscover and preach the biblical gospel in Christendom both in Nigeria, Africa and the world at large.

I, no doubt, commend the author and recommend the book to all honest Christians who seek to promote the healthy development of the church through the feeding of the flock (1 Pet 5:1-4). This is a wise counsel to heed because the CHIEF Shepherd will no doubt come to reward his under-shepherds for what they did and how and why they did them. Samuel's is a voice worthy to be added to existing ones. His words need to be heard and heeded.

Rowland S. Babatunde Ph.D.
Founder and Chairman, Providence Leadership
Development Foundation (PLeDeF)
Minister Emeritus, 2nd ECWA,
Ilorin, Kwara State
Fellow, Human and Natural Resources of
Nigeria (FHNRN), Kwara State, Nigeria

Preface

This book is a burden on my heart that has spanned several years. As far back as 1997, I have keenly been observing some questionable trends among Nigerian Neo-Pentecostals (i.e., the Nigerian New Pentecostal denominations). But at the time, my knowledge of biblical theology was still a piecemeal. Although I was born into the family of an evangelical preacher, I freed myself from all forms of bias and prejudice to get closer to Neo-Pentecostals with the aim of knowing and understanding more. As a matter of fact, when I graduated with a B.A. from my first seminary, one of my seminary professors tried to connect me with a Neo-Pentecostal church leader so that I could begin my pastorate with him. Because of his knowledge of me, this professor had confidence that I could function anywhere, regardless of the denominational appellation. But after much wrestling in prayer, the Spirit of the Lord wouldn't allow me to go in that direction.

At one time, a pastor friend wanted me to serve as pastor in his Neo-Pentecostal denomination. Again, the Lord hindered me from doing so. The last offer came when I graduated with my master's degree in 2009. An old friend of mine, with whom I grew up in an evangelical church, relocated to a city, and there he moved his membership to one of the largest Neo-Pentecostal denominations in Nigeria. This friend told me of the great offers available to me if I joined the pastorate of this denomination with my master's degree. One of the pastors in this church came in person to my house to have a lengthy discussion with me just to ignite my interest. He told me,

> When we absorb you into our commission [i.e., his church denomination], see, here, we don't preach about what will make people sad or feel guilty. We preach what will lift up the people's

spirits. We preach about the principles of success, principles of creating your own wealth, principles of working faith, principles of breakthrough, principles of healings, signs and wonders, etc.

His words looked captivating and enticing. He added that my starting salary would be about ₦70,000 per month, with some other remunerations, prophetic seed-offerings, and gifts from members. My wife would also be paid a salary if she was a graduate (which she was). As of then, the evangelical church with which I was aiming to work would be paying me a peanut or a stipend. A friend of mine told me to go for the former ₦70,000 offer, and he added that this was an open door. Again, and as usual, I prayed to the Lord, and the Spirit of the Lord convinced me that this is an open cage (a trap), saying, ***"I have not sent you there; don't allow your destiny and calling to be caged or trapped."*** Finally, I began my pastoral work with the evangelical church, receiving a ridiculously small amount as monthly salary, but I found joy and fulfillment in my work.

There are different motives with which many are preaching the gospel today. Some of these motives shall be expounded in this book. The plague of the "pseudo-gospel" is indeed a part of contemporary theological issues in Christianity. However, some of these deviations, without any iota of doubt, began in the 1980s by the importation of some foreign religious and theological ideologies from overseas into African Christianity (especially Nigeria). Hence, this book does not speak to African Christianity alone but to the whole body of Christ, especially in the Western world. It is plausible that some African Christian leaders have ignorantly fallen into some erroneous practices. Nevertheless, evidence reveal that some of them enjoy the 'goodies' that come with the paths they have chosen, and they are not ready to repent. Hence, it is no longer a matter of ignorance but a matter of choice. This situation calls for the urgency of responding to the

"Macedonia call" to compliment efforts in liberating Africa from pseudo-Christianity. This book is not intended to be condemnatory in any way. Indeed, who am I to condemn anyone? It is, however, a book on reality and truth. As such, the truth exposes, rebukes, enlighten, encourages, and corrects in love. Apart from being an eye-opener and a wake-up call for Christians all over Africa (and elsewhere), this book is also a good tool for a would-be missionary in any part of the African continent.

A. Tunde Samuel
Doctor of Missiology
May 27, 2021

Chapter 1
Africa: God's Own Continent

"For the kingdom is the LORD›S: and he is the governor among the nations" (Ps 22:28)

Readers must not think that I have a negative view of my own continent, Africa, or of my own dear country, Nigeria. Hence, the following facts are put forward. These facts are derived from biblical and historical narratives. Africa was never a cursed land; it has been an integral part of the biblical story from the beginning. For example, God allowed Israel, His covenant nation, to sojourn on African soil for about four hundred years, waiting for the fullness of time to cast out the Canaanites, the original inhabitants, so that the Israelites could move in and occupy their land. It was in Africa that Israel grew large enough to become a nation.[1] An African man was the only one audacious enough to rescue the prophet Jeremiah from the dungeon (Jeremiah 38:7). Africans were prophesied as people who would be God-seekers from the beginning: "*Envoys out of Egypt and Ethiopia will seek the Lord*" (Psalm 68:31).[2] According to Deji Ayegboyin and F. K. Asonzeh Ukah, "Ambassadors will come from Egypt, Ethiopia will stretch out her hands to God (Psalm 68:31) is understood to be a prediction of the incursion of the Ethiopians (that is black Africans) into the household of God."[3] The Queen of Sheba, a friend to King Solomon,

[1] According to the biblical account, the Israelites spent over four hundred years in Egypt (Gen 15:13-14; Ex 12:40-41; Lev 18:28; Ps 105:23-24). The prophet Hoshea foretold this episode in the life of our Savior: "When Israel was a child, I love him, and out of Egypt I called my son" (Hos 1:1; cf. Matt 2:15).

[2] Unless otherwise noted, all Scripture quotations come from the King James Version and New International Version.

[3] J. S. Pobee explains that this prophecy is construed by some Africans to mean a shift of Christianity's center of gravity from the North (Euro-America) to the south (Africa)." Deji Ayegboyin and F. K. Asonzeh Ukah, "Taxonomy of Churches in Africa: The Case in Nigeria," *Ogbomoso Journal of Theology* 13, no. 1 (2008): 5. The truth that Africans will seek God was always the center of Billy Graham's evangelistic message in the African continent. See *Huffington Post*, "Billy Graham Preached 'Jesus Was Not a White Man' in South Africa in 1973," last modified December 19, 2013, video (2:02), https://www.huffingtonpost.com/2013/12/19/billy-graham-white-jesus_n_4474404.html.

was from Africa (see 1 Kings 10).

There is a direct link between Africa and the land of Israel in fulfillment of biblical prophecies about the Messiah (cf Matthew 2: 15). The baby Jesus was also hidden in Africa for safety when Herod was seeking to kill him. As Matthew 2:15 reads, "*I called my Son out of Egypt* [i.e., Africa] ...." Several biblical scholars attest to the foregoing facts.

In their reference to Matthew 27:32 and Mark 5:21, Darrow Miller and Scott Allen write, "At the other end of his earthly life, God used another African, Simon the Cyrene (Cyrene is modern-day Libya), to aid Jesus at His moment of suffering."[4] Roland Werner, William Anderson, and Andrew Wheeler further stress,

> Therefore, it seems clear that it was a Meroitic court official who heard the gospel of Jesus from the deacon Philip, and brought back his new-found faith to the Meroitic capital of Napata. This Sudanese man was therefore the first known non-Jewish believer in Jesus Christ—before the Roman centurion came to faith (Acts 10), and long before the gospel reached Europe. So it can be said that the message of Jesus was sown in Sudanese soil only a few years after the crucifixion and resurrection of Jesus Christ certainly before the year 40.[5]

The well-known Nigerian scholar, Byang Kato, also discussed the involvement of Africa as a continent in God's salvific agenda for the world:

> On the day of Pentecost, Africa was represented. Settlers of Cyrene in North Africa were there when the Holy Spirit inaugurated the Christian Church (Acts 2:10). An African—

[4] Darrow L. Miller and Scott Allen, *Against All Hope: Hope for Africa* (Phoenix: Disciple Nations Alliance, 2005), 18.

[5] Roland Werner, William Anderson, and Andrew C. Wheeler, *Day of Devastation Day of Contentment: The History of the Sudanese Church across 2000 Years* (Nairobi, Kenya: Paulines Publications of Africa, 2000), 23.

> the Eunuch of Ethiopia was one of the first converts outside the Jewish circle (Acts 8). When the first "missionary conference" was held, an African was there (Acts 13:1) a reference to Simon named Niger cf. Living Bible). Africa in the first four centuries of Christian's era produced outstanding theologians like Augustine, Tertullian, Cyprian, Athanasius, Arius and Origen. In the first 200 years of the existence of Christianity, North Africa and the modern-day Turkey had the strongest churches.[6]

At this point, it is no longer a hidden truth concerning how the good news of Jesus Christ came to the people of Africa.

In addition to the involvement of Africa in early Christianity, history maintains that the Septuagint—the first Greek translation of the Old Testament—was done in Alexandria, Egypt. Christianity entered Europe twenty years after Christ's death and resurrection—when Lydia was converted (Acts 16:10f.). Christians from North Africa and Turkey evangelized Western Europe and the British Isles.[7] As Miller and Allen state, "What a thrill to read that the gospel went first, by way of Aithiopia [sic], along the umbilical cord of the continent of Africa, before it extended to the Gentiles of Europe by a Jew named Paul in the late forties and early fifties."[8]

Christianity spread from the Middle East (Jerusalem) to Africa, Europe, and then the Americas. Converted Christians later returned to many unreached areas of Africa.[9] Christianity has, therefore, been present on the African continent for centuries. The trends of Christian history are now shifting, placing Africa again at the forefront of the spread of

---

[6] See more in Byang Kato, "Africa under the Cross" (Typescript of Voice of Kenya at Nairobi Baptist Church, Nairobi, Kenya, November 16, 1975), 1-3. See also Stephen Neill, *A History of Christians Missions* (New York: Penguin, 1964), 46.

[7] Miller and Allen, *Against All Hope*, 19

[8] Miller and Allen, *Against All Hope*, 19.

[9] Kato, "Africa under the Cross,"3.

Christianity worldwide. Further, Allan H. Anderson remarks, "West Africa, and in particular Nigeria and Ghana, has been the scene of an explosion of a new form of Pentecostalism since the mid-1970s, to such an extent that it may become the future shape of African Christianity, which turns increasingly Charismatic."[10] In response to Anderson's point of view, it must be stressed here that the Nigerian Pentecostalism of the late 1960s to early 1980s was still a bit orthodox (i.e., biblical) in their theological worldview. But it will be questionable to project the current Nigerian Neo-Pentecostalism as a role model or an ideal Christianity—and this is the central argument of this book.

Several observers have noted a demographic shift in the present world of Christianity. The center of gravity has shifted from the global North to the global South and East. These observers believe that the exponential growth of Christianity in Africa, Asia, Latin America and the Pacific is behind this shift.[11]

According to Philip Jenkins, a professor of religious history,

> We are currently living through one of the transforming moments in the history of religion worldwide. Over the past five centuries or so, the story of Christianity has been inextricably bound up with that of Europe and European-derived civilizations overseas, above all in North America. Until recently, the overwhelming majority of Christians have lived in White nations, allowing

[10] Allan H. Anderson, *An Introduction to Pentecostalism: Global Charismatic Christianity* (New York: Cambridge University Press, 2004), 160.

[11] B. Moses Owojaiye, *Speech: ECWA Yesterday, Today and Tomorrow* (Delivered at ECWA IDCC Convention, Ilorin, Nigeria), November 14, 2015.Owojaiye is a young brilliant African researcher and scholar on World Christianity. He is presently a PhD graduate from Africa International University, Nairobi, Kenya. For further readings, Owojaiye point attention to the works of other scholars. Like Philip Jenkins, *The Next Christendom: The Coming of Global Christianity* (Oxford: Oxford University Press, 2002); Daryl Balia and Kristeen Kim, eds., *Edinburgh 2010: Witnessing to Christ Today*,vol. 2 (Eugene, OR: Regnum Books International, 2010), 11; Matthews Ojo, *The End-Time Army: Charismatic Movements in Modern Nigeria* (Trenton, NJ: Africa World Press, 2007); Ogbu Kalu, *African Pentecostalism: An Introduction* (Oxford: Oxford University Press, 2008); Mark Noll, *The New Shape of World Christianity* (Downers Grove, IL: IVP Academic, 2009); Mark Shaw, *Global Awakening: How 21st-Century Revivals Triggered a Christian Revolution* (Downers Grove, IL: IVP Academic, 2010).

> theorists to speak smugly, arrogantly, of "European Christian" civilization. Conversely, radical writers have seen Christianity as an ideological arm of Western imperialism. Over the past century, however, the center of gravity in the Christian world has shifted inexorably southward, to Africa, Asia, and Latin America.[12]

The impact of global Pentecostalism, and especially of African Neo-Pentecostals, in this magnificent shift cannot be over emphasized. Jenkins adds,

> Already today, the largest Christian communities on the planet are to be found in Africa and Latin America. Some 2 billion Christians are alive today, about one-third of the planetary total. The largest single bloc, some 560 million people, is still to be found in Europe. Latin America, though, is already close behind with 480 million. Africa has 360 million, and 313 million Asians profess Christianity. By 2050, only about one-fifth of the world's 3 billion Christians will be non-Hispanic Whites. Soon, the phrase "White Christian" may sound like a curious oxymoron, as mildly surprising as a "Swedish Buddhist." Such people can exist but a slight eccentricity is implied.[13]

Jenkins paints a vivid picture of the demographical reconstruction currently occurring. He indicates that the era of Western Christendom as the geographical epicenter of Christianity has already been altered by this shift, and he goes on to say, "The trend in the phenomenal shift will continue to apace in the decades ahead."[14]

Furthermore, amidst severe persecution, "China now boasts of a fast-growing Church, with an estimated 16,500 new Christians every day.

[12] Jenkins, *The Next Christendom*, 1-3. See Mark A. Noll and Carolyn Nystrom, *Clouds of Witnesses: Christian Voices from Africa and Asia* (Downers Grove, IL: InterVarsity Press, 2011), 9.

[13] Jenkins, *The Next Christendom*,1-3.

[14] Jenkins, *The Next Christendom*,2.

Africa, once called 'the missionary graveyard,' now represents the fastest growing Church for any continent as a whole: 24,000 new Christians every day (sic)."[15] The largest Christian gatherings are now found in the global South,[16] while the largest churches in Western Europe, according to Timothy Tennent, are "pastored by African Christians."[17] Aided by the trends of globalization and glocalization, this era of Christianity is not limited by geographical borders, cultures, languages, academic differences, or racial prejudices. Christianity is now being expressed in diverse cultural flavors. Renowned scholar R. C. Sproul predicted this very reality:

> I believe that within thirty years the largest and strongest branch of Christendom will be in Africa and that it is absolutely critical that the church in the United States right now pour as many resources as possible into the emerging churches of the Third World, particularly in Africa. We have the materials; we have things that these people need, to be grounded and strengthened for future generations. They cannot provide it, but we can.[18]

It appears that all hope for the future sustainability of global Christianity is shifting toward the global South. The significant presence of Christians in Africa, Asia, Latin America, and the Pacific demonstrates that Christianity is truly a global phenomenon. Lamin Sanneh contends that God designed the Christian faith to be a global movement rather than a faith of a particular people, place, or region. Although Christianity began within the Palestinian world, Sanneh states that the events in the New Testament—in the ministries of the apostles of Christ and the early

[15] Timothy Tennent, "The Translatability of the Christian Gospel" (convocation speech delivered at Asbury Theological Seminary, Wilmore, KY, 2011).

[16] C. Peter Wagner and Joseph Thompson, *Out of Africa: How the Spiritual Explosion among Nigerians Is Impacting the World* (Ventura, CA: Regal, 2004), 8-18.

[17] Tennent, "The Translatability of the Christian Gospel."

[18] R. C. Sproul, *Acts*, St. Andrew's Expositional Commentary Series (Wheaton, IL: Crossway, 2010), 28.

church—prove that God intended to spread Christianity from its original geographical and socio-political contexts to other parts of the world.[19]

Randy Arnett points out the current impacts of Pentecostalism on African Christianity:

> Within a century, Pentecostalism has risen from obscurity to ascendancy in global Christianity. There percussions of this movement may not be dismissed easily. The movement shapes today's Christianity. A significant center of Pentecostalism's global footprint lies in Africa. Pentecostalism projects a vision that captures the imagination of Africans, especially West Africans.[20]

Today, the Nigerian church occupies a significant place in this dramatic global shift. As Babatunde Oladimeji observes, "The Christian church in Nigeria has become a major force in global Christianity. Nigeria has produced a number of highly influential figures in Christianity."[21] Further, Babatomiwa M. Owojaiye writes,

> Nigeria is sub-Saharan Africa's most populous country and is home to the region's largest Christian population. This Western African nation has more than 80 million Christians, who accounts for about half of the country's total population. There are more Christians in Nigeria than in traditional Christian Western Europe. In fact, Nigeria's Christian population is nearly the same size as the total population of Germany.[22]

Twenty-first-century Nigerian Christianity includes a missionary vision

[19] Lamin Sanneh, *Disciples of All Nations: Pillars of World Christianity* (Oxford: Oxford University Press, 2008), 54.

[20] Randy Ray Arnett, "Pentecostalization: The Changing Face of Baptists in West Africa" (PhD diss., The Southern Baptist Theological Seminary, 2012), 3.

[21] Babatunde Oladimeji, "A History of Charismatic Influence on the Anglican Church in Nigeria," *Asian American Theological Forum* 6, no. 2 (May 29, 2017).

[22] Babatomiwa M. Owojaiye, "ECWA Yesterday, Today and Tomorrow" (speech delivered at ECWA IDCC Convention, Ilorin, Nigeria, November 14, 2015). Owojaiye is a young brilliant African researcher on world Christianity. He graduated as PhD candidate at Africa International University, Nairobi, Kenya.

that challenges and reshapes expressions of Christianity around the world. According to Allen Effa, "We have to regard African Christianity as potentially the representative Christianity of the twenty-first century. While in the previous centuries Northern Atlantic developments dominated global Christianity, the Christianity typical of the twenty-first century will be shaped by the events and processes that take place in Africa."[23] Effa agrees that the above prediction is already a reality: "You want to see where Christianity is heading? Come, look at Nigeria. It's already here."[24] In sketching a quick map of Africa, the map has a shape similar to a gun's revolver. Nigeria is said to occupy the position of the trigger, where the gospel is being shot out to other parts of Africa and the world at large.[25]

It is evident that the significant expansion of Nigerian Neo-Pentecostalism requires careful examination. As a close observer, I have noted that the mass movement of people from mainline churches to Neo-Pentecostal churches has been enormous in recent years. In this book, the main reasons behind the explosive growth of Nigerian Neo-Pentecostal churches will be examined. Additionally, because it is the duty of every Christian to present the gospel in keeping with the message of Scripture, Nigerian Neo-Pentecostalism' understanding of the practical role of the Holy Spirit vis-à-vis their presentation of the gospel will also be engaged.

---

[23] Allan L. Effa, "Releasing the Trigger: The Nigerian Factor in Global Christianity," *International Bulletin of Missionary Research* 37, no. 4 (October 2013): 214-17.

[24] Effa, "Releasing the Trigger: The Nigerian Factor in Global Christianity,"215.

[25] Effa, "Releasing the Trigger: The Nigerian Factor in Global Christianity," 216-17.

Chapter 2
We Need to Get it Right

"*But even if we or an angel from heaven should preach a gospel other than the one we preached to you, let them be under God's curse!*" (Gal 1: 8)

As seen in the previous chapter, to claim that Christianity was first brought to Africa by white missionaries some two hundred years ago is historically inaccurate. So also, the old cliché, "Christianity is a white man's religion." The contemporary involvement of the African continent with Christianity is by no means recent. Interestingly, today again, the history of Christianity is winding back to where it began.[1] As of today, the center of gravity of world Christianity is located somewhere in the corner of West Africa. It is certain that the devil himself knows the havoc that African Christianity can wreak upon his kingdom if the African land is able to discover the spiritual wealth, socio-economic prosperity with which God lavishly endows this continent. Hence, the struggles and tussles for existence in Africa are not without satanic undertones (and the blindfold of ignorance), which attempt to wage war against the earthly extension of the kingdom of God.

As pointed out earlier, besides the covenant people of the Bible Land (i.e., the Jews), Africa and Asia seem to be the closest continents to, and thus the first recipients of the gospel outside of, the Jewish land. In these critical times, it is very interesting to see history winding its way back to where it began. For instance, taking a country as a case study, Nigeria for instance. Nigeria was predominantly evangelized by evangelical missionaries from America and Canada and by Protestant and Roman Catholic missionaries from Europe during the colonial era. Talking about

[1] Missiologists today are talking more on 'Reversed Missions' See more in Van Engen, Charles. Mission on the Way: Issues in Mission Theology. Grand Rapids, MI: Baker, 1996.

the frontier exploits of Nigerian Christianity in missions' endeavors, it has been observed that African Christianity potentially is representative of Twenty first century Christianity. While in the previous centuries, Northern Atlantic developments dominated global Christianity, the Christianity typical of the twenty-first century will be shaped by the events and processes that take place in Africa.[2]

All these realities are accolades to Christianity Movement in Africa, most especially as some Christian nations in the West are presently in a drastic backslidden state. However, there is a reality and a big challenge that needs or should be addressed. What is the use of boasting about thc growth of Christianity that goes along (or ladened) with all forms of corruption and carnality? What is the use of producing 'Christians' who are experts at embezzling government treasuries and who are not, by any means, better than unbelievers—or even worse? It was in Antioch that the early disciples of Christ Jesus were first called Christians—that is, Christ-like people (Acts 11:26).[3] What is the use of producing so-called Christian believers whose lifestyle belie the teachings of Christ? We now have church leaders who are good at deceiving people in the name of the gospel to make themselves the richest men in town. The mass conversions characterized by syncretism in most places in Africa coupled with the delusions of Neo-Pentecostalism about a materialistic gospel cannot be denied.

There is no doubt about it—something is evidently wrong with the brand of Christianity that is preached and practiced today, especially among the Neo-Pentecostal and charismatic movements in many areas of Africa. Nevertheless, orthodox and evangelical Christians have their

---

[2] B. Moses Owojaiye, *Speech: ECWA Yesterday, Today and Tomorrow*

[3] It worth mentioning, however, that the term "Christians" both in Antioch and in the first century was derogatory not commendation (cf 1Peter 4:14-16).

own axes to grind in this end-times apostasy. Africa scored high by the numbers but rate low by practice or lifestyle. Many have already fallen into the charade that the apostle Paul called "***the gospel which is not gospel***" (Gal 1:6-9).

Let's Fix the Mess

The impact of the Nigerian Neo-Pentecostalism in making Christianity widely known in Nigeria can by no means be overestimated. Most of them have first-class patterns of worship (i.e., church services). The contextualization of their worship coupled with inspirational songs that appeal to the souls of millions worldwide demand *kudos*. The passionate zeal of Nigerian Neo-Pentecostals is worthy of emulation, and their liturgical practices strive for relevance in different contexts. There is no doubt that Nigerian Neo-Pentecostals have designed an effective means of attracting young people. For instance, a Nigerian Neo-Pentecostal denomination has a captivating caption that reads, "Discover, Develop and Deploy your talent."[4] Captions like this one draw many youths who are jobless due to the economic instability in Nigeria. Like the attractional churches, Nigerian Neo-Pentecostals use music and creative elements that appeal to the desired audience as well as teachings that are designed to be inspirational and motivating and thus have a powerful magnetic influence upon today's young generation.[5] However, one of the issues frankly addressed in this book concerns the biblical quality, not just the numerical conversion of Nigerian Neo-Pentecostal followers. To put it straight to Nigerian Neo-Pentecostals concerning their gospel proclamation—What is the theological foundation of the gospel they preach? How genuine is the faith of their converts? How biblical is the

[4] Nigeria Neo-Pentecostals are good at innovating enticing and captivating ideas.

[5] Jared C. Wilson, *The Gospel-Driven Church: Uniting Church-Growth with the Metrics of Grace* (Grand Rapids: Zondervan, 2019),24.

pattern of their growth?[6] Consider, for instance, the following data presentation by Pew Research Center:

> Nigeria is the seventh most populous country in the world, with 206 million people. By 2100, it is projected to be the world's third most populous country—ahead of the U.S.—with 733 million people, according to United Nations estimates. Nigeria is expected to add more people than any other country during that span. . . . Nigeria's population is almost evenly split between Muslims (50%) and Christians (48.1%), as of 2015. It has the world's fifth-largest Muslim population (90 million) and the world's sixth-largest Christian population (87 million).[7]

From the demographics above, one would expect that the 87 million Christians in Nigeria are enough to set the nation ablaze with fire of revival compared to the handful of early church believers that were reckoned to have turned the world upside down (upside right) in the first century.[8] The journey of the gospel that made an indelible mark upon the history of the entire world began with about 120 early believers who gathered in the 'upper room' in Jerusalem. Unfortunately, an internal observer has pointed out that today, "the more the churches, the more the corruption in Nigeria." The answer to this issue is not far-fetched; people embrace the Neo-Pentecostal gospel as an alternative means of getting out of poverty and a quick way of amassing wealth. Hence, the conversion of many who call themselves Christians in Nigeria is questionable. When the content of the gospel that people receive and believe is erroneous, that same content will also affect people's way of living.

[6] To date, many of the Pentecostal Christians are migrants from traditional mainline churches. See more in John O. Aina, *How to Cub Youths Exodus from the Church* (Jos, Nigeria: ECWA Challenge Book, 2015), 28-32.

[7] John Gramlich, "Fast Facts about Nigeria and Its Immigrants as U.S. Travel Ban Expands," Pew Research, February 3, 2020, https://www.pewresearch.org/fact-tank/2020/02/03/fast-facts-about-nigeria-and-its-immigrants-as-u-s-travel-ban-expands/.

[8] For more, see Harvey Cox, *Fire from Heaven: The Rise of Pentecostal Spirituality and the Reshaping of Religion in the Twenty-First Century* (Cambridge, MA: Da Capo Press, 2001),3.

To avoid the temptation of bias in delving into the subject under discussion, a survey is conducted, and key books written by renowned Nigerian Neo-Pentecostal leaders are also consulted. The focus here is that Nigerian Christianity needs to get the gospel message and gospel proclamation right. As global attention is shifting toward the global South as the hope of global Christianity in these end times, it is important that we do not export to other nations or import a gospel that is unbiblical, and which will not be able to stand the test of time. The core of the gospel message is the plan of the Holy Trinity to save humanity (Hebrew 10:9), the love of God that established the plan of salvation (John 3:16), the execution of God's plan for the salvation of humankind (1 Corinthians 15:3-4), and the proclamation of the finished work of Christ on the cross for the redemption of sinners (Luke 24:46-47).[9] Hence, the true gospel must be preached to encompass the establishment of God's kingdom (Luke 16:16), repentance that leads to the knowledge of the truth (2 Timothy 2:25-26), repentance from sin that is accompanied with a godly sorrow (2 Corinthians 7:10), repentance for the forgiveness of sins (Luke 24: 46-47), repentance towards God by confessing Jesus Christ as Lord, and repentance that leads to life eternal by putting one's faith in Christ (Acts 11:18).[10] There is no need to produce Christians whose lifestyles are far away from the life of Christ and who do not resemble him in their conduct. The next chapter will be a short diversion to a brief background of the world of Pentecostalism in general before turning to the history of Pentecostalism in Nigeria vis-à-vis Nigerian Neo-Pentecostalism.

---

[9] Evangelical Church Winning All, *2019 Sunday Manual for Adults*, 28:34. For further reading, see John Stott, *The Cross of Christ: Study Guide Edition* (Downers Grove, IL: IVP Books, 2006), 23-30; Mark Dever, *The Gospel and Personal Evangelism* (Wheaton, IL: Crossway, 2007), 10-17.

[10] Evangelical Church Winning All, *2019 Sunday Manual for Adults*, 28:34-35.

Chapter 3
The Three Waves of the Holy Spirit

"And my speech and my preaching was not with enticing words of man's wisdom, but in demonstration of the Spirit and of power: That your faith should not stand in the wisdom of men, but in the power of God." (1 Corinthians2: 4-5)

The doctrine of the supernatural gifts has been a subject of much disagreement and controversy among believers for centuries. As Timothy Tennent explains, "Some argue that the apostolic miracles served to grant authority to the ministers in the church, whereas others claim they were given only to attest to His Word."[1] There is also no unified position on why and when the supernatural gifts stopped—if they ceased at all. Some maintain that the operation of these gifts ended when the canon of the Scripture was completed, whereas others hold that these gifts ceased when all the apostles died. Still others maintain that these gifts were still in operation until the persecution of Christians officially ended and the Roman government officially granted Christianity full legal status. Some argue that even though the operation of these gifts is no longer normative to today's church, God can still decide to manifest them whenever he deems appropriate. But there are those, mainly of the Neo-Pentecostal movement who rigidly maintain that the supernatural gifts have been operative just like in the Apostolic times.

However, for some decades, the Holy Spirit has been moving in miraculous ways beyond the imagination of many scholars as believers engage in active witnessing. There have been three distinctive waves of the Spirit from late-nineteenth century until now. The first wave is the Pentecostal movement, characterized by the powerful ministry of

[1] Tennent, *Invitation to World Missions*,418.

the Holy Spirit in the realm of miraculous manifestations that some Christians found to be abnormal or unusual. According to Peter Wagner, "Prominent among the miraculous works were what have been called the baptism in the Holy Spirit, speaking in tongues, healing the sick, and casting out demons."[2] In this regard, and different from the second and third waves of the Holy Spirit, Pentecostals believe in a second work of grace after conversion, which they term "baptism of the Holy Spirit," a work subsequent to regeneration and evidenced by speaking in tongues. Concerning the first wave, Wagner writes,

> The majority of the Christians were not prepared for this outpouring of the Holy Spirit. For one thing, they had no theology for handling it. For many, the miraculous signs and wonders that we read about in the New Testament were restricted to that period of history . . . Because there was no theological grid for understanding what the Holy Spirit was doing through the Pentecostals, movement, evangelicals did the only thing they knew how: They declared Pentecostals heretics.[3]

Although the Pentecostals have their own share of errors, not everything they do and believe constitutes heresy.

The "charismatic movement" is the second wave of the Holy Spirit. As a fulfillment of the dream of Pentecostals, the charismatic movement broke out in the twentieth century from among the mainline denominations.[4] Though second-wave proponents looked into the Scriptures with evangelical lenses, they also validate the relevance of the miraculous working of the Holy Spirit for Christianity today. Charismatics believe in the baptism of the Holy Spirit and speaking in tongues, but they do not

[2] Wagner, *The Third Wave of the Holy Spirit: Encountering the Power of Signs and Wonders Today* (n.p.: Servant, 1988), 16.
[3] Wagner, *The Third Wave of the Holy Spirit*, 16.
[4] Wagner, *The Third Wave of the Holy Spirit*, 17. Such denominations include the Roman Catholic Church as well as Protestant churches (e.g., Episcopal, Lutheran, Presbyterian, United Methodist).

see the baptism of the Holy Spirit as a second work of grace subsequent to salvation nor do they maintain that speaking in tongues is evidence for such a work.

The third wave of the Holy Spirit comes from among evangelicals who, for one reason or another, have chosen not to be identified with either the Pentecostal or the charismatic movement. This last group simply retains the name "Third Wavers."[5] Emerging in the 1980s, third-wave proponents believe that the gifts (including the sign, or miraculous, gifts) of the Holy Spirit are very relevant for today's church and are needed for effective witnessing.[6] They never see speaking in tongues as necessary for all believers, but they maintain that the Holy Spirit gives gifts as he wills. Some of the champions of the third wave include C. Peter Wagner, Charles H. Kraft, John Wimber, and Dick Bernal.[7] It must be stressed, though, that the focus here is not to prove that one wave is better than another. However, when each wave is examined with an open mind, a lot can be gleaned to improve the effective presentation of the gospel. Wagner sheds light on this point when he writes,

> All three [waves are] committed to one Body, one Spirit, one hope, one Lord, one faith, one baptism and one God and Father of all (see Ephesians, 4:4-6). All hold a high view of the authority of Scripture and believe in the urgency of world evangelization. All are convinced that the power of God described in the Gospels and Acts is in effects as God's kingdom is manifested around the world today. The similarities are much greater than the differences. But there are important differences, for each group feels that God

---

[5] Harvey Cox, *Fire from Heaven: The Rise of Pentecostal Spirituality and the reshaping of Religion in the Twenty-First Century* (Cambridge: Da Capo Press, 1995), 281-2.

[6] For more, see Wagner, *How to Have a Healing Ministry in Any Church* (Ventura, CA: Regal Books, 1988), 15-17. The argument in this book remains that God may choose to interfere in the ways he wants as men and women take the gospel to the unreached parts of the world. No one can limit His interventions.

[7] See more in Cox, *Fire from Heaven, 283-5*; and Wagner, *The Third Wave of the Holy Spirit*, 16f.

has chosen to minister through them in a particular way.[8]

When Jesus promised to send "another Comforter" (i.e., the Holy Spirit) to believers, his ultimate goal was not to create division in his body, the church. Unfortunately, one of the most misconstrued teachings today in Christendom is the teaching on the Holy Spirit. Today, the body of Christ is divided into various factions based on the various positions concerning the workings, and gifts of the Holy Spirit. Regarding the miraculous gifts of the Spirit, there seems to be three prominent positions. The first is the "cessationist" position, which maintains that the sign and miraculous gifts of the Holy Spirit were for the early apostles and, therefore, ceased upon the completion of the New Testament. The cessationists vary in their positions. Some today deny subjective forms of the Holy Spirit's guiding or leading individuals to make certain decisions or to interpret particular passages of the Scripture. On the other hand, there are some partial cessationists who deny the exercise of some revelational gifts (such as prophecy, speaking in tongues, and the interpretation of tongues) but are not opposed to praying for the sick and are open to the possibility that the Holy Spirit still leads people to make certain decisions.[9]

The second position is the "continuationist" (or non-cessationist) view, which maintains that all the gifts of the Holy Spirit, as well as the miraculous power portrayed in the New Testament, are meant for today. This position emphatically says that the signs gifts of the twentieth century are simply the sign gifts of the first century. The signs gifts are everywhere, says the adherents; they have continued unabated from day one until today. The third position is the "open-but-cautious"[10] view, which argues for the possibility that miracles can and do still happen

[8] Wagner, *How to Have a Healing Ministry in Any Church*, 18.

[9] Tennent, *Invitation to World Missions*,418.

[10] For more, see Richard B. Gaffin, *Perspectives on Pentecost: New Teaching on the Gift of the Holy Spirit* (Philipsburg: Presbyterian and Reformed Publishing Company, 1979), 109; Thomas Schreiner, *Spiritual Gifts: What they & why they Matter* (Nashville, TN: B & H Publishing Group, 2018), 165.

today according to how God purposes things to be by His own sovereign will. However, this position is primarily concerned with how to curtail the potential abuse of biblical truth.[11]

To go into further detail regarding these positions will detract from the goal. However, summing up the effects of these various positions, especially as they influence the Western theological point of view, Tennent writes, "But regardless of which of these schemes are followed, the point is that theological reflection in the West gradually became dominated by a range of theological systems that denied that the full exercise of the supernatural gifts of the Holy Spirit was a normative, much less essential, part of the church's ongoing life and witness in the world."[12] Nonetheless, and contrary to the Western evangelical point of view,

> Pentecostals [everywhere as well as Nigerian Neo-Pentecostals] believe that the full range of the gifts and the miraculous manifestations of the Spirit present in the New Testament are available for believers today. Pentecostals reject any notion that Acts is merely descriptive and no longer applicable to believers today. They reject the idea that the gifts of the Holy Spirit are either limited to the first century or passed away with the apostles.[13]

In practical terms, several Western missionaries in the past have explained away as superstitions some of the spiritual realities for which their theological background does not provide adequate answers.[14] Seasoned anthropologist and missionary Paul Hiebert sheds more light unto the plight of the "excluded middle" when he analyzes how Western missionaries with a Christianized version of a two-tiered universe often fail to see the spiritual battle with which local people wrestle.[15] As John

[11] Robert L. Saucy, "An Open But Cautious View" in *Are Miraculous Gifts for Today?* 97-103

[12] Tennent, *Invitation to World Missions*, 418.

[13] Tennent, *Invitation to World Missions*,422.

[14] John Wimber and Kevin Springer, *Power Evangelism* (Bloomington, MN: Chosen Books, 2009), 74.

[15] Paul G. Hiebert, *Anthropological Reflections on Missiological Issues* (Grand Rapids: Baker Book

Wimber and Kevin Springer summarize,

> The "excluded middle" includes the influence of angels and demons on everyday life, the Holy Spirit's intervention in divine healing, signs and wonders, and spiritual gifts. Non-Western worldviews make room for all kinds of supernatural intervention in everyday life, so the idea that a Christian God can heal is easy for them to accept. But we Western Christians, by excluding this middle zone, usually make little or no room for what in Scripture is considered normal: the regular activity of both God and Satan in human life.[16]

Oftentimes, when people close their hearts to the reality of the supernatural realm, they quickly fall into the dangers of "selectivism" and "reductionism" in their biblical hermeneutics. In biblical hermeneutics, "selectivism" involves picking certain portions of the Scripture and omitting other parts, while "reductionism" involves an approach to biblical interpretation that fails to do total justice to the holistic interpretation of a particular passage of Scripture. "There are two ways," Wimber and Springer suggest, "a hard heart affects our worldview. A hard heart may incline us toward a worldview that excludes the supernatural, or it may prevent us from altering a faulty worldview to include the supernatural."[17] The fact remains that every worldview has its own "blind spots," which are usually the areas of life that people often do not take into consideration or that they assume do not work. Blind spots frequently have devastating repercussions in any given society, especially when people with blind spots enter another culture. It would be wise to mention that "many Western Christians neatly package their lives into two categories, 'natural' and 'supernatural,' with the latter quite removed

House, 1994), 189f.

[16] Wimber and Springer, *Power Evangelism*,133.

[17] Wimber and Springer, *Power Evangelism*,145.

from their everyday lives. Unusual or unexplainable experiences are attributed to 'chance' or 'coincidence.'"[18] This secularized kind of mindset does not completely align with all that the Scriptures reveal concerning the mystical relationship between the material and the spiritual worlds.

Despite its own theological flaws, the fact remains that the stupendous growth of Pentecostalism (including Neo-Pentecostalism) all over the world has had a dramatic impact on people's understanding of pneumatology and global evangelization. Besides, contrary to the conventional evangelical point of view, "increasingly, missions practice around the world understands the book of Acts not only as an accurate *description* of the Holy Spirit's work through the early churches, but also as a *prescription* paradigm that should guide church's practice today [especially as it relates to evangelism]."[19] Right from the start of the twentieth century, Pentecostals have awakened the global church of Christ to the normative roles of the Holy Spirit in evangelism. To this point, Samuel Escobar contends, "Evangelical Protestantism emphasized the 'continuity in truth by the Word,' whereas, Pentecostalism has emphasized the 'continuity in life by the Spirit.'"[20] No doubt, the combination of these is needed for an effective and efficient witnessing.

Some areas of Clarification

The argument of this book on the Holy Spirit agrees with the Pentecostal and third wave positions on the following areas. First, Pentecostals ask,

> Is Jesus Christ the Great I Am? or is He the Great I was? Pentecostals believe that the Holy Spirit continues to make available to the church the full range of Jesus' miraculous ministry, as well as the apostolic signs and wonders. . . . Pentecostals

[18] Wimber and Springer, *Power Evangelism*,138.

[19] Tennent, *Invitation to World Missions*, 428.

[20] Samuel Escobar, "A Missiological Approach to Latin America Protestantism," *International Review of Mission* 87, no. 345 (April 1998), 172.

> understand that if someone is demon possessed, then having the demon cast out in the name of Jesus is still part of the good news and the practical extension of Christ's triumphant victory over the principalities and powers (Col. 2:14-15; Eph. 6:12). In other words, if the Holy Spirit is alive and real, then He must have the power and the means to extend his Dynamic life in the real and concrete ways into the lives of those who are suffering [under Satanic influence].[21]

As believers endeavor to take the gospel of Christ to places it has not yet reached, the Holy Spirit is still in the business of attesting to the gospel with signs and wonders as he pleases. The Spirit is actively working today in power, and I have witnessed spectacular acts of God's power again and again. When anyone maintains this position, he risks being tagged as liberal, especially in the West. (For further reading on the activities of the Holy Spirit see my book, *The Baptism of Power: Engaging Charismatic, Evangelical and Pentecostal on the Holy Spirit*).

Second, classical Pentecostals believe in the imminent return of Jesus Christ. Hence, their activities are marked with aggressive witnessing for Christ throughout the world. The distinctiveness of Pentecostals' pneumatology accounts for their passion and effectiveness in evangelism. According to Pentecostals, the Holy Spirit is not only a full person of the Godhead, a member of the Trinity; He not only inspired the Holy Scriptures and regenerates us; but He also empowers us for effective evangelism. Pentecostals are convinced that the Holy Spirit confirms the preaching of the gospel and the declaration of the resurrection of Jesus through the giving of sign and wonders, just as He did through those unlearned fishermen and tax collectors who were His first apostles.[22]

---

[21] Tennent, *Invitation to World Missions*,422.
[22] Tennent, *Invitation to World Missions*,422-23.

Hence, to restrain or limit the workings of the eternal Spirit of God within a particular timeframe may not be accurate when Christians step out of their comfort zones to evangelize. As mentioned in chapter 1, today, Pentecostals are no doubt at the forefront of "global Christianity." The fact remains that "Pentecostals learned the principle of *sola scriptura* from the Reformation but then used it as a basis for celebrating a supernatural, apostolic faith that predated the historical divisiveness of denominationalism. The result was a new basis for cooperation and collaboration in missions, which facilitated the spread of Christianity around the world."[23]

However, this book disagrees with the Pentecostal position on the pattern of "baptism with the Holy Spirit" that claims speaking in tongues is for all and sundry (See my book *The Baptism of Power: Engaging Charismatic, Evangelical and Pentecostal on the Holy Spirit*). The work of Gregg R. Allison on this issue will prove very useful at this juncture. To shed more light on this subject, Allison identifies two major baptisms that believers participate in at one time or another in life, namely, water baptism and Spirit baptism. For the two types of baptism, he identifies four elements that are critical to each. Water baptism has (1) the pastor as the baptizer, (2) the new convert as the baptizee or baptizand, (3) water as the medium, and (4) the purpose of indicating one's confession of faith, incorporation into the church, membership or identification with Christ, and obedience to the Scriptures. Spirit baptism has (1) Jesus as the baptizer, (2) the new convert as the baptizee, (3) the Holy Spirit as the medium, and (4) the main purpose of adding a new convert to the body of Christ (as reinforced by the apostle Paul in 1 Corinthians 12:12-13 and in several other passages of the Scripture).[24] For this second baptism, Allison maintains that it occurs as sinners believe in Jesus Christ for salvation.

[23] Tennent, *Invitation to World Missions*,424. Tennent adds that "the growth of the global church in the wake of the Pentecostal witness was so profound that Henry Van Dusen coined the expression 'Third Force' to describe it."

[24] Gregg R. Allison, "Baptism with and Filling of the Holy Spirit," *Southern Baptist Journal of Theology* 16, no. 4 (2012): 8.

To this point, Allison writes,

> One of the aspects of God's work of saving sinful human beings is Jesus Christ's baptism of new converts with the Holy Spirit, by which they are incorporated into his (Christ's) body, the church. Such a baptism is (1) initiatory, occurring at the beginning of salvation (along with effective call, regeneration, justification, union with Christ, adoption, and initial sanctification); (2) universal, being a divine work in the life of every Christian; (3) purposeful, incorporating new believers into the church of Jesus Christ; and (4) indelible, being a permanent membership in the body of Christ, from which defection is not possible.[25]

It is therefore very clear at this point that no one can belong to the body of Christ without being baptized into it by the Holy Spirit. Hence, salvation and Spirit baptism take place simultaneously; there is no delay after salvation for the baptism of the Holy Spirit, which, as some take it, is to be received by the laying on of hands.[26]Billy Graham writes,

> I am convinced that many of the things some teachers have joined to baptism with the Holy Spirit really belong to the fullness of the Spirit. Thus, the purpose of the baptism with the Holy Spirit is to bring the new Christian into the body of Christ. No interval of time falls between regeneration and baptism with the Spirit. The moment we received Jesus Christ as Lord and Savior we received the Holy Spirit. He came to live in our heart.[27]

The apostle Paul says, "*And if anyone does not have the Spirit of Christ, they do not belong to Christ*" (Rom 8:9c), and, "*No one can say Jesus is Lord, except by the Holy Spirit*" (1 Corinthians12:3). Therefore, every believer is

[25] Allison, "Baptism with and Filling of the Holy Spirit," 8.

[26] Zacharias Tanee Forum, *You can receive the Baptism into the Holy Spirit Now* (Lagos: Conquest Communication Ltd, 2007), 45-64.

[27] Graham, *The Holy Spirit*,71.

baptized into the body of Christ at the point of conversion: "*For we were all baptized by one Spirit so as to form one body—whether Jews or Gentiles*" (1 Corinthians 12:13). In addition, the argument of this book disagrees with Pentecostals who see the baptism of the Holy Spirit as a second work of grace that is subsequent to salvation and is evidenced by some miraculous demonstration (e.g., speaking in tongues).[28] However, I am not against the gift of tongues. (I have dealt with this in detail in my book *The Baptism of Power: Engaging Charismatic, Evangelical and Pentecostal on the Holy Spirit*).

Just as the Apostle Paul clearly says in Ephesians 4:18, Allison's explanation on the filling with the Holy Spirit is very instructive. According to him, a person may be indwelt by the Spirit of God but may not optimize the inherent blessings of the Spirit until later in life. Allison goes on to direct attention to the examples of people who were already indwelt by the Spirit but were uniquely filled at particular times so that they could perform certain unusual tasks. In the book of Acts, these examples include Peter (4:8), the Jerusalem church (4:31), Stephen (7:55), Barnabas (Acts 11: 24), Paul (13:9), and others. To be constantly "full of the Holy Spirit" brings every Christian to a state of being effective, fruitful, and productive in life and in fulfilling the Great Commission. Wayne Grudem, in accord with Allision, presents four notable, practical marks, or works, that the fullness of the Holy Spirit produces in a yielded life: empowerment, purification, revelation, and unification.[29] Hence, the continuous filling of the Holy Spirit is needed for continuous empowerment, and this empowerment is vital for effective evangelism. More remarkably, the baptism of the Holy Spirit takes place at the point

[28] Late Byang Kato, a renowned African theologian once said, "young Christians today are being urged to seek "a second blessing" or a "second baptism" especially among the Pentecostals. This kind of teaching defies thorough and true biblical interpretations." See, Byang Kato, "The Power of the Holy Spirit," in *Today's Challenge* (Jos: Challenge Publication, September/October 1974), 4.

[29] Wayne Grudem, *Systematic Theology: An Introduction to Biblical Doctrine* (Grand Rapids: Zondervan, 2000), 635.

of regeneration, but the continuous filling of the Holy Spirit produces power in believers for victorious and effective Christian living.

Again, let have a brief clarification on the subject 'healing,' which is part of the controversial issues in Christendom. I'm neither a Pentecostal nor a charismatic believer (as mentioned earlier). But by inductive studies of the scriptures, couple with personal encounters with the Holy Spirit, as an evangelical, I believe that when you are under the fullness of the Holy Spirit, any gift or various gifts of the Holy Spirit can manifest through you as the Spirit deems fit! For examples, I believe in praying for the sick through the gift of faith (Mark 11:22-26; 1 Corinthians 12: 9), the gift of healing (1 Corinthians 12: 9) or just by simple obedience to the Scripture (James 5: 13-17)! I, however, do not oblige to the teaching that everybody must be healed as some Pentecostals claimed. We read of cases in the scriptures of believers or people of God that remained unhealed. For instance, prophet Elisha died of sickness (2 Kings 13: 14f). Paul was not healed from his thorn after he prayed several times. Timothy was not healed from his stomach illness. Trophimus was not healed when Paul prayed for him. "*Erastus remained at Corinth: but Trophimus I left at Miletus sick*" (2 Timothy 4:20). (One thing is certain though, regardless of their challenges, these men fulfilled their callings). But at the same time, I really do not know how those who claim that the age of the supernatural is gone with the apostles read their Bible to arrive at this conclusion. It is very easy to come to this conclusion though if only we do our theology within the four-walls of an office, within the four-walls of a classroom, and within the close walls of churches. Unlike many professors of theology today, the early apostles were always on the fields witnessing to the lost souls. Paul theology was not a theoretical one, but a product of his missional activities. Anytime we take the gospel out there where sinners are, we will witness the power of God at work, as powers and principalities of darkness bow for Jesus Christ through the workings of the Holy Spirit.

Nevertheless, our faith in Christ Jesus should not be based on healing and miraculous signs. Healing and miraculous signs cannot stand the test of time. People who get healed either medically or miraculously still or will one day die; only the salvation of souls lasts till eternity. For examples, Smith Wigglesworth was popularly known as healing apostles in his days, yet he died of kidney stone at the age of 78. Catheryn Kuhlman was an American healing lady evangelist, yet she died of heart disease at the age of 69. Some years back, I personally witnessed the move of God's power in healings, signs and wonders as Reinhard Bonnke staged a crusade in Kwara State, Nigeria. But Bonnke went back to heaven through lung cancer at the age of 79. Archbishop Benson Idahosa, a famous Nigerian Television-evangelist, was reported to have raise people from dead. But he too passed away suddenly before his 60th birthday. Myles Munroe experienced several miraculous acts of God in his ministry, he preached much on the 'Kingdom' (Heaven on earth). Yet, he passed away at the age of 68 in plane crash, with his wife and a daughter. Why? This world is not heaven yet, rather, the entire creation is still groaning waiting for its redemption (Romans 8: 21-22). On the other hand, Billy Graham was a reputable evangelist who retained an unprecedented life of integrity throughout his life span. He was not known to center his gospel's message on healings and miracles. Graham central gospel's message is, '***you must be born again.***' Graham outlived many of his contemporary preachers, he died at the age of 98. This is not an argument to discredit healing ministry or to downplay the miraculous power of God, who is forever the same yesterday, today and forever. But the emphasis here is, ***the salvation of souls must be prioritized above all other things***. Jesus once told his disciples not to rejoice because they performed some healings and witnessed miraculous moves; but to rejoice because their names are written in heaven (Luke 10: 20 paraphrase mine).

Chapter 4
The Emergence of Nigerian Pentecostalism

"According to the grace of God which was given to me, as a wise master builder I have laid the foundation, and another builds on it. But let each one take heed how he builds on it" (1 Corinthians 3: 10 NKJV)

Nigerian Pentecostalism has multiple origins. James O. Adeyanju maintains that the emergence of Pentecostalism in the geographical entity now regarded as Nigeria was not immediately occasioned by the expansion of the Pentecostal religious phenomenon that ensued in the United States. Pentecostalism could aptly be described as the third wave of Nigerian Christianity—the two prior waves being the Catholic and the Protestant mission endeavors.[1] In other words, the Catholic and Protestant missionaries and their activities had already taken their due courses, which Pentecostals took advantage of as they later emerged.[2] Both the Catholic and Protestant churches resulting from their mission endeavors had registered their presence in Nigeria in the 1400s (Catholics) as well as in the 1800s (Protestants).

Nigerian Indigenous and Classical Pentecostalism

Due to its own unique historical origin, the emergence of Pentecostalism in Nigeria has been variously dated by scholars.[3] Although Nigerian classical Pentecostalism was glowing in its prime in the late 1960s

[1] James O. Adeyanju, "A Critical Examination of the Emergence of Pentecostalism and the Diversity of its Practices in Nigeria," (A Paper Presentation to the Faculty of Christian Education, ECWA Theological Seminary, Igbaja, Nigeria, March/April 2018), 2.

[2] Gary S. Maxey, *Capturing the Lost Vision: Can Nigeria's Greatest Revival Live Again?* (Lagos, Nigeria: WATS Publication, 2016), 29-30.

[3] See A. A. Ausaji, "The Pentecostal Transformation of Nigerian Church Life 1," *Asian Journal of Pentecostal Studies* 5, no. 2 (2002): 189-204.

to early 1980s, it may not be historically correct to imagine that the Pentecostal movement began in Nigeria in the 1970s or 1980s, as A. A. Ausaji claims,[4] because a primitive or indigenous Pentecostal movement was already present and active before it was later linked with foreign global Pentecostalism. Allan Anderson highlights the fact that the entrance of Pentecostalism into Nigeria brought transformation within the independent churches that gave birth to local forms of Pentecostal churches, called "Spiritual Churches." These churches place much emphasis on the power of the Holy Spirit, which manifests in healing, prophecy and speaking in tongues.[5]According to Samson O. Ijaola,

> Interestingly, the beginning of African Pentecostalism has no link to Western Pentecostalism. It emerged from the missionary churches, first as charismatic movements before they finally gained autocephaly—as an African response to the perceived cold spirituality, and a rebuttal, of the Western spiritual hegemony. Apparently, in the long run it synergized with Western Pentecostalism to gain theological footing and prominence among the Catholic and evangelical dominated churches and to escape the persecuting colonialists in Africa.[6]

In the same way, Gary S. Maxey and Peter Ozodo point out,

> The tracing of history behind this in West Africa would require a careful look at emerging models of native Christian leadership in Africa starting with Liberia's William Wade Harris (1860-1929), and including Nigeria's Garrick Sokari Braide (1862-1918) and Joseph Ayo Babalola (1904-1959). All three of these

[4] Ausaji, "Pentecostal Transformation of Nigerian Church Life," 204.

[5] See Allan Anderson, *Spread the Fires: The Missionary Nature of Early Pentecostalism* (Maryknoll, NY: Orbis Books, 2007), 162-3.

[6] Samson O. Ijaola, "Pentecostalism, the Prosperity Gospel, and Poverty in Africa," in *Pentecostalism and Politics in Africa*, ed. Adeshina Afolayan, Olajumoke Yacob-Haliso, and Toyin Falola (Ibadan, Nigeria: Springer International, 2018), 141.

> African "prophets" gained massive followings among people who were on the marginal fringes of Christianity and who at best were superficially engaged in the biblical view. They apparently knew relatively little about biblical standard of holiness or about what it meant to be sanctified people.[7]

During this period of time, the key factor that determined the popularity of these prophets was their ability to wade off—via power encounters—the imminent forces of evil, not necessarily their exhibition of Christ-like holiness. To set the record straight, Ijaola writes,

> The earliest Pentecostal movements in Africa can be described as classic African Pentecostal movements known for their conservativeness, and a gospel without an emphasis on prosperity. Some of the pioneers, such as Joseph Ayo Babalola of Christ Apostolic Church, Bayo Sadare of The Precious Stone Church, John Aluko Babatope and Samuel Adegboyega of The Apostolic Church, were known for their conservativeness, whereas Moses Orimolade of Cherubim and Seraphim was known for his asceticism.[8]

Again, the historical root of what may be properly designated classical Pentecostalism in Nigeria could be dated back to the latter part of the twentieth century. A crude form of Pentecostalism, which manifested in healing practices coupled with result-oriented prayers, began during an influenza pandemic in the southern part of Nigeria in 1918. Members of established churches at that time (e.g., Christ Army Church, the Anglican Church) seceded to form spiritual groups called Prayer Societies.[9] Adeyanju

[7] Gary S. Maxey and Peter Ozodo, *The Seduction of the Nigerian Church* (Lagos, Nigeria: WATS Publication, 2017), 169-70.

[8] Ijaola, "Pentecostalism, theProsperity Gospel, and Poverty in Africa," 142.

[9] These earliest charismatic movements were viewed as schismatic groups by the established churches. They were derided and given derogatory appellations, such as break-away movements and separatist groups. See B. C. D. Diara and N. G. Onah, "The Phenomenal Growth of Pentecostalism in the Contemporary Nigerian Society: A Challenge to Mainline Churches," *Mediterranean Journal of Social Sciences* 5, no. 6 (April 2014): 395.

writes,

> A typical example of such Prayer Societies was the Precious Stone Society members of which became prominent as they ministered healing to influenza victims in 1918. In 1920, Precious Stone Society metamorphosed into Faith Tabernacle Congregation (FTC). FTC was an international Christian religious body; its headquarters was in Philadelphia, USA. Apostle Joseph Ayodele Babalola (1904-1959) soon became a staunch member of FTC, leading the great Oke Ooye, Ilesa Revival in the 1930s. Miraculous signs and wonders expressed through raising of the dead, healing of sick, restoration of blind sights, reactivation of the womb of barren women among others. In their thousands, inquirers thronged the venue of the Revival from different places all over the country and beyond so as to get cured from their psychosomatic problems.[10]

Prophet Moses Orimolade Tunolase (c. 1879-1933) was said to have ministered in a charismatic way in other regions of Nigeria then. The gospel proclamation of Tunolase about the kindness of God, leading sinners to repentance, was marked with "supernatural" occurrences. His efforts resulted in many miraculous happenings.[11] Eventually, with the assistance of Abiodun Akinsowon, the charismatic movement led to the formation of the Cherubim and Seraphim Church movement. To this day, Tunolase is still viewed as the father of Aladura churches[12] in Nigeria.[13] This appellation is because his

[10] Adeyanju, "Emergence of Pentecostalism in Nigeria," 7..

[11] Anderson writes, "Another Anglican member, Moses Orimolade Tunolashe began preaching in about 1915 after partially recovering from a long illness. Crowds came to him for prayer for healing during the influenza epidemic of 1918. His emphases caused him to be known as Baba Aladura ('prayer father)—a tittle used by subsequent leaders of the church that he founded. See Allan Anderson, *Spreading Fires: The Missionary nature of Early Pentecostalism* (Maryknoll, NY: Orbis Books, 2007), 166.

[12] The 'Aladura Churches'in their formation displayed a crude form of indigenous Charismatic appearances. They placed focus on prayer and fasting as means to experience the supernatural move of God.

[13] The Nigeria Indigenous Pentecostal movement, which started as "Aladura churches," has its own stark weakness of being syncretic in its beliefs and practices. Today, this syncretism has been massively inherited by Nigerian Pentecostals and Neo-Pentecostals.

ministerial campaigns were characterized by signs and wonders that endeared many people to him.[14] From the above discussion, even though some indigenous charismatic practices had already been in existence, one could safely aver that the Pentecostal movement in its early form began in Nigeria as an offshoot of the relationship between the African indigenous churches (AICs) and mission churches.

The first classical Pentecostal church to have evolved from the relationship above in Nigeria is The Apostolic Church (TAC). In 1931, TAC began in Nigeria, and the allegiance of FTC (Faith Tabernacle Congregation) members in Nigeria transferred to TAC as "the decade long relationship between the Faith Tabernacle America and Nigeria abruptly came to an end [in 1925] when Clarke the leader of Faith Tabernacle in America was accused of adultery."[15] The Christ Apostolic Church (CAC), the second group of classical Pentecostals, came out of TAC around 1941 due to (1) the insistence of the British leaders of TAC not to indulge in any form of medication in the church and (2) the British Anglican church doctrine of infant baptism.[16] Intermittently, the intrusion of foreign Pentecostal denominations (e.g., the Assemblies of God in 1939, the Foursquare Gospel Church in 1954) complemented homegrown Pentecostal efforts. Such efforts included those of Pa Josiah Abiodun Akindayomi, a former member of the Cherubim and Seraphim Church (C&S), who later founded the Redeemed Christian Church of God (RCCG) in 1952. Significant to this period is the charismatic movement of the Civil War Revival from mid-1960s to early 1970s.

The period from 1967 to 1970 was one of the darkest moments in Nigeria in the modern era. During this time, there was an outbreak of a bloody civil war that almost wiped out certain ethnic groups in the nation.

[14] Samson A. Fatokun, "Women and Leadership in Nigerian Pentecostal Churches," *Studia Historiae Ecclesiasticae* 32, no. 3 (2006): 193-205.

[15] Anderson, *Spreading the Fires*, 166.

[16] Anderson, *Spreading the Fires*, 166.

However, God, in His sovereignty, transformed that same period by one of the greatest movements of His power in Nigeria. The Pentecostal and charismatic outpouring that began during this period of war is popularly called the Civil War Revival. The revitalization power of this time was characterized by a call to persistent prayer, holiness, inductive Bible study, the awareness of God's presence, and passionate evangelism.

Accompanying these features were phenomena like the infilling of the Holy Spirit, evidenced by speaking in tongues, and manifestations of spiritual gifts (especially healing and prophecy). The spark of revival fire began primarily in high schools and higher institutions, but like wildfire, it soon cut across every segment of the nation. This phenomenon ultimately led to spontaneous evangelism, church planting, and rapid church growth.[17] Worth mentioning is the fact that both the imported Western and the African classical Pentecostal movements were known to focus largely on end-time teachings, especially the imminent second advent of Jesus Christ, which has often led to soul-searching. Although they believed in the power of the Holy Spirit to combat witchcraft and dark forces, they gave less emphasis to prosperity as a special kind of gospel, which later evolved among Neo-Pentecostals in the late 1970s.[18]

To be truthful to Nigerian history of Christianity, it must be admitted at this juncture a total justice has not be done to the history of Pentecostalism in Nigerian in its entirety in this book for the purpose of focus. For instance, the reputable and formidable impact of Pa Sydney G. Elton (who was one of the early fathers of Classical Pentecostalism in Nigeria), and the birth of Pentecostalism in the Eastern and Northern States of the country, all worth venturing into. To mention but few, men like Edozie Mba (Riches of Christ), Paul Nwachukwu and Augustine

[17] See Austen Ukachi, *The Best Is Yet to Come: Pentecostal and Charismatic Revivals in Nigeria 1913-1990s* (Lagos, Nigeria: Summit Press, 2013), 22-25.
[18] Ijaola, "Pentecostalism, the Prosperity Gospel, and Poverty in Africa," 142.

Nwaodika (Grace of God Mission, GGM), Uma Ukpai, Bishop Mike Okonkwo, Evang O. Ezekiel (Christian Pentecostal Mission, CPM) and host of others, have made tremendous contribution to the establishment and expansion of Pentecostalism in the Eastern States of Nigeria. Similarly, Evangelist Mathew Ojo, Paul Gindiri, and many others work in the North.[19] However, the works of Austen Ukachi, and Gary S. Maxey and Peter Ozodo, and others have done thorough justice to this already. Interested readers can go for their books to read more on historical analysis.

[19]. See Austen Ukachi, *The Best Is Yet to Come: Pentecostal and Charismatic Revivals in Nigeria 1913-1990s.*

Chapter 5
The Birth of Nigerian Neo-Pentecostals (Part 1)

"*We understand that some men from here have troubled you and upset you with their teaching, but we did not send them!*" (Acts 15 :24 NLT)

There is no doubt that both Nigerian classical Pentecostals began with a good drive of the Holy Spirit as they carried out evangelism and experienced a "historic revival," until the mid-1970s, when their focus began to drift. Gary S. Maxey attests to this drift, saying,

> By the mid-1970s, there were clear signs that the Civil War Revival was beginning to wane. The dissipation became evident first in the east. The Hour of Freedom Evangelistic Association was rather quickly discontinued after Stephen and Raphael Okafor left for further studies in the United Kingdom. The vacuum was filled to significant degree by the rise of the first neo-Pentecostal churches, and before long there were charges and counter-charges of false doctrine, of moral looseness and of vying for leadership supremacy.[1]

The question now concerns how the old Nigerian Pentecostal movement morphed into Neo-Pentecostalism. Gary Maxey and Peter Ozodo's book, *The Seduction of the Nigerian Church* sheds more light on this metamorphosis.

Already, there were some questionable beliefs and practices evident among Nigerian Pentecostals toward the end of the 1970s, after the Civil War Revival. The indelible impact of Nigerian Pentecostals and the

[1] Maxey, *Capturing the Lost Vision*, 211.

charismatic movements during this revival fire cannot be overemphasized. Even though revival was short-lived due to various factors, it cut across several geographical locations from the late 1960s to early part of the 1970s.[2] At that time, three major factors characterized the Nigerian classical Pentecostal movement. First, this movement, as a result of the assumption of the imminent return of Jesus Christ, centered on passionate evangelism. Second, the message of the classical Pentecostal movement during the Civil War Revival centered on salvation that must be evidenced by genuine repentance and holiness. Third, there was an emphatic stress on Holy Spirit baptism evidenced by tongues, signs, and wonders. Through this movement, thousands of churches were planted in different parts of Nigeria as revival spread like wildfire. As a matter of fact, there was no emphasis on material prosperity during this time, as members were eagerly awaiting the second coming of Christ.[3] However, a few factors interrupted the longevity of this revival (as explained in the last section of this chapter).

However, in the 1970s, a new wave of Pentecostal revival broke out among college students, bolstering more new Pentecostal denominations. Benson Idahosa, Nigeria's most influential Pentecostal preacher, established his Church of God Mission (CGM) in 1972. Samson Ijaola writes, "The earliest link of the prosperity gospel to Nigeria dates back to 1971, when Benson Idahosa, a lay preacher in the Assemblies of God attended Christ for All Nations Bible College in Dallas, Texas, through the connection and sponsorship of Gordon Lindsay. . . . The Bible College was a prosperity gospel-based school."[4] The fact remains, "Idahosa had his first experience of prosperity theology, which aptly 'fit his

[2] See Maxey, *Capturing the Lost Vision*,45-7.

[3] The DNA of this movement focuses on repentance, new birth, holiness, evangelism, deeper study of the Bible, and devotion to prayers. While miracles definitely happened during the Civil War Revival, they were almost never the central focus. See Maxey, *Capturing the Lost Vision*,169-171; Maxey and Ozodo, *The Seduction of the Nigerian Church*, 57-58.

[4] Ijaola, "Pentecostalism, the Prosperity Gospel, and Poverty in Africa," 147.

entrepreneurial nature.' Idahosa did not complete his course in the school but equipped with the tool of the prosperity gospel, returned to Nigeria to spread it in 1971; having dazzled his teachers with the knowledge he acquired within a short stay."[5] From that time, classical Pentecostalism was defaced by the introduction of a materialistic (prosperity) gospel. At this point, Nigerian classical Pentecostalism began its metamorphosis into "**Neo-Pentecostalism**." Per Ijaola, "The late Archbishop Benson Idahosa indubitably changed the face of Christianity, and in particular classical Pentecostalism, in Africa."[6] Observers believe that the exposure of Idahosa to foreign teachings on material prosperity did a lot of damage to his initial evangelistic passion. From a notable report,

> Beside his aggressive planting of the Church of God Mission, Idahosa ran the first Christian TV evangelism program, known as "Redemption Hour," in Nigeria, like Oral Robert did in the United States. He also established the All Nations for Christ Bible Institute attended today by most prominent prosperity preachers, including non-Nigerians like Duncan Williams of Action Chapel, Ghana, and Suleiman Umar of Niger; others who have attended the school include 15 students from Ghana, seven from Chad, four from the Ivory Coast, three from Kenya, two from Cameroon, and one each from Sierra Leone and Togo. Those from Nigeria include Ayo Oritshejafor, David Oyedepo, Felix Omobude, Fred Addo, and Chris Oyakhilome. These protégés of Benson Idahosa have followed his footsteps to advance the prosperity gospel beyond the shores of Africa to the global North.[7]

[5] Ijaola, "Pentecostalism, the Prosperity Gospel, and Poverty in Africa," 147. See also Ron MacTavish, "Pentecostal Profits: The Prosperity Gospel in the Global South" (master's thesis, University of Lethbridge, 2013).

[6] Ijaola, "Pentecostalism, the Prosperity Gospel, and Poverty in Africa," 147.

[7] Ijaola, "Pentecostalism, the Prosperity Gospel, and Poverty in Africa," 147 See also Efe Ehioghae and Joseph Olarewaju, "A Theological Evaluation of the Utopian Image of Prosperity Gospel and the African Dilemma," *IOSR Journal of Humanities and Social Science* 20, no. 8 (2015): 66-75 (esp. 71).

Another Pentecostal denomination, The Grace of God Mission (GGM) began in the eastern part of the country in the late 1970s. In Addition, William Funso Kumuyi began a Bible Study group in the early 1970s, which later became the Deeper Life Bible Church (DLBC). The evolution of the leadership of Enoch A. Adeboye in RCCG in 1980 (which today has a shared nature of both classical Pentecostalism and more of Neo-Pentecostalism) has since boosted the status of Pentecostalism in Nigeria such that the denomination may be reckoned as one of the fastest-growing denominations in the country.[8] Christian Pentecostal Mission (early 1980) of Evang O. Ezekiel also played a prominent role in the growth and spread of Pentecostalism. These Pentecostal denominations were later followed by the founding of other new Pentecostal churches, such as Living Faith Church (a.k.a. Winners' Chapel) in 1986 and Mountain of Fire and Miracle Ministries (MFM) in 1989. Today, Neo-Pentecostal churches in Nigeria have increased astronomically; the number is in the hundreds, if not in the thousands.[9] Unfortunately, the newer the Pentecostals churches being birthed in Nigeria, the further they are drifting away from what Nigerian classical Pentecostals were known for.

Classification of Nigerian Neo-Pentecostals

It is challenging to accurately classify the numerous Neo-Pentecostal denominations in Nigeria today because the number of new parishes continues to expand by the day. Borrowing ideas from James O. Adeyanju and the taxonomy of Deji Ayegboyin and F. K. Asonzeh Ukahon, the nomenclature of Pentecostalism, a classification of Nigerian Neo-Pentecostalism would include,

1. Neo-Pentecostal churches that are evangelistic in nature. Despite of some inaccurate biblical interpretations (due to ignorance), they make

[8] Philip Jenkins, *The Next Christendom: The Coming of Global Christianity* (Oxford: Oxford University Press, 2011), 94, 260-61.

[9] Adeyanju, "Emergence of Pentecostalism in Nigeria," 11.

soul-wining and the sanctification and edification of the saints their priority (this group still retains some elements of classical Pentecostalism).

2. Neo-Pentecostal churches that strive to handle the Word of God correctly but appear to be more concerned with signs and miracles in their camps and conference centers and evidence some seemingly syncretistic practices with a few doctrinal errors (due to biblical illiteracy).

3. Neo-Pentecostal churches that present themselves as spiritual warriors in their outlook. These churches give much attention to fiery prayer, deliverance, attacks against both physical and spiritual enemies, and the like. Their pattern of prayer is "die! die!! die!!!"

4. Neo-Pentecostal mega churches that are using the template of thoroughgoing prosperity theology to advance their cause.

5. Neo-Pentecostal churches that attract members to themselves as they employ motivational talks and comedians.

6. Neo-Pentecostal parishes whose founders are "called" into Christian ministry because of the poor economic condition of Nigeria and are, therefore, given to spiritual extortion and other fraudulent practices in their folds.[10]

7. Neo-Pentecostal churches with founders that engage in occultic, magical, and fetish practices

Characteristics of Nigerian Neo-Pentecostals

Today, there are common beliefs and practices among these Pentecostals that bring about the new nomenclature of "Nigerian Neo-Pentecostals" that is employed throughout this book. In the course of writing this

[10] Adeyanju, "Emergence of Pentecostalism in Nigeria," 12-14; Deji I. Ayegboyin and Kennedy Asonzeh-Ukah, "Taxonomy of Churches in Africa: The Case of Nigeria," *Ogbomoso Journal of Theology* 8, no. 1 (2008): 1-15. See also Ezekiel A. Bamigboye, "Pentecostalism and Cross-Cultural Mission in the 21st Century Nigeria," *Ogbomoso Journal of Theology* 8, no. 1 (2008): 167-70.

book, questionnaire administered. Hence, coupled with some of the belief systems discussed above, the responses obtained from research questionnaire will help to shed more light on some of the beliefs and practices of Nigerian Neo-Pentecostals.[11] Many of the Nigerian Pentecostals that began in the late 1970s and continued to exist today, even though most of them came out of Nigerian classical Pentecostalism, exhibit more of the characteristics of Neo-Pentecostalism. The reason for their aberration will be considered when discussing "The Seduction of Nigerian Pentecostals" in the next chapter. Similarly, the new Pentecostal denominations that are coming up today in Nigeria all fit into the new name "Nigerian Neo-Pentecostals." At this juncture, it will be good to itemize some of the characteristics of Nigerian Neo-Pentecostals. (I have elaborately discussed some of these characteristics in my next book *Church or Human Empire*, which is sequential to this book (about to be published).

In more general terms but with slight variations, like classical Pentecostals, Neo-Pentecostal churches are those who inherently emphasize the role of the Holy Spirit in the life and mission of the church, particularly with reference to phenomenal ecstasy noticeable in prophecy, speaking in tongues, healing and other miraculous signs. The explosion of Neo-Pentecostalism in Nigeria and elsewhere attests to this reality, as H. C. Achunike observes.[12]But more than this, below are some noticeable characters of Nigerian Neo-Pentecostals leaders.

First, Nigerian Neo-Pentecostals leaders operate a one-man-show type of church system. The general overseers (GOs), or founders, and their wives rule over the members. Second, most of the general overseers control the financial system of the church without anyone being able to question

[11] The alternative name being used to describe this new brand is "Nigerian New Pentecostal." See Ayegboyin and Ukah, "Taxonomy of Churches in Africa,"12.

[12] H. C. Achunike, "The Challenges of Pentecostalism to the Mainline Churches in Nigeria," *Koinonia* 2, no. 2 (December 2004): 21.

their authority. Third, they are quick to threaten members or anyone else who challenge their authority with curses. Fourth, to justify their manipulative way of life, the general overseers quickly quote Scriptures like "*Touch not my anointed and do my prophet no harm*" (Ps 105:15) and "*By a prophet the LORD brought Israel out of Egypt, and by a prophet was he preserved*" (Hos 12:13). Fifth, they emphasize their ability to heal the sick and their ability to predict the future through their prophetic offices. Sixth, most of the general overseers live questionable, and flamboyant lives through the donations and money they have received from their members, which they have invested over some periods of time. Seventh, they are full of sweet and motivating words that make it difficult for the simple or gullible minds to know that they are being exploited. Unfortunately, some of the innocent followers think that they are giving their money and material possessions to advance the gospel of Christ; little do they know that they are only giving their money to feed the greed of these insatiable ministers of the gospel. In the chapters ahead, I will delve deeper into some of these characteristics.

Chapter 6
The Birth of Nigerian Neo-Pentecostals (Part 2)

"*And many false prophets shall rise, and shall deceive many*" (Matt 24: 11)

The Seduction of Nigerian Pentecostals

The impact of the Civil War Revival will eternally remain relevant to Nigerian Christianity. However, concerning the factors that influenced Nigerian Pentecostal fervor, the delay of Christ's return formed the first factor that dwindled the passionate commitment of classical Pentecostal churches. Church members who hoped that Christ would return any moment began to lose hope in the latter part of the twentieth century. Second, after Nigeria experienced prosperity in the 1970s, a social and economic crisis began to assail the country in the 1980s. Unfortunately, the church had not done enough to provide the moral guidance needed to uplift and safeguard its members.[1] With the socio-economic chaos, Nigerian Christianity began to change drastically in the mid-1980s when some Nigerian Pentecostal leaders began to form an alliance with some Pentecostals leaders in the West. This alliance was formed by the Nigerian leaders' physically visiting and adopting some of the writings of foreign Pentecostal preachers. The alliance formed the third factor concerning the seduction of Nigerian Pentecostalism. As Gary Maxey and Peter Ozodo write,

> By the late '70s Pentecostal churches as a whole were abandoning the gains of the Civil War Revival, especially as they struggled with the rising socio-economic challenges before them. At the

[1] Maxey and Ozodo, *The Seduction of the Nigerian Church*,51.

> same time, they were beginning to import and drink the spiked Kool-Aid of the American Health and Wealth Gospel. It was to prove a fatal move as these newly minted churches sold a precious birthright of revival orientation for a mess of self-focused pottage.[2]

The close alliance between Nigerian and Western Pentecostal leaders resulted in a sudden change of bearing for Nigerian Pentecostal churches. Samson O. Ijaola rightly observes,

> Just as classical Pentecostalism was a renewal movement that emerged from the Protestant Holiness movement, with an emphasis on prayer and the Holy Spirit's power and gifts, neo-Pentecostalism is a movement that replenishes the classical Pentecostal beliefs with an optimism derived from faith that defines prosperity as a part of the redemption package for Christians. Therefore, the prosperity gospel hails from a long history of Pentecostalism. Its roots in the Western Pentecostal prosperity gospel movement are incontrovertible. From North America to Africa, the prosperity gospel preachers are attracting throngs of people from the mainline churches and are churching the unchurched. However, this movement has been heavily criticized by both classical Pentecostals and some mainline churches for what is conceived as its material inclination.[3]

The first doctrinal error imported to Nigeria by Pentecostal and Neo-Pentecostal leaders has to do with the Word of Faith teaching from the Word of Faith movement in the U.S. "A significant part of the background for the introduction of Word of Faith teaching into Nigeria was the distribution of the writings of E. W. Kenyon."[4] According to Charles Lola,

---

[2] Maxey and Ozodo, *The Seduction of the Nigerian Church*,51-52.

[3] Ijaola, "Pentecostalism, the Prosperity Gospel, and Poverty in Africa," 138.

[4] Gary S. Maxey, *The WATS Journey: A Personal Narrative* (Lagos: WATS, 2014), 44-45, 50-51; Maxey and Ozodo, *The Seduction of the Nigerian Church*,85.

the "Word of Faith" is not a church; it is a movement that has become the most dominant in impact and influence on the twenty-first-century Christian church, particularly across the global South. The Word of Faith movement came out of the Pentecostal movement in the late twentieth century (1950-1970s). Its founder was E. William Kenyon, whose own work is based on another man's work—that of Phinehas Quimby.[5]

The clear difference between the teachings of Quimby's "New Thoughts" and Kenyon's "Word of Faith" is that Quimby's teaching was based on the power of the mind, not on religion, whereas Kenyon applied the same principles to the heart of the Christian faith. At the heart of Kenyon's Word of Faith movement is the belief in the "Force of Faith." With the "Force of Faith," (or "New thought"), it is believed that words can be used to manipulate the "Faith-Force" in order to obtain all of the promises contained in Scripture. It is from this belief in "Faith-Force" that comes the "name it and claim it" teaching, which is seen as the power of positive confession. At this point, I will be making a constructive criticism of the teachings of some men of God both in Nigeria, in Africa as a whole, and in other nations—including many of them that I have a good regard for. I am not set in destroying their reputations and personalities at all. The target is to juxtapose their teachings with the Scripture since they too are quoting from the Scriptures to back up their claim. The personalities of these men are to be respected, but unbiblical and misleading teachings must be contended against in the Spirit of Christ.

Bishop David O. Oyedepo, one of the champions of the preachers of faith in Nigeria (who is the founder of Living Faith Church; a.k.a. Winners' Chapel), boldly writes of himself,

[5] Charles Lola, Google Form survey, January 10, 2020. See Hank Hanegraaff, *Christianity in Crisis: The 21st Century* (Nashville: Thomas Nelson, 2009), 253-54.

> There are still dispensationalists on the earth today, men that are sent to serve their generation by opening new chapters of depth in God's Word. The Holy Ghost has sent me to open a new chapter to this generation. He has sent me with the powerful Word of faith, and has also delivered into my hands mysterious instruments that have been used over the years to raise the dead, destroy HIV/AIDS, dissolve cancers, establish liberty, provoke success, and command favor, all for the uplift of Zion![6]

The second doctrinal error imported to Nigeria by Pentecostal and Neo-Pentecostal leaders emanates from the Word of Faith movement and centers on the "health and wealth gospel" (a.k.a. the prosperity gospel).[7] Maxey and Ozodo remark,

> We are saying that the major Characteristic of the contemporary Nigerian Church in which it differs markedly from its antecedent is the pronounced focus on *material prosperity*. Material prosperity is certainly an important focus, and especially for Nigerians who have progressively found themselves at wits end to know how to physically survive. But the pendulum has swung too far in the wrong direction. In much of the contemporary Nigerian Church, hunger for a holy God has been replaced by hunger for material prosperity. Dedication to God has been replaced by dedication to financial success. As the emphasis has continued doors have been opened to bring in unethical, corrupt and worldly elements, all in the name of prosperity.[8]

---

[6] Oyedepo, *Signs and Wonders Today*, 58.

[7] Kenneth Hagin had studied the works of William Kenyon and became the foremost admirer of Kenyon and the founder of the Word of Faith movement. Hagin largely made the Word of Faith movement what it is today. He was the foremost leader and proponent of the prosperity (or health and wealth) gospel. There are others who later joined in the pursuit of these falsehoods under the disguise of receiving a "Revelation of Knowledge." This is not to say that all that these men taught is wrong but that some certain teachings of theirs need to be brought under biblical scrutiny.

[8] Maxey and Ozodo, *The Seduction of the Nigerian Church*,82-83 (emphasis added).

According to the doctrinal stand of the health and wealth gospel, sickness and suffering should not be parts of the Christian faith.[9]

The third doctrinal error imported to Nigeria centers on the hyper grace movement, which teaches faith without obedience, grace without restriction and accountability, liberty without responsibility.[10] The teachers of "hyper grace" maintain that all of Jesus' teachings were prior to Calvary and therefore are a reflection of the Old Testament dispensation. As a matter of fact,

> The resulting message of the hyper freedom and hyper grace is a modern form of antinomianism, *perverting the grace of God into a license for immorality* (Jude 4). Antinomianism comes from the Greek roots meaning lawlessness. An antinomian is someone who believes that under the gospel dispensation, the moral law is no longer relevant because salvation is obtained through faith alone (*sola fide*) . . . . So, what the proponents of this new "grace revolution" or "grace reformation" are advocating is nothing but a revival of the much older heresy of antinomianism, which goes all the way back to Bible time.[11]

Just like his subtle tactics of luring people away from the truth, Satan seems to approach Nigerian Pentecostals with crafty deception. "None of the deceptive teachings that have led the Nigerian Church astray over the past forty years have come to us without significant elements of truth. All of them have appealed to deeply felt needs within the hearts of hungry and thirsty Nigerians."[12] Hence, many people gullibly defend

---

[9] Roland S. Babatunde, *The Faith of our Fathers: Feared Not Sword and Fire* (Ilorin, Nigeria: Tanimola Press, 2014), 20.

[10] Maxey and Ozodo, *The Seduction of the Nigerian Church*,181-82.

[11] Maxey and Ozodo, *The Seduction of the Nigerian Church*, 183 (emphasis added). See also Michael L. Brown, *Hyper Grace: Exposing the Danger of the Modern Grace Message* (Lake Mary, FL: Charismas House, 2014), 284-6. The apostle James's warning is very clear: "faith by itself, if it does not have works, is dead"(Jas 2:17).

[12] Maxey and Ozodo, *The Seduction of the Nigerian Church*, 81.

those deceptions with the mindset that those teachings are scriptural. The old Nigerian classical Pentecostals never focused on material prosperity.[13] The power of positive thinking (Word of Faith) did not factor into their theology, and the message of holiness (though with its tail of legalism[14]) characterized their evangelistic zeal—unlike today's hyper grace teaching. But from the late 1970s onward, Nigerian Pentecostals began to derail gradually due to the aforementioned issues.

Today, Nigerian Neo-Pentecostalism seems to have revived the errors that existed in Nigerian Pentecostalism to the extreme. There is, however, presently a clear line of demarcation between Nigerian classical Pentecostals and Neo-Pentecostals. The difference primarily centers on the alarming rate of increase in Neo-Pentecostals' ethical and moral decadence as a result of their inordinate pursuit of power and materialism in the name of "prosperity." As Ijaola observes,

> That the claim of Neo-Pentecostalism to be part of the Pentecostal movement rests in its belief in the exhibition of charisma of the Holy Spirit, including speaking in tongues, faith, signs, and wonders. However, it distinguishes itself by the doctrine of wealth and health. The prosperity gospel is often defined against the backdrop of the nexus between the experience of a spiritual rebirth—salvation—and the existential reality of poverty.[15]

Mike Oye rightly points out, "When the materialistic gospel was first imported to Nigeria in the 80s, somebody like me and some other concerned brothers in the Lord stood to oppose it. But some insensitive preachers and uninformed followers called us backsliders and lukewarm who are no longer hot for God. But today, time has proven what is right."

---

[13] Sunday Bwanhot, interview by the author, Chicago, IL, December 7, 2019.

[14] Both the older Pentecostal churches and the holiness movement in general have been heavily plagued by legalism for decades. See Maxey and Ozodo, *The Seduction of the Nigerian Church*, 82.

[15] Ijaola, "Pentecostalism, the Prosperity Gospel, and Poverty in Africa," 143.

Well-known professor of Christian theology, ethics, and public policy Sunday B. Agang expresses this decadence well:

> Christians in Nigeria should be afraid of something more dangerous than the Islamization agenda; the ethical and moral decadence eroding Christian public life . . . . I worry more about the serious moral decadence and ethical decline which now characterize Christianity in Nigeria and the African continent at large. Today, many Christians are deeply involved in corruption and flaunt decadent and immoral lifestyles . . . . Christians in Nigeria are dancing on the brink of moral and ethical collapse.[16]

Unfortunately, the vast majority of Nigerian Pentecostals are not exempt from this moral and ethical degeneration.

The fourth challenge to Nigerian Christianity is a home-based error of syncretistic practices—that is, the mixture of elements from two or more distinct religious belief systems.[17]In my research, about 77 percent of the survey respondents agreed that Nigerian Neo-Pentecostals have Christian beliefs and practices that portray the practices of African Traditional Religion (this subject will be elaborated later). Fifth, in the late 1970s and early 1980s, there came a loss of inner character, or Christ-likeness, that resulted in a form of worldliness among early Nigerian Pentecostal leaders and members. According to Maxey and Ozodo, "Worldliness involves taking on more and more of the coloring of the world around us until there is little distinction between those who are a part of the body of Christ and those who are not. Standard[s] for ethical conduct are relaxed."[18]

---

[16] Sunday Bobai Agang, "The Greatest Threat to the Church Isn't Islam—It's Us," *Christianity Today*,April 21, 2017, https://www.christianitytoday.com/ct/2017/may/radical-islam-not-nigerian-churchs-greatest-threat.html.

[17] Robert J. Schreiter, *Constructing Local Theologies* (Maryknoll, NY: Orbis Books, 1985), 144-58.

[18] Maxey and Ozodo, *The Seduction of the Nigerian Church*, 58.

Finally, although Scripture establishes the priesthood of all believers in Christ Jesus, African cultural practices involve a penchant for title-based hierarchies. Hence, the clamor for titles also works its way into the midst of Nigerian church leaders. As Maxey and Ozodo correctly point out,

> The gradual emergence of an increasingly self-centered quasi-biblical and quasi-ethical Christianity was clearly evident as we moved into the '80s and '90s. The proliferation of titles most visibly modeled and spurred by Benson Idahosa's elevation as the first Pentecostal archbishop in Africa became the order of the day. . . . The resulting unbridled quest for titles within the Nigerian Church was the regrettable outcome. Pride gradually became one of the most unrebuked sins within the Church.[19]

At this point in the history of the Nigerian wing of Pentecostalism, self-glorification set in as self-centeredness began to manifest through self-advancement and self-governance. Again, Maxey and Ozodo aver, "The minimal title of 'Rev Dr' became increasingly commonplace for literally thousands, no matter how questionable the ordination or how unmerited or illegitimate the doctorate. Very sub-standard theological schools began to emerge, in too many cases offering doctorates in exchange either for money or for a few days of uncreditable resident study."[20] Among Nigerian Neo-Pentecostal leaders today, it is very common to see one man holding up to five to seven titles (e.g., Most Snr Apostle/Prophet/Evangelist or Arch-Bishop/Prophet).

---

[19] Maxey and Ozodo, *The Seduction of the Nigerian Church*,59.
[20] Maxey and Ozodo, *The Seduction of the Nigerian Church*, 59.

Chapter 7
The Theological Presuppositions of Nigerian Neo-Pentecostal Churches

"Every man's work shall be made manifest: for the day shall declare it, because it shall be revealed by fire; and the fire shall try every man's work of what sort it is" (1 Corinthians 3: 13)

The Nigerian Neo-Pentecostals' theology plays a prominent role in the content of their gospel presentations. In the same way, the growth of Nigerian Neo-Pentecostal churches also lies majorly on some of their theological inclinations. I will highlight few of these theological predispositions. According to Richard Burgess, "Since the 1970s, Nigeria's religious landscape has been transformed by the emergence of new, locally instituted, Pentecostal churches, with a more modern and global orientation than their Aladura predecessors."[1] Burgess, in his desire to know the theology of Nigerian Neo-Pentecostals, has completed in-depth research that will be helpful at this juncture. He begins by asserting,

> Due to rapid expansion and adept use of media technologies, these churches have recently attracted the attention of scholars from a variety of disciplines. Nigerian theologian Deji Ayegboyi identifies three broad categories: "Holiness Movements," "Prosperity Organizations," and "Deliverance Ministries," though there is considerable overlap between the three.[2]

As one of the largest Pentecostal bodies, Deeper Life Bible Church has planted over six thousand branches all over Nigeria. With another bigger

[1] Richard Burgess, "Nigerian Pentecostal Theology in Global Perspective," *Penteco Studies* 7, no. 2 (2008): 30.

[2] Burgess, "Nigerian Pentecostal Theology," 31.

auditorium under construction, Living Faith Church (a.k.a. Winners' Chapel), opened the Faith Tabernacle church auditorium, containing 50,400 seats in Lagos. The Dunamis Church International, founded by Paul Eneche, recently opened a new church auditorium in 2019 with seating capacity for 100,000 people. Because of its aggressive missionary ambitions and the migratory habits of its members, in addition to the present trend of globalization, Nigerian Neo-Pentecostalism has spread to various parts of the world.[3] As Burgess writes,

> Redeemed Christian Church of God (RCCG), for example, has congregations in more than one hundred nations. In London, which has by far the largest Nigerian community in the U.K., there are over eighty Nigerian initiated denominations and independent churches. The largest single congregation in Western Europe is the London-based Kingsway International Christian Centre (KICC), founded by Pastor Matthew Ashimolowo, which has grown to around 12,000 in fifteen years. The largest Nigerian initiated denomination in Britain is RCCG, which has planted more than 250 congregations in under twenty years. Its flagship congregation, Jesus House, has over three thousand members.[4]

Burgess also observes that "as local Christian communities, African Pentecostal churches are now recognized as an important source for African theological reflection. Theirs is an enacted theology that emerges through reflection and practice, in contrast to the more formalized written theology of the European mission churches."[5] However, the practical focus and concerns of African Pentecostals tend to center on issues like healing, economic security, and fertility, with theologies that reflect a concern for identity construction and contextual relevance. In

[3] Burgess, "Nigerian Pentecostal Theology," 30.
[4] Burgess, "Nigerian Pentecostal Theology," 31.
[5] Burgess, "Nigerian Pentecostal Theology," 30.

addition, many of the ingredients that sum up the religious repertoire of Nigerian Pentecostal churches are found within African Pentecostalism generally. For instance, Burgess writes,

> Nigerian Pentecostals claim to derive their theology directly from the Bible. While they may handle (biblical interpretation) in an uncritical way by neglecting its historical context, it is partly because they wish to make it relevant to local contexts. It is also because they are reluctant to divest the Bible of its supernatural character. Like liberation theology, Nigerian Pentecostals seek to understand local contexts and culture in the light of Scripture, but they do so by retaining a literalist approach to biblical hermeneutics. They look for correspondences between their own life situations and the Bible, and expect Biblical texts to have practical relevance and problem-solving potential.[6]

Contrary to the proper principles of biblical interpretation (or hermeneutics), Nigerian Pentecostals seem to follow "post-modern theories" of reading and interpreting the Bible.[7] Burgess further adds,

> Nigerian Pentecostals also have a fondness for narrative texts and find particular affinities between the biblical world and their own. This leads to a preference for the Old Testament and the narrative portions of the New Testament, especially the Gospels and the Book of Acts. Old Testament characters, such as Abraham, Moses, Elijah, Elisha, Hannah and Ruth, are especially popular as illustrations of the fruits of God's blessings and miraculous intervention. Their pragmatic hermeneutical approach sometimes leads to allegorical readings of biblical narratives. Without abandoning a commitment to biblical literalism, they

[6] Burgess, "Nigerian Pentecostal Theology," 32.

[7] Philip Jenkins, *The New Faces of Christianity: Believing the Bible in the Global South* (Oxford: Oxford University Press, 2006), 41.

> find multiple layers of meaning in the text, which satisfy African Pentecostal aspirations for a practical and experiential form of Christianity.[8]

According to Stephen S. O. Y. Baba,

> The Nigerian Neo-Pentecostals need to improve on their Hermeneutics. The Nigerian Neo-Pentecostals approach of socio- cultural context of the people in engaging biblical texts needs review. Their method of interpreting the bible has a weakness. It begins with man and ends with man. The Nigerian Neo-Pentecostals stress the end results instead of emphasizing the starting point. In my own opinion, it is impossible for such a gospel they preach or teach that is apart from repentance and faith in Christ to bring a desired result. My submission is that they need to stop stressing the end results apart from the necessary starting point which is Salvation in Christ first—individual repentance and faith in Christ.[9]

Baba adds that Nigerian Neo-Pentecostals need to stop preaching an "escapism gospel" and employing hermeneutics of suspicion. According to Baba, an "escapism gospel" is any preaching of Christ that says there is no suffering. This is a new kind of prosperity gospel that substitutes positive thinking for salvation and presents the gospel as an escape route by teaching the congregation methods of removing pain and suffering from their lives as believers. The people who are doing this need to go back to the basics and use the valid standard principles of biblical interpretation, which teach punishment for sinners and present redemptive grace for fallen human beings through Christ, who brought proper reconciliation. The gospel of salvation—rather than an escapism

[8] Burgess, "Nigerian Pentecostal Theology," 33.

[9] Stephen S. O. Y. Baba, Google Forms survey, October 26, 2019.

gospel—must be emphasized.

As a result of the pragmatic approach of Nigerian Neo-Pentecostals to biblical interpretation, a selective hermeneutical method eventually becomes their order of things.[10] This method has the potential to wrench biblical texts out of their contexts in order to support Nigerian Neo-Pentecostals' predetermined arguments. "This 'proof-texting' approach," says Burgess, "can result in 'truncated, if not erroneous, views on theological issues.' This is especially apparent in the way Nigerian Pentecostals construct their theologies of deliverance and prosperity."[11] Popular Africa theologian Ogbu Kalu critiques Pentecostal theology, labeling it "bumper sticker" hermeneutics or "experiential literalism," where "personal and corporate experiences are woven into the hermeneutical task," fusing the horizons of the past and present with a "pragmatic hermeneutical leap."[12]

Concerning the result of this pragmatic leap, John O. Enyinnaya writes, "In their elevation of experience over Scripture, and unquestioning acceptance of dreams, visions and spontaneous prophetic utterances, over and above the teaching of the Bible, Pentecostals err in their valuation of the authority of the Bible."[13] Either as a result of hermeneutical illiteracy or intentional personal gratification, most Pentecostal preachers always focus their teaching and preaching on what their followers would like to hear. As Enyinnaya notes, "This shifting membership base of some of these churches make the preachers tend to preach what will suit the taste of listeners so they would come back next Sunday. This listener-friendly disposition or public relations concern of much of Pentecostal preaching makes it open

[10] Charles Lola sees this as error of "selective private interpretation" of the Scriptures rather than biblical interpretation—comparing Scripture with Scripture. Charles Lola, Google Forms survey, January 30, 2020.

[11] Burgess, "Nigerian Pentecostal Theology," 33.

[12] Ogbu Kalu, *African Pentecostalism: An Introduction* (Oxford: Oxford University Press, 2008), 266-67. See also Burgess, "Nigerian Pentecostal Theology," 33.

[13] John O. Enyinnaya, "Pentecostal Hermeneutic and Preaching: An Appraisal," *Ogbomoso Journal of Theology* 8, no. 1 (2008): 149.

to much suspicion."[14]

Most Nigerian Neo-Pentecostals never believe in the ***assurance of salvation*** for believers in Christ Jesus; thus, worshippers bind themselves to their leaders, whose instructions they must strictly adhere to so as to "make heaven."[15] Ter Haar observes that in African Christianity, the prophet-healer-miracle worker is strongly appealing and wields great authority, and he maintains that Enoch A. Adeboye fits this image.[16] In addition,

The authority that is ascribed to Adeboye by some of his ardent followers is questionable because it may be construed as appropriating divine prerogatives. His authority is regarded as "supreme, his orders final, and his power and supremacy considered next to Christ." One of his Assistant General Overseers has said, Adeboye is the God we now see in human flesh; what he tells us we take as coming from God directly. We do not argue with it. Such statements may be identified with the cult of hero-worship.[17]

Several Pentecostal leaders wrongly misinterpret Scriptures, such as 2 Chronicles 20:20, which reads, "And they rose early in the morning, and went forth into the wilderness of Tekoa: and as they went forth, Jehoshaphat stood and said, Hear me, O Judah, and ye inhabitants of Jerusalem; Believe in the LORD your God, so shall ye be established; believe his prophets, so shall ye prosper" (KJV). These Nigerian Neo-

[14] Enyinnaya, "Pentecostal Hermeneutic and Preaching," 151.

[15] The phrase "to make heaven" reveals that many of the Pentecostal Christians are still striving with their own power and strength to be able to get to heaven. This reveals their theology of work-based salvation, not salvation by grace alone (Ephesians 2:8). Most of the Nigerian Neo-Pentecostal leaders preach vehemently against the doctrine of eternal security.

[16] Gerrie Ter Haar, "A Wondrous God: Miracles in Contemporary Africa," *African Affairs* 102 (2003): 409-28.

[17] Afolarin Olutunde Ojewole and Efe Monday Ehioghae, "Leadership and Power in the Pentecostal Movement: Selected Case Studies," in *Pentecostalism and Politics in Africa*, ed. Adeshina Afolayan, Olajumoke Yacob-Haliso, and Toyin Falola (Ibadan, Nigeria: Springer International, 2018), 326. See also Enoch A.Adeboye, *As Pure as Light* (Lagos, Nigeria: CRM Book Ministry, 1999), 327; Adeboye, *How to Turn Your Austerity to Prosperity* (Lagos, Nigeria: CRM Book Ministry, 1989), 283.

Pentecostal leaders interpret the passage above as referring to *themselves* as the prophets who will bring their followers to heaven—the "promised land."[18] In his message to his audience, and talking about himself and his ministry, David O. Oyedepo writes,

> I do believe that you are going to partake of the fullness [full blessings] of this commission. You must diligently hearken to the voice of the Lord your God, and observe to do whatever He commands you through my mouth. Then, the Lord your God will set you on high, above all nations of the earth. "Believe in the Lord your God, so shall ye be established; believe his prophets, so shall ye prosper. I say this over and over again, God sent me. He said, 'Go and make my people rich!'" That is an assurance that wherever I stand, poverty must not survive.[19]

The belief always is that if people want to get to heaven after death, they must follow their pastor's words to the letter.[20]

Another equivalent Scripture is Hosea 12:13: "And by a prophet the Lord brought Israel out of Egypt, and by a prophet was he preserved" (KJV). According to the Pentecostal and Neo-Pentecostal interpretation of this passage, "the prophets" are now the church leaders responsible for leading their followers to success on earth and to heaven as well. In the doctrinal liturgy of any Pentecostal or Neo-Pentecostal assembly, disobedience to a Pentecostal leader attracts curses that can cause any follower to eventually miss out on heaven.

Some members of Nigerian Neo-Pentecostal churches have yielded total control of their lives to these so-called "men of God." Some

---

[18] David O. Oyedepo, *Walking in Dominion* (Lagos, Nigeria: Dominion, 2006), 165-69. See also Oyedepo, *Understanding Your Covenant Rights* (Canaan Land, Lagos: Dominion, 2003)1-5.

[19]Oyedepo, *Breaking Financial Hardship* [Lagos, Nigeria: Dominion, 1995], 54-55.

[20] Pastor Enoch Adejare Adeboye, "Anyone Not Paying His Tithes Will Not Get to Heaven," YouTube video, 6:04, April 13, 2018,https://www.youtube.com/watch?v=PX4T9teq97o..

denominations have prayer grounds, prayer camps, or prayer cities, where people go to pray and fast for days, weeks, or months, as instructed by their pastors or as they are motivated.[21] Many Nigerian Neo-Pentecostal leaders always warn their followers, "Be not deceived by the teaching of eternal security."[22] Hence, most followers live in perpetual fear of hell since they are not sure if they will get to heaven after death. Some Pentecostal denominations contain a lot of "dos" and "don'ts." By this, Nigerian Neo-Pentecostal leaders always have a strong grip over their followers.

Both the Neo-Pentecostal and charismatic movements of Nigeria hold to the continuation of the prophetic office. Babatomiwa Moses Owojaiye writes,

> According to charismatic theology, as one of the leadership offices of the Old Testament (1 Samuel 9:9, 11, 19; 2 Sam 15: 27) and New Testament (Ephesians 4: 11), the prophetic office is available to selected men and women (Acts 2:17). Charismatics teach that women such as Miriam (Exodus 15:20), Deborah (Judges 4:4), Huldah (2 Kings 22:14; 2 Chronicles 34:22), Noadiah (Nehemiah 6:14), and Anna (Luke 2:36) joined the ranks of men called to direct, build up, and mature the people of God as a God-fearing community.[23]

In African Traditional Religion, there is always a quest to know what will happen in the future. Hence, when people are not well discipled after

[21] See Victor Oludiran, *The 7 Levels of Prayer: A Tested Formula for Approaching the Throne of Grace* (Smyrna, GA: LICAIM, 2015), 69-71. Prayer and fasting are always in patterns of 7 days, 14 days, 21 days, 40 days, 60 days, 90 days, and 120 days—depending on the mandate given by the "man of God" (MOG). People stay on the prayer mountains' prayer camps uninterruptedly for the duration of the prayer-and-fasting period. At the MFM Prayer City on the Lagos-Ibadan Expressway, prayer is said to go on 24hours a day, 7days a week, non-stop, all year round. See Abimbola Adelakun, "Pentecostal Panopticism and the Phantasm of the Ultimate Power," in Afolayan, Yacob-Haliso, and Falola, *Pentecostalism and Politics in Africa*, 102.

[22] Kumuyi, *Adultery Forbidden*, 29.

[23] Babatomiwa Moses Owojaiye, "The Problem of False Prophets in Africa: Strengthening the Church in the Face of a Troublesome Trend," *Lausanne Global Analysis* 8, no. 6 (November 2019): 2.

their conversion, they usually carry this same worldview and practice into Christianity—resulting in religious syncretism. Such syncretism happens a lot among Neo-Pentecostal followers. Byang Kato's old observation has come into the limelight: "The defunct gods of African traditional religions are now rearing their heads. . . . The devil has many other avenues for fighting against Christ and His church and he knows where best to succeed. Christo-paganism appears to be the area of attack within the next generation. The battle has started."[24] Nigerian Neo-Pentecostal prophets who are able to foretell future events have multitudes of people following them as they turn themselves into little "gods."[25] Bisola H. Johnson, who says she was once a captive of fake popular Nigerian prophet T. B. Joshua, writes extensively about her fourteen-year ordeal under the bondage of the "prophet."[26] She gives various examples of fake prophecies given by Joshua, none of which ever came to pass. For example, Johnson writes,

> T. B. Joshua's false prophecies include this about the 200-plus schoolgirls kidnapped by Boko Haram in April 2014; T. B. Joshua said, "unless I am not called by God. I place my career and calling on the line. That these 200 plus school children kidnapped, they have to be released immediately, unharmed and unhurt." Over three years later, they remain captive, with some of them possibly converted to Islam and carrying out terrorist murders. Therefore, T. B. Joshua is condemned by his own words as a false prophet. He also falsely predicted the 2014 Ebola crisis was over, as against its wildfire spread, which actually got much worse; and that the missing Malaysia Airline jet would be found in 2014. Today, in 2017 the plane is still missing [sic].[27]

[24] Byang Kato, *Theological Pitfalls in Africa* (Nairobi, Egypt: Evangel, 1975), 175.

[25] M. Ademola Adebiyi, interview by the author, Louisville, KY, January 25, 2020. Danny McCain sheds more light on this issue in his book *Tough Tests for Top Leaders: God's Strategy for Preparing Africans to Lead Global Christianity* (Jos, Nigeria: Capro Media, 2000),37-42.

[26] Bisola H. Johnson, *The T. B. Joshua I Know: Deception of the Age Unmasked* (Lagos, Nigeria: n.p., 2018), 1-3.

[27] Johnson, *The T. B. Joshua I Know*, 310.

Scripture clearly points out the litmus tests for a true prophet of God. One of these tests is that the predictions that come from the prophet must come to one-hundred-percent fulfillment. Failure to measure up to this standard attracts the death penalty under the Old Testament law (see Deuteronomy18:21-22). Johnson adds that "this fake prophet frequently talks about the visions God gives him, he claimed before that he sees the future as clearly as if he is watching Emmanuel TV."[28] Johnson continues,

> A few days to the election in the USA, on Sunday the 5th November 2016, in a bid to be relevant, T. B. Joshua claimed that God had shown him the new president of the United States of America .... The Lord said, there is a State that enormously (cast 99%) vote for this woman, and the woman has a narrow win. This prophecy was nothing more than stating what the polls were saying on CNN and everywhere that it would be a narrow win for Hillary Clinton. As we all now know, it wasn't nearly as close as predicted, and the winner is most definitely not "the woman" as T. B. Joshua forecasted.[29]

There are numerous other fake prophets and prophetesses among Nigerian Neo-Pentecostals who are spreading fake teachings all over Nigeria and Africa today.

According to Burgess,

While the intention of Nigerian Pentecostals is to be biblical, their theology is also shaped by local concerns and contexts—all theology is culturally conditioned. Despite a tendency to demonize traditional culture and to present themselves as modern individuals, Nigerian Pentecostals interpret Christianity through the lens of existing religious categories and especially the traditional search for spiritual power, a pervasive theme in

[28] Johnson, *The T. B. Joshua I Know*,310.
[29] Johnson, *The T. B. Joshua I Know*,310

societies such as the Yoruba and Igbo. For the Yoruba, the quest for power (*agbara*) to enhance life is the hermeneutical key to understanding their attraction to all religion, including Pentecostalism. In Yoruba culture (for instance), the "good life" is summed up in the state of *Alafia* or "peace," which embraces protection, practical guidance, health, fertility, success and material prosperity, all fruits of power looked for in Christianity.[30]

As pointed out above, it is never an exaggeration to say that in an attempt to contextualize biblical theology, some vital truths of the biblical Christianity have been compromised by Nigerian Neo-Pentecostals. Relevance should never lead to the reduction of gospel truth; otherwise, one may fall into the error of presenting a different gospel. Either out of ignorance or to intentionally enslave their followers further, Nigerian Neo-Pentecostal leaders get angry at anyone who challenges their prowess of biblical interpretation:

> Nigerian Pentecostals are sometimes intolerant of alternative readings of Scripture by those outside their particular constituencies and are liable to accept without question the interpretations of their leaders . . . . The opinion of the General Overseer or local pastor is rarely challenged publicly, presumably in recognition of their status and their role as power brokers. This is also reflected in the choruses of "amens" and "hallelujahs" that follow their declarations from the platform during church services and conferences. This reluctance to tolerate alternative readings may be connected to the idea that the actual words of the Spirit-anointed leader are loaded with spiritual power.[31]

Many of the Neo-Pentecostals preachers can preach to their congregations for an hour or hours without opening the Scripture more than one time. In their preaching, these men can be making references

[30] Burgess, "Nigerian Pentecostal Theology," 34.
[31] Burgess, "Nigerian Pentecostal Theology," 33-34.

to people they healed elsewhere, or others who received breakthrough, deliverance, promotion etc, through their prayers. In the minds of their members, when these leaders speak, God has spoken. For example, according to Sunday Adelaja, most Africans cannot travel unless they first go to their pastors and obtain permission and garner their prayers for safe travels. The people see it as a miracle to travel and arrive safely at their respective destinations. Many give their pastors prophetic seed-offerings (i.e., money) so that they will pray for the miracle of a safe journey.[32] However,

> amidst all those prayers and dependence on miracles, Africa still has one of the highest rates of road accidents in the world. Statistics from World Health Organization revealed that the risk of dying as a result of a road traffic injury is highest in the African Region, and lowest in the European Region. Most Europeans don't depend on miracles for safe driving, they don't go to their pastors to ask for prayers before they travel and in fact, most of them don't believe in God, yet they still have a far lower rate of road accidents than in Africa.[33]

Men and women do not always need a miracle from heaven to drive safely; they need to take on the responsibilities of constructing good roads, learning road safety rules, and obeying those rules. Most of what many Africans are asking God to do are the kinds of things that they can do by themselves if they exercise prudence. Some of these miracles can be done without dependence upon pastors. The craving for miracles allows many Nigerian Neo-Pentecostal leaders to exercise "unquestionable authority" over the people they lead. Afolarin Olutunde Ojewole and Efe Monday Ehioghae write,

---

[32] Sunday Adelaja, *How the Church Creates Economic Recession* (Kiev, Ukraine: Golden Truth, 2018), 30.

[33] Adelaja, *How the Church Creates Economic Recession*, 30-31.

The divine mystique which Adeboye presents allows his followers to implicitly believe that he is in direct touch with God. He seems to have reinforced this perception by the phrases that are common in his sermons and books, such as "God told me," "My Father says," [my Daddy said], and "The Lord instructed me." Indeed, there are those among his parishioners who believe that God speaks to him in plain language, unlike others whom God may choose to communicate with through dreams and visions. There are equally many others who perceive him as a miracle worker, believing that whatever he touches ceases to be ordinary.[34]

Most Nigerian Neo-Pentecostal leaders are addressed as "Father," "Daddy," "Papa," "Daddy GO," and the likes. The same honor given to these leaders must equally be accorded to their wives.[35] With the kind of precipitating theological worldview discussed above in place, attention will now be drawn to the contents of Neo-Pentecostals' gospel. Nevertheless, Nigerian Neo-Pentecostals' undue emphasis on some of the following elements of their presentation of the gospel calls for critical scrutiny. These elements also form the content of the gospel being presented by the Nigerian Neo-Pentecostals.

[34] Ojewole and Ehioghae, "Leadership and Power in the Pentecostal Movement," 326. See also Adeboye, *As Pure as Light*, 326-27.

[35] According to one Neo-Pentecostal pastor, "A Neo-Pentecostal leader's wife is addressed as 'Mummy,' 'Mother,' 'Mummy GO,' 'First Lady,' and the like. She is always seen as second in command after her husband." Isaac Kolade, interview by the author, Louisville, KY, November 20, 2019.

Chapter 8
Ten Major Factors Characterizing Nigerian Neo-Pentecostals' Gospel (Part 1)

"*But though we, or an angel from heaven, preach any other gospel unto you than that which we have preached unto you, let him be accursed*" (Gal 1: 8)

In this chapter and the next, the argument of this book will dig deep into the ten major characteristics that constitute the core of Nigerian Neo-Pentecostals' gospel presentations. To arrive at these characteristics, a survey was carried out, targeting various members of both Neo-Pentecostal and evangelical denominations in Nigeria. In all, there were about sixty respondents, thirty evangelical participants and thirty Neo-Pentecostal participants. In addition, a questionnaire was distributed to church founders (i.e., independent church owners),[1] pastors, unit leaders, and members in select Neo-Pentecostal and evangelical churches for them to respond concerning Nigerian Neo-Pentecostals' emphases in evangelism and the practical ways in which they conduct evangelism.

Emphasis on Signs and Wonders

The Neo-Pentecostal respondents all agree that the manner in which Nigerian Neo-Pentecostals present the gospel makes people believe that signs and wonders are waiting for them once they embrace the gospel. When the gospel is presented in a way that makes recipients focus on signs and wonders, there is the likelihood that people will receive the

[1] Most Nigerian Pentecostal churches are founded and owned by individuals. In these types of churches, the founders are always called GOs or Superintended.

wrong gospel, which is not the gospel of our Lord Jesus Christ. The fact remains that it is possible to win people to signs, wonders and miracles without actually winning them to Christ. In fact, performing or receiving miracles in the name of Jesus is never a criterion for salvation.[2] One of the signs that Nigerian Neo-Pentecostals always emphasize is the ability to speak in tongues. Acts 2:1-4 reads,

> When the Day of Pentecost had fully come, they [i.e., the disciples of Christ] were all with one accord in one place. And suddenly there came a sound from heaven, as of a rushing mighty wind, and it filled the whole house where they were sitting. Then there appeared to them divided tongues, as of fire, and *one* sat upon each of them. And they were all filled with the Holy Spirit and began to speak with other tongues, as the Spirit gave them utterance (NKJV).

This narrative recount the Holy Spirit's descent on the earliest apostles and followers of Christ on the same day as the Jewish religious festival of Pentecost in Jerusalem. From an ancient ecclesiological perspective, "Pentecost" occurred fifty days after Jesus' two climatic events: forty days after Christ's resurrection plus ten days after his ascension into heaven.[3]

In Pentecostalism, the day of Pentecost, when the Spirit came upon early believers to baptize the early church, is significant—hence, the movement's nomenclature. The phenomenological experience displayed in Acts 2:1- 4 arguably culminated in an event in which the Spirit of God paid a special visit to the world scene for the sole purpose of empowering the members

---

[2] Christ Jesus warns against charismatic displays that do not lead to genuine salvation: "Many will say to me on that day, 'Lord, Lord, did we not prophesy in your name and in your name drive out demons and in your name perform many miracles?' Then I will tell them plainly, 'I never knew you. Away from me, you evildoers!'" (Matt 7:21-23).

[3] Elmer Towns and Douglas Porter, *From Pentecost to the Present: The Ten Greatest Revivals Ever* (Nashville: Thomas Nelson, 2000), 13-15; Williams J. Larkin Jr., *Acts*, IVP New Testament Commentary Series (Downer Grove, IL: InterVarsity Press, 1995), 48-50.

of Jerusalem's earliest apostolic community.[4] The descent of the Spirit came as a fulfillment of the promise of Jesus Christ that the Holy Spirit would succeed him after the consummation of his career on earth through his resurrection and ascension (Luke 24:46-49; Acts 1:4-8). In John 14-16 (often referred to as the Upper Room Discourse), Jesus taught a great deal about the ministerial nature of the Holy Spirit after the completion of his (i.e., Jesus') mission.[5] With this teaching in mind, contemporary Pentecostals consistently emphasize spiritual power, spiritual gifts, and teachings concerning the Holy Spirit.

In Pentecostalism, therefore, predominant emphasis is afforded to the personal experience of God through the Holy Spirit. Specifically, Pentecostal groups seek to reenact the descent and baptism of the Spirit upon the early disciples as recorded in Acts 2:1-4. E. A. Livingstone defines Pentecostalism as "a religious movement whose members . . . share a common belief in the possibility of receiving the same experience and gifts as did the first Christians on the day of Pentecost in Acts 2:1-4."[6] H. C. Achunike shares Livingstone's definition when he maintains that the term "Pentecostalism" refers to certain elements of the Christian life often associated with the experience of the power of the Holy Spirit that manifested strongly at the feast of Pentecost in the Bible and in the consequent gifts of the Holy Spirit by Christ.[7]

The Acts 2:1-4 periscope, depicted and referred to by Livingstone and Achunike above, is central to the claims of Pentecostal Christians, who desire to reenact the spiritual event as it originally occurred in the apostolic church at Jerusalem in the first century. Even though

[4] R. Kent Hughes, *Preaching the Word Acts: The Church Afire* (Wheaton, IL: Crossway, 1996),29.

[5] Adeyanju, "A Critical Examination of the Emergence of Pentecostalism and the Diversity of its Practices in Nigeria," 13.

[6] E. A. Livingstone, ed., *The Concise Oxford Dictionary of the Christian Church* (Oxford: Oxford University Press, 1977), 86.

[7] H. C. Achunike, *Catholic Charismatic Movement in Igboland 1970-1995* (Enugu, Nigeria: Fourth Dimension, 2009), 35.

Pentecostals place emphasis on speaking in tongues as they try to reproduce this event exactly, they do not emphasize the "sound from heaven, as of a rushing mighty wind," which they have not been able to produce.[8] Achunike describes Pentecostalism as referring to "the emphasis on the Third Person of the Trinity and His manifestations in the individuals and corporate lives of Christians."[9] Hence, the Pentecostal emphasis here is that every believer—all over the world—should have the same experience with glossolalia (i.e., speaking in tongues). Glossolalia plays a communicative and demarcative role in the lives of Pentecostal Christians. It is used among Pentecostal members to testify to the "conformity" of the believer to the community's requirements and for individual members' involvement in their relationship with God.[10]

In African Traditional Religion, the concept of speaking in other tongues when in the "high-spirit" during worship and celebration times is well known. Of course, the source of these tongues is surely not the Holy Spirit. Hence, when the Nigerian Neo-Pentecostal gospel emphasizes speaking in tongues as a must for everybody, most converts seem to find a substitute for the old practice.[11] For example, Chris Oyakhilome, the president of Christ Embassy (a.k.a. Believers' Love World), in his teaching on speaking in tongues, maintained that "there are miracles you cannot receive from God until you are able to speak in tongues." He added, "Human prayer in human language cannot go far enough. Because, human languages are corrupted, and will not appeal to the holy God."[12] Daniel Iselaye, in his own opinion, points out that Oyakhilome's teaching here is heretical because, in the early church during the days of the apostles, everyone did not speak in tongues (1 Corinthians 12:29-30).[13]

[8] See Achunike, *Catholic Charismatic Movement in Igboland 1970*-1995, 35-37.
[9] Achunike, *Catholic Charismatic Movement in Igboland*, 35.
[10] Adeyanju, "The Emergence of Pentecostalism in Nigeria," 17.
[11] Adebiyi, interview by the author, Louisville, KY, January 25, 2020.
[12] Chris Oyakhilome, "The Benefits of Speaking in Spiritual Tongues," *Online Teaching* accessed April 28, 2020 at https://www.youtube.com/watch?v=MhhXazexrM8.
[13] Daniel Iselaye, interview by the author, October 25, 2019.

Michael Green writes, "A Tongue is a gift from the good Lord to some people. . . . But as we have seen, there is no suggestion in any of the initiation teaching of the New Testament that it is the invariable mark of the presence of the Spirit."[14] Hence, to consider speaking in tongues as a mark of genuine conversion or a sign of spiritual maturity lacks biblical support. Most Nigerian evangelicals see speaking in tongues as the least of the spiritual gifts, and it does not define one's true Christian identity, as Neo-Pentecostals suppose. According to Ponle Segun Alabi, the director of Covenant of Peace Evangelistic Association (COPEA), in his exegetical analysis on speaking in tongues,

> The Corinthians have been told they were carnal (1 Cor. 3:3), immature or babies (1 Cor. 3:1), AND not wise (1 Cor. 1:26)—yet they could speak in tongues. What part of their lives was being edified and how much of that edification is glorifying to the Church? So, before you make yourself out to be a super Christian because you speak in tongues—see it here, it does not the Church in Corinth superior to the Berean's Church. We do not forbid speaking in tongues, but we seek the greater gifts that edifies the Church and promote that when speaking. Speaking and non-speaking in tongues is not our gospel—Jesus Christ who died and rose again. Did all speak in tongues in the New Testament Church? Listen to the Bible answer: "All do not have gifts of healings, do they? All do not speak with tongues, do they? All do not interpret, do they?"—1 Cor. 12:30. It's in your Bible—check it.[15]

Iselaye maintains that what some people claim to be the workings of the Holy Spirit are actually those things that are falsifiable, yet people

[14] Michael Green, *Thirty Years That Changed the World: A Fresh Look at the Book of Acts* (England: InterVarsity Press, 2002),259.

[15] Ponle Segun Alabi, "The Exegesis of Jude 20: Speaking in Unknown Tongues and Praying in the Spirit" (lecture, Ajilete Discipleship Center, Ogbomoso, Nigeria, February 6, 2020).

think they can use such claims as yardsticks to measure one's spirituality, such as in the case of speaking in tongues and anointing. Such practices are similar to African Traditional Religion, so many worshippers feel at home.[16]

Emphasis on Healing

Similarly, 100 percent of Neo-Pentecostal respondents agree that when presenting the gospel, Nigerian Neo-Pentecostals over-emphasize physical healings. Furthermore, renowned Nigerian evangelical scholar Roland S. Babatunde has challenged the Nigerian Neo-Pentecostal doctrine that maintains that a believer must not be sick or experience any suffering because Christ has paid it all:

> Many Christians so persistent in teaching that if you are sick or economically poor, it must be a result of your personal sin. It can be but it is not always so because this world detests the things and people of God. The more intentional and persisted a person serves God; the more trials he would face. Fortunately, we always triumph in the name of the Lord whether in life or death. Either of the two will bring glory to God if he so desire (Rom 8:18-39). No Christian has the mandate to use a biblical passage to support his view at the detriment of relevant passages on the subject.[17]

To Nigerian evangelicals, whenever Christians pass through the challenges of physical ailments, such challenges are not the result of a lack of faith or a lack of the Holy Spirit in them; instead, oftentimes, God permits such situations as trials of faith. Moreover, apart from being tried and persecuted for aligning with Christ, Christians share in suffering with the entire creation in anticipation of future glory (Rom 8:18-27).[18]

[16] Daniel Iselaye, Google Forms survey, October 25, 2019.
[17] Roland S. Babatunde, *The Faith of our Fathers: Feared Not Sword and Fire* (Ilorin, Nigeria: Tanimola Press, 2014), 20.
[18] Babatunde, *The Faith of our Fathers: Feared Not Sword and Fire*, 20.

Moreover, Conrad Mbewe observes that in Africa, the noise of miracles and healings has been blown beyond proportion among Neo-Pentecostals than the reality of miracles and healings that are witnessed. In light of this, Mbewe seems to make a sarcastic statement with respect to the present COVID-19 pandemic:

> I know I'll get into trouble for saying this, but as a shepherd over my sheep, I need to point out the elephant in the room while the COVID-19 pandemic lasts. One of the loudest calls in the last few years has been that of so-called faith healers who have claimed to have the power to miraculously heal the sick "in the name of Jesus." Their voices have been very loud on radio, on television, on the internet, and on billboards, despite the lack of verifiable evidence. Here comes COVID-19 and they have all gone deathly quiet, while over 100,000 people have died due to the pandemic. What kind of Christian love is this? Surely, this is the time for them to go to the epicenters of this disease and miraculously heal those who are on ventilators fighting for their lives. They cannot just go quiet.[19]

Further challenging so-called faith healers (that is, the elephant in the room), Mbewe points attention to the compassionate heart and healing ministry of Jesus:

> When Jesus was on earth, leprosy was contagious and incurable. You did not touch lepers. They were quarantined outside the community and could only be allowed back into society upon being verified as healed by local priests. Jesus touched the lepers and miraculously healed them. He would then send them to priests for verification and reintegration in society. In the name of love, may those who claim to have similar powers go and heal

[19] Conrad Mbewe, *19 Pastoral Thoughts on COVID-19* (Luzaka, Zambia: Ever Green, 2020), 21.

the COVID-19 victims! If the health workers do this alone—at great risk to their lives—let us not hear anyone claiming to have miraculous powers to heal the sick after COVID-19 is over.[20]The truth remains that the news of healing is too louder than the reality of healing among the African Neo-Pentecostals. Hence, Christendom must return to the true and thorough teachings of the Bible. Christian teachers must stop promoting vices, such as riches, at all costs (1 Tim 6:1-10) and, instead, should promote worthy character and godliness.[21]

Emphasis on Miracles

According to my research findings, Nigerian Neo-Pentecostals always present the gospel by making people believe that signs and wonders are waiting for them once they embrace the gospel. Hence, 100 percent of Neo-Pentecostal respondents agree that in the course of presenting the gospel, Nigerian Neo-Pentecostals convince people of the miracles that await them once they come to Christ. When the gospel is presented in a way that makes recipients focus their minds on miracles, there will be high rate of false converts who do not desire to know the true Savior. Scripture does not encourage believers to concentrate on signs, wonders, and miracles when they are presenting the gospel.[22] While not denying the reality of miraculous occurrences in Christendom as God deems them necessary, Nigerian evangelicals disagree with Nigerian Neo-Pentecostals on two points concerning this issue: the normativism of miracles (as they were in the days of the apostles) and the placement of miracles as the central focus in evangelism.

[20] Mbewe, *19 Pastoral Thoughts on COVID-19*,21.

[21] Babatunde, *The Faith of Our Fathers*, 20.

[22] In the Gospel of Luke, the disciples of Jesus return from a witnessing exercise filled with amazement because of the signs and wonders they experienced while on the field, but Jesus blatantly tells them, "Do not rejoice that the spirits submit to you but rejoice that your names are written in heaven" (10:20).

Sunday Adelaja, a renowned Nigerian charismatic pastor in Ukraine, challenges Nigerian Neo-Pentecostals on the issue of seeking after miracles. He brings up research conducted in America in 2016 that claimed that more than 661,000 Americans have kidney failure. Of these, 468,000 individuals are on dialysis, and roughly 193,000 live with a functioning kidney transplant. In Nigeria, statistics revealed that 25 million Nigerians have kidney failure, and out of this number, about 18,000 will need dialysis every year. If these 18,000 Nigerians needing dialysis or a kidney transplant decide to go to miracle-workers to seek healing, instead of going to the hospital, they will surely die of kidney failure—not because God cannot heal but because God has given wisdom to doctors to be able to manage diseases with modern medical procedures. (This, too, is a display of God's mercy and miraculous working). Now, one may say, 'But I know one pastor who heals people.' Well, that may be true, but how many does he heal per year? If one does the statistics and compares them with how many people are treated in hospitals by doctors per year, one will be amazed by the difference. The simple reason simply is that spiritual miracles are not an everyday occurrence; hence, one should not spend one's whole life seeking after them. It is wise to trust the doctors to whom God has given the wisdom to heal.[23]

Again, miracles are God's interventions. It is what God does at will. No man or woman can hold God to ransom for doing or not doing a miracle. One may receive a miracle and yet may not know or understand God. The people of Israel, more than any nation, received miracles from God, yet they failed to know God. For forty years, they ate miraculous food from God and still did not know him. God showed His acts to them, but His ways were only discovered by one man, Moses.[24]

---

[23] See Adelaja, *How the Church Creates Economic Recession*, 29-30.
[24] Adelaja, *Damaged by Religion*, 90-91.

Emphasis on Breakthroughs

Nigerian Neo-Pentecostal churches highly esteem prayers for breakthroughs, which are seen as sudden fortunes or riches that come upon people in response to the prophetic prayers of spiritual leaders on behalf of their members.[25] Hence, breakthrough messages center on acquiring massive riches without stress or sweat (i.e., instant gratification); they are messages that expect an effect without a cause.[26] Some churches have weekly, bi-weekly, or monthly anointing services for breakthroughs. According to Amiable Abiodun, "During these services, members queue in front of the pastors, who come with olive oil (anointing oil) in bottles to anoint members as a way of connecting them with their breakthrough. Moreover, getting visas to travel to foreign countries, such as the US, UK, and Canada, is seen as a huge breakthrough."[27]Gary Maxey and Peter Ozodo clearly write,

> It is to be feared that in the modern Nigerian Church much of the membership have come to the conclusion that Christianity is basically about material prosperity. Wealth is in many sectors projected as a sign of spirituality. Faith in Christ is quantified most readily in material terms. On the other hand, poverty is a curse. Churches with those messages are attracting ever-larger audiences as they focus messages on how to "prosper" and to get their next "breakthrough." Scriptures that focus on self-sacrifice, self-denial, the cross, sin and holiness are seldom used. When members of such churches "prosper," almost never does anyone ask after the genuineness of their sources of wealth.[28]

For instance, the followers of several prosperity preachers in Nigeria

[25]Akin Aniyikaiye, interview by the author, Louisville, November 21, 2019.
[26] For more discussion on this issue, see Sopuru, *Modern Theology versus Biblical Theology*, 6-9.
[27] Amiable Abiodun, interview by the author, Egbe, Nigeria, October 19, 2019.
[28] Maxey and Ozodo, *The Seduction of the Nigerian Church*, 115.

have been convinced by their general overseers' teaching that "the anointing paves the way for wealth."[29] Of the Neo-Pentecostal survey respondents, 96.7 percent maintain that converts are attracted to Nigerian Neo-Pentecostal churches because of their passionate desire to experience breakthroughs in life. Indulgence in this regard not only has affected the quality of church growth in Nigeria but also has had a negative effect on the economic growth of the nation. Nigerian Neo-Pentecostalism is breeding followers who run after instant gratification instead of accepting hard work and personal responsibility. If this trend continues, it will result in a nation of indolent people who desperately run from one church to another in search of miracles.[30] Nigerian pastors who convince their members to wait for miracles of money (i.e., financial breakthroughs), when such members do not work or engage in any business transactions, are simply saying that people can reap where they have not sowed. It is a message of effect without a cause, which encourages idleness and laziness.

As Adelaja correctly writes,

> There is hardly a church in Africa and especially in Nigeria today that does not organize miracle and breakthrough services. Some churches have what is called "31 days' miracle and breakthrough services." Others have services like "one-month prophetic encounter service" and so on. All of these attract a lot of people including civil servants, businessmen, laborers and various citizens from different sectors of the nation. Some of these miracle seeking individuals actually abandon their jobs and works to attend these miracle and breakthrough services . . . . Can you imagine how many inventions would have been invented if we spent those thirty or sixty days of miracle services

[29] To these members, when one is anointed by the Holy Spirit, wealth is a companion of this anointing. See David Oyedepo, *Anointing for Breakthrough* (Lagos, Nigeria: Dominion, 2014), 150.

[30] Adelaja, *How the Church Creates Economic Recession*, 33.

in the laboratories doing research?[31]

If millions of Christians in Nigeria invested some of these days in research exercises to discover solutions and cures to some of the problems plaguing the nation, then Nigeria, as a whole, would have been better off.[32]Adelaja writes, "Miracles and Breakthrough are good, but unfortunately, researchers have found out that after many years of research, that neither of them is part of the factors that enhance the economic growth of a nation."[33]

In emphasizing the necessity of breakthroughs, Nigerian Neo-Pentecostals are proclaiming the gospel as the means to a life of earthly success. The Nigerian Neo-Pentecostal gospel promises its adherents success. In his book *Success Strategies*, Oyedepo describes God's kind of success this way:

> A faith-based journey through the scripture makes it abundantly clear that the God-kind of success enjoyed by the patriarchs (riches without sorrow; Proverbs 10:22) is the kind of success that is available and only attainable in the kingdom. It is having the good life without any strain, no stress or strife—success that only comes from above. It does not come with nightmares, but with good sleep, *for the Lord giveth his beloved sleep* (Psalm 127:2).[34]

If one goes by this definition of success (that is, a state free of any strain, stress, strife, or nightmare), then all of the apostles of Jesus Christ who faced persecution and, therefore, died were a bunch of failures. In 2 Corinthians 11:23-27, the apostle Paul highlights some of ordeals he faced during his attempts to spread the gospel:

---

[31] Adelaja, *How the Church Creates Economic Recession*, 36.

[32] Over eight-five million people in Nigeria belong to various church denominations. Sadly, the majority of them spend most of their time praying and asking God for miracles and breakthroughs daily and weekly. See Adelaja, *How the Church Creates Economic Recession*, 35.

[33] Adelaja, *How the Church Creates Economic Recession*, 33.

[34] David Oyedepo, *Success Strategies* (Lagos, Nigeria: Dominion, 2003), 6 (emphasis original).

> Are they servants of Christ? I'm talking like a madman—I'm a better one: with far more labors, many more imprisonments, far worse beatings, many times near death. Five times I received the forty lashes minus one from the Jews. Three times I was beaten with rods. Once I received a stoning. Three times I was shipwrecked. I have spent a night and a day in the open sea. On frequent journeys, I faced dangers from rivers, dangers from robbers, dangers from my own people, dangers from Gentiles, dangers in the city, dangers in the wilderness, dangers at sea, and dangers among false brothers; toil and hardship, many sleepless nights, hunger and thirst, often without food, cold, and without clothing. (CSB)

Even the patriarchs themselves faced lots of challenges in their journeys. Over the first three centuries of the Christian era, it is estimated that as many as two million Christians died for their faith. Journalist John Allen reports that Christians today are indisputably the most persecuted religious body on the planet. One scholar estimates that 90 percent of all people killed on the basis of their religious beliefs are Christians.[35]

> The climax of Nigerian Neo-Pentecostals' teaching on success assures followers that they can reach a certain stage in their journey of faith when they will no longer experience any struggle or strife—a state of perfect ease.[36] In addition, Oyedepo maintains,the struggle, which actually started in Genesis, has since continued and will only terminate when you are redeemed. Therefore, struggle for survival is a curse that came upon mankind after the fall. Man was not created for struggle, but became a victim of struggles as a result of the curse of God placed upon him

[35] Jim Denison Forum, "The latest on the building collapse in Florida: Three biblical ways to prepare for an uncertain future", June 25, 2021.

[36] See more in Gbeminiyi Eboda, *Accelerate Your Success Rate* (Lagos, Nigeria: Move Your World International, 2013), 79-81.

> at the fall. Sweat is a curse and it represents struggle for survival. In the book of Genesis 3:17-19 (where the word *sweat* first came to light) sweat connotes hardship . . . . If you are born again, you have been redeemed from the curse of struggles.[37]

Contrary to the way Nigerian Neo-Pentecostals view success, success is fulfilling God's intended purpose on earth, which may sometimes consist of hardship and strife, but the help of the Holy Spirit brings assurance and victory.[38] Coupled with Nigerian Neo-Pentecostals' misconstrued teaching on the biblical concept of success is their teaching on the "kingdom of God," Oyedepo, in his book, *Exploits of Faith*, maintains that the mission of faith is to bring heaven down to earth. In his faith confession, Oyedepo writes,

> I would like to make this confession of faith: I'm set to create my heaven, to make Jesus real on the earth in His resurrected form, where sickness, disease and failure couldn't touch Him, giving Him a name above all names. Whatever cannot depress, molest or oppress Jesus cannot come near me, because the Word is near me in my mouth and in my heart, even the Word of faith. I am here on earth to make Jesus real in character, charismas, results and in signs and wonders.[39]

There are many other preachers of the "heaven-on-earth gospel." Chris Oyakhilome's teachings center on the ability of believers to live exactly like Christ and to create another heaven on earth, where there are no pains, no sicknesses, and no troubles of any kind. Late Myles Munroe, from the Bahamas, was another popular preacher of the "heaven-on-earth gospel," and his theological point of view has influenced a lot of Nigerian Neo-Pentecostal leaders. Munroe's popular emphasis was that

[37] Oyedepo, *Success Strategies*, 17-18.

[38] Babatunde, *The Faith of our Fathers*, 21-23.

[39] David O. Oyedepo, *Exploits of Faith* (Lagos, Nigeria: Dominion, 2005), 215-16.

believers can establish the perfect kingdom of Christ on earth exactly as it is in heaven. This remained his central message before he passed away in a plane crash in 2014.[40]

The truth is, however, that if we could create our own heaven on earth as perfectly as it is in heaven, then there would be no need for the new heavens and new earth as mentioned in Revelation 21. But the fact remains that we are all living on the earth that is still groaning, waiting for its redemption (Romans 8:21-23). Furthermore, Jesus rightly says, "I have told you these things, so that in me you may have peace. In this world you will have trouble. But take heart! I have overcome the world" (John 16:33). As long as we still live here in this fallen world, we are equally not excepted from its ripple's effect.

Deliverance-Focused Gospel

According to my research findings, 100 percent of Neo-Pentecostal survey respondents agree that Nigerian Neo-Pentecostals place much emphasis on deliverance in their gospel presentations. The reason for this emphasis is not far-fetched. African Traditional Religion has a concept that the whole world is full of spirits. The only good spirit is that which comes back to be born again. So, the entire life cycle is dominated by fear. The graveyard is believed to be filled with the spirits of the dead roaming about. Since people bury their dead inside their compounds or backyards, places of fear are numerous.[41] Some rocks, mountains, rivers, and certain trees (e.g., baobab and mahogany) are believed to have spirits dwelling in them. Sacrifices are offered to these objects to pacify the spirits since people live at their mercy.

---

[40] See Myles Munroe, *Rediscovering the Kingdom: Ancient Hope for our 21st-Century World* (Shippensburg, PA: Destiny Image, 2004), 139-141.

[41] Byang Henry Kato, "A Critique of Incipient Universalism in Tropical Africa," (PhD diss., Dallas Theological Seminary, 1974), 78. For further reading, see Richard J. Gehman, *African Traditional Religion in Biblical Perspective* (Kaduna, Nigeria: Baraka Press, 2000), 34f.

In some communities, at the beginning of the harvest season people place their first fruits at tombs or at the bottom of spirit-indwelt trees before consumption begins. Failure to carry out this practice can cause a person or community to incur the wrath of the spirits (gods), who, in return, can bring about afflictions such as diarrhea, measles, and drought. The spirits not only bring sicknesses upon a community; they also possess certain persons in a community and enable them to carry out certain—usually evil—supernatural acts.[42] Hence, the average person in most places throughout Nigeria (or Africa) is always seeking deliverance and protection from evil forces. As a result of a lack of discipleship after conversion, the same concept of fear of spirits is present within Christian churches.[43]

Hundreds of thousands of people flood the churches of some of the pastors who specialize in deliverance. One of the most well-known and well-respected deliverance pastors in Nigeria is Daniel K. Olukoya, the founder and president of Mountain of Fire Ministry (MFM). As Richard Burgess writes,

MFM describes itself as a "do-it-yourself Gospel Ministry" and promotes "violent prayer" as the solution to "stubborn problems." According to Olukoya, "the only language the devil understands is the language of violence and resounding defeat," and he exhorts his followers to "fight until every foe is vanquished and Christ is Lord indeed." Because of its emphasis on protecting and delivering people from the activities of malicious spirits, Afe Adogame, suggests that it should be classified under the rubric of the "security gospel" rather than the "prosperity gospel" movement.[44]

[42] Kato, "A Critique of Incipient Universalism in Tropical Africa," 78-79.

[43] In the worldview of African religion, life is often explained with reference to religion and the spirit world. See John S. Pobee, *West Africa: Christ Would Be an African Too* (Geneva: World Council of Churches, 1996), 10.

[44] Burgess, "Nigerian Pentecostal Theology," 37. See also Daniel Olukoya, "Praying for a New Beginning," in *The Prayer and Deliverance Bible* (Lagos, Nigeria: MFM Ministry, 2007), 1-157.

Many of MFM's prayer captions always center on warfare, battle, deliverance, and the like:

> One of Olukoya's many publications, entitled "Prayers to destroy diseases & infirmities," is described as a "spiritual warfare manual specifically targeted at destroying diseases and infirmities." Another, entitled "Dominion Prosperity," promises to lead believers "out of the dungeon of poverty" and place them "on the mountain top of prosperity." . . . Other titles, such as "Dealing with Local Satanic Technology," "Overcoming Witchcraft," "Power against Marine Spirits," and "Dealing with the Evil Powers of your Father's House," reflect the church's preoccupation with deliverance from witchcraft and evil spirits, as well as past associations with "occult" powers and traditional religious culture.[45]

MFM's publications are full of elaborate liturgies of prayers specifically designed to liberate Christians from demonic powers and afflictions and to remove obstacles to individuals' progress, success, and prosperity.[46] This type of ministry can sell best in places like Nigeria and some other parts of Africa where there is no access to good hospitals, high levels of illiteracy, and systemic abject poverty. According to Burgess, "In several occasions, members are encouraged to combine repetitive recitation of prayers with violent bodily movements in order to dislodge evil spirits that have gained access through ancestral covenants, witchcraft or idols."[47] At MFM's headquarters in Lagos, a single worship service can host over 200,000 people. However, from the

[45] Burgess, "Nigerian Pentecostal Theology," 37. See also Daniel K. Olukoya, *Strange Enemies, Strange Prayers* (Lagos, Nigeria: MFM Press, 2019), 1-100; Olukoya, *Mountain Top Life: Daily Devotional* (Lagos, Nigeria: MFM Press, 2019), 1-376; Olukoya, *The Hour of Freedom* (Lagos: Battle Cry Christian Ministries, 2014), 1-60; Olukoya, *Prolong Your Life* (Lagos, Nigeria: MFM Press, 2013), 1-29; Olukoya, *Power for Explosive Success* (Lagos, Nigeria: MFM Press, 2005), 1-74.

[46] When addressing the need of deliverance after salvation for the ministers of the gospel themselves, Daniel Olukoya writes, "You cannot minister effectively and have your services approved by God, if you fail to obtain deliverance in certain vital areas of life and ministry. . . . Ministers of the gospel should also be made conscious of the indispensable nature of personal and ministerial deliverance as a criterion for success and holistic living." See Daniel K. Olukoya, *When the Deliverer Needs Deliverance: Deliverance Manual for Ministers and Church Workers* (Lagos, Nigeria: MFM Press, 2007), 7.

[47] Burgess, "Nigerian Pentecostal Theology," 37.

biblical point of view, the power to set free anyone who has received the gospel lies in the gospel message itself. Jesus emphasizes this point in John 8:32: "You shall know the truth, and the truth shall set you free." When the gospel is well presented and accepted, it brings deliverance from sin and the oppression of Satan without any need for the laying on of hands by any professional deliverance minister.

Unfortunately, people lose their lives daily by going to pastors for deliverance and engaging in ruthless religious activities. For instance,

> While some people are told to fast endlessly for deliverance, others are forced to eat things that are not healthy for them. Some are forced to live in churches for an extended period of time. People do crazy things that they are told to do by their pastors in the name of deliverance. In the process, many people have lost their lives. I have deliberately included newspaper reports and police reports of some incidences of churches in Nigeria as evidence. . . . You can begin to see the extent of damage that have been created by religion in Africa, especially in Nigeria. On July 4, 2017, a popular Nigerian newspaper reported the death of three people in a church in Warri Nigeria during deliverance.[48]

People are full of every form of ignorance and fail to know that no church leader, preacher, or evangelist has in him the monopolistic power to deliver people from curses and the menaces of life. Christ alone accomplished this feat on the cross. Hence, Christ Jesus must be the central focus of every gospel proclamation. Daniel Sopuru remarks that as evangelicals, "we preach the gospel by saying, accept Christ as your Lord and Personal Savior, then your sins will be forgiven, and you will have the indwelling of the Holy Spirit who will enable you to live Christ-like life."[49]

---

[48] Adelaja, *Damaged by Religion*, 33-34.
[49] Daniel O. Sopuru, Google Forms survey, October 18, 2018.

Chapter 9
Ten Major Factors Characterizing Nigerian Neo-Pentecostals' Gospel (Part 2)

"*. . . For such people are not serving our Lord Christ, but their own appetites. By smooth talk and flattery, they deceive the minds of naive people*" (Romans 16: 17-18)

Emphasis on Anointing and Power

According to Nigerian Neo-Pentecostals, tarry meetings are needed for the endowment of anointing and power from the Holy Spirit. For example, on a monthly basis, the Redeemed Christian Church of God (RCCG) observes what is called a "Holy Ghost Service," where hundreds of thousands of members gather at the RCCG Redemption Camp to keep a vigil, with the expectation of receiving the power and anointing of the Holy Ghost, as "Daddy Adeboye" administers them to attendees. During this kind of gathering, which happens among all Nigerian Neo-Pentecostal churches, people are anointed with oil. They also participate in "Holy Communion," which is expected to break all yokes and curses of life. This oil (olive oil) is popularly known as anointing oil simply because the ministers have prayed upon the oil, which makes it carry special power for all possibilities. Of course, coming from a fetish background, most converts enjoy visible substances being added to their faith.

Most Nigerian Neo-Pentecostals prefer the name "Holy Ghost" (as seen in the KJV Bible) rather than the name "Holy Spirit."[1] People are

[1] This accounts for why many NNP leaders will not allow their members to use any other translation but the KJV.

anointed with oil on their foreheads as a means of connecting with the power of the Holy Spirit. In his argument on the mystery of the anointing oil, David Oyedepo refers to the anointing oil as "God's life" in a bottle:

> The anointing oil is a mystery of the end time, packaged by God for the endless victory of the saints. . . . It is the Spirit of God, mysteriously packaged in a bottle. It is designed to communicate the power of God, bodily. It is the power of God in your hand, in the person of the Holy Spirit. The anointing oil is the power of God placed in a tangible form in man's hand, to make an open show of the devil. It is what it takes to be out of every grave.[2]

Tunde Bakare, (even though he is being tagged of being a political pastor, who is affiliated with 'All Progressive Congress'—APC), openly criticizes the idea of projecting the 'anointing oil' as 'God's life in a bottle.' According to Bakare, God cannot be caged in a bottle. This practice depicts another vivid form of religious syncretism. The Holy Spirit himself is the giver of power, and he has no need for human or other physical agents to convey this power.[3] In a similar manner, Chris Oyakhilome also opposed the practice of referring to the anointing oil as 'the Holy Ghost in the bottle.' Oyakhilome writes,

> I read a book the other day and the author said that the anointing oil is the Holy Ghost in a bottle. It's not true; it's simply ridiculous. He said that the oil is not a symbol, that it is not figurative. He emphatically declared that the oil is the Holy Ghost in a bottle. I was shocked, "Oh there's no evil force that can come against the oil", he said. "If you have enemies, when they

---

[2] David O. Oyedepo, *Winning the Invisible Battles* (Lagos, Nigeria: Dominion, 2006), 173-74.

[3] Tunde Bakare openly condemned Oyedepo's book as heretical. See Wale Odunsin, "I Tore Oyedepo's Book Because He Said Anointing Oil Is God's Life in a Bottle – Tunde Bakare," *Daily Post* (Nigeria), September 7, 2014. See also Victorson Agbenson, *Moment of Truth: The Compelling Story of Pastor Tunde Bakare* (Ibadan, Nigeria: Safari Books, 2014), 262-66; Chris Oyakhilome, *The Oil and the Mantle* (Lagos, Nigeria: LoveWorld Publications, 1997), 43-6.

come face to face with the oil, something is going to happen." Somebody needed a job and had been rejected. According to the testimony, he anointed his application letter with oil and they accepted him.[4]

In presentation of the gospel, most Nigerian Neo-Pentecostals capitalize on the laying on of hands, material prosperity, speaking in tongues, deliverance, and power. But the abuse of the acclaimed power of the Holy Spirit among Nigerian Neo-Pentecostals has resulted in a quest for "power by all means," money, and popularity. The early apostles never used such tricks and magic in spreading the gospel. Nigerian Neo-Pentecostal religiosity, on the other hand, is full of this kind of belief and practice.

Breaking Generational Curses

Of the Nigerian Neo-Pentecostal survey respondents, 94 percent teach that after conversion, every Christian needs to go to their leader(s) in order to be set free from generational curses.[5] But to evangelicals, when Christ died on the cross, he became a curse for us (Gal 3:3) in order to remove the curse of the law from us. Deuteronomy 28 contains lists of curses attached to the failure to live according to the law. There are curses in the law, but Christ took away those curses when he was hung on the cross. Christ's work erases the fear that a Christian can suffer because of any sin committed by one's ancestors. Every curse was broken by the death of Jesus on the cross.[6] As Zac Poonen correctly avers, "When we

[4] Chris Oyakhilome, *The Oil and the Mantle* (Lagos, Nigeria: LoveWorld Publications, 1997), 38. "People have done to the oil what the children of Israel did to the brazen serpent of Moses. God did not intend for them to use it every time they had a problem. It was his appointed means of healing and delivering them on a particular occasion. But they abused it and began to call on it for every problem." See Oyakhilome, *The Oil and the Mantle,* 38.

[5] Daniel Iselaye, Google Forms survey. See more in Moses Rahaman Popoola, *Freedom from Generational Curses* (Ilorin, Nigeria: Modern Impressions, 2011), 1-19.

[6] John R. W. Stott, *The Cross of Jesus: Study Guide Edition* (Downers Grove, IL: InterVarsity Press,

received Christ as our Lord, every curse was broken. We don't have to live in fear of a generational curse any longer. Instead, we have the opposite—the blessing of Abraham (Gal 3:14). That is why we can now receive the Holy Spirit through faith."[7] Moses Rahaman Popoola puts it this way:

> And through faith in his finished work on the cross, all who believed are redeemed from all "curses" from God and man. Jesus Christ, the Son of God, is the only Redeemer, and Deliverer. There is no man or woman of God who has the anointing or oil to deliver (Luke 4:18-19). Believers are to exercise authority on demonic power based on what Jesus has done on Calvary. Never live your life in a bondage anymore, as if the cross has never taken place.[8]

An African pastor once said in his teaching, "No matter how born again you are, there are some curses in your life that will still remain unbroken unless you go for deliverance." By this statement, he is convincing his audience that they need to come to him for prayer because he is an expert in deliverance ministry. To the Nigerian Neo-Pentecostals, only some special spiritual functionaries are authorized to break some special curses in people's lives. Some of these belief systems are the reason some Nigerians can be seen on mountains tops, prayer camps, and the like praying for their enemies to "die! die!! die!!!"

In addition, some Nigerian Neo-Pentecostal pastors are very quick in attributing the causes of some sicknesses that could be treated in hospitals to 'curses' or 'spiritual attacks (attacks by demons and witches).' People that could have received treatments in hospital are directed to prophets or places of prayers for anointing oil, holy water,

---

2006), 147-48, 335-38. See also Gehman, *African Traditional Religion*, 13-14.

[7] Zac Poonen, *Through the Bible: A Message for Today from Every Book of the Bible* (Bangalore, India: CFC Production, 2016), 744.

[8] Popoola, *Freedom from Generational Curses*, viii.

prayer mantles etc. People need to be reoriented better to be wise in knowing the causes of their ailments as to know the best way to handle them. Many of the prophets and pastors won't use the same anointing oil or prayer mantles they sell to people to treat themselves when they are sick. Rather, they go to the best hospitals around them, or fly out of the country for better treatments. A recent research reveals the life expectancy of Hong Kong as 85 years, Japan as 84 years, Tunisia as 73 years, Morocco as 73 years, Ghana as 64 years. But Nigeria, which is known to be topmost in the list of the most religious countries in the world, and prays more than the countries listed above, has life expectancy of 54 years.[9] Why are demons attacking and killing more people in Nigeria than in Hong Kong and Japan that do not pray as Nigerians do? The truth is ignorance and lack of knowledge kill more than curses, demons, and witches. Someone was right when he said, "China produces over 2 million engineers every year. Africa produces over 10 million pastors every year, yet witches are still disturbing us in Africa."

Emphasis on "Working Faith" (or "Name It and Claim It")

Almost all (94%) of survey respondents agree that Nigerian Neo-Pentecostals place much emphasis on working faith—that is, "name it and claim it." This is similar to the power of positive confession. This type of faith is not necessarily a trust in the living Word of God but an imagination of good things in one's heart; people picture something in their mind and then begin to confess it with their mouth until it manifests. Like the *modus operandi* of yoga transcendental meditation, this type of faith lies in exercising the power of the human soul. This is not the power of the Holy Spirit. People are told to imagine seeing themselves in their dream mansions or latest car. When they register the

[9] Dr Richard Okoye of 'Doctor Savealife Foundation Vision 2025.

picture successfully in their minds, people are told to sow seeds of faith for what they have pictured as they begin to claim it by "faith." Thousands of people have become frustrated after several years of sowing and claiming, yet nothing is forthcoming. People need to be taught how to be more creative so as to contribute to the nation's economy rather than be told to hang onto the empty "name it and claim it" formula that defies the dignity of labor.

Emphasis on Material Prosperity

Majority (about 90%) of survey respondents buttress the point that Nigerian Neo-Pentecostals present the gospel in a way that assures people of material prosperity. Joseph Ezeigbo maintains that "Nigerian Neo-Pentecostals portray evangelistic activity as a means of obtaining wealth and overcoming economic poverty. Many Nigerian Neo-Pentecostals see ministry as a business and employment opportunities,"[10] whereas evangelical churches view evangelism as a means of proclaiming the gospel to the lost and to the dying world. Again, Bakare, a Neo-Pentecostal preacher who always tries to strike a balance in his teachings, writes, "Many [pastors] are not called by God but by their bellies. . . . The church cannot help fighting corruption in the country because it is itself corrupt. If the river is polluted from the fountain it is flowing from, everyone who drinks it will drink poison. The Pastors say what the people want to hear, they no longer talk about sin.[11]" Further Paul Alexander righty observes,

> Pentecostal prosperity preachers on television shows and from behind pulpits around the world claim that a $10 gift will yield $1000. As Gloria Copeland, one of the main proponents of the prosperity gospel, has claimed, "You give $1 for the gospel's sake and $100 belongs to you. You give $10 and receive $1000. Give $1000 and receive $100,000. Give one airplane and receive an equivalence

[10] Joseph Ezeigbo,Google Forms survey, October 23, 2019.

[11] Tunde Bakare, "Pastors Are Turning to Traders," *Sunday Sun* (Lagos), September 25, 2005, 2, 47. See also Maxey and Ozodo, *The Seduction of the Nigerian Church*, 17.

of ten airplanes." She should know; she and her televangelist husband have a $6 million mansion and a $20 million jet.[12]

This misconception has dominated the gospel presentations of Nigerian Neo-Pentecostal preachers. Their emphasis is on a "seed-sowing" gospel as a means of obtaining financial prosperity. Bishop David Oyedepo, who is a close disciple of Kenneth Hagin and Kenneth Copeland,[13] remains one of the promoters of this kind of gospel in Nigeria. In his chapter titled "The Covenant of Prosperity," Oyedepo affirms,

> In the early morning of August 27, 1987, I heard the Lord speak to me while I was on a mission trip to USA. "Get back home and make my people rich." It was so clear, so vivid, so strong that I was on the next available flight back to Nigeria, I had to cancel every engagement that I had in US because I heard that clear word from the Lord. It was not an advice, it was a command; "***Get back home and make my people rich.***" I said to myself, "Who am I? What do I have to enrich anybody? How would they even believe that I am sent to enrich them?" Then God said from His word, "As poor making many rich" (2 Cor. 6:10). "Never mind how you look, go and say what I said." The world is a living witness today that, that mandate was not fake, it came from heaven and its effect shows in the lives of multitudes [sic].[14]

---

[12] Paul Alexander, *Signs and Wonders: Why Pentecostalism Is the World's Fastest Growing Faith* (San Francisco: Jossey-Bass, 2009), 61. Many of the Nigerian Neo-Pentecostals preachers agree with the Copeland's theology of material prosperity and esteem him as their hero.

[13] The New American Pentecostal movement—as championed by Hagin, Copeland, and host of others—has already left indelible marks on the Pentecostal movement in Nigeria. According to Oyedepo, Having been a student of Kenneth E. Hagin for over 20 years, and excitedly following his ministry through his books, one day the Lord showed me a picture of Hagin while in my study room at 5 am and said to me, "Look at this man," and I looked up. He then went on to say, "Pattern your ministry after this man . . . ." I craved the unction upon Hagin so badly that when I was at his meeting in 1986, I said, Lord, whatever makes Hagin Hagin, I want it . . . . As I was looking at him ministering from the gallery where I sat, the power of God fell on me! I broke down in tears, weeping profusely and uncontrollably, and the Lord said, "My son, David, the baton has been passed over to you." (David Oyedepo, *Exploits in Ministry* [Lagos, Nigeria: Dominion, 2006], 269-70)

[14] Oyedepo, *Understanding Your Covenant Rights*, 145-46.

The main issue remains that if the primary purpose of the gospel of Jesus Christ is to make people materially and financially rich, then all of the apostles and early believers in Jesus Christ were a bunch of failures because they were never millionaires and they did not produce millionaires. Throughout the New Testament, the primary focus of the gospel of Christ is never to make people materially and financially rich (see, e.g., Matt 1:23). According to Gary Maxey and Peter Ozodo, "The fact that there are scores of pastors and church leaders within the Nigerian Church who measure personal wealth in millions of dollars, and not less than a half dozen who own private jets, is a staggering and embarrassing indictment against all of us. Virtually none of them have transparent financial accountability to their followers."[15]

Many Nigerian modern days' preachers hold that as soon as you are born again, you have entered into a state of perfect physical health throughout your life. "The state of perfect health is the will of God for all his covenant children. People pride themselves in having private doctors and family doctors but when Jehovah Rapha becomes your personal physicians, you become a living wonder. As far as God is concerned, you are not entitled to either sickness or pains."[16] As one of the respondents pointed out, the vast majority of followers among Nigeria Neo-Pentecostalism are needs-oriented Christians. The faith of these people is anchored on getting "bread" from Jesus. This is similar to what happened in John 6, where a multitude of people were following Jesus with false intentions. Jesus blatantly tells them, "Very truly I tell you, you are looking for me, not because you saw the signs I performed but because you ate the loaves and

[15] Gary S. Maxey and Peter Ozodo, *The Seduction of the Nigerian Church* (Lagos, Nigeria: WATS, 2017),112. Oyedepo is being hailed as the wealthiest pastor in Nigeria (with a total net worth of above $150 million). He has large properties that include about four private jets and foreign houses in countries like the United States, the United Kingdom, and elsewhere. Presently, more than ten NNP pastors have at least one private jet.

[16] Oyedepo, *Understanding Your Covenant Rights*, 117, 120. To the followers of Oyedepo, when one is baptized in the Holy Spirit, one receives the divine power that will liberate him or her from poverty and all manner of sicknesses.

had your fill. Do not work for food that spoils, but for food that endures to eternal life" (vv. 26-27). Among the notable Neo-Pentecostal preachers who always like to strike a balance is Joseph Ali. In his Macedonian call for sound biblical theology and doctrine among his colleagues, Ali notes, "There are some wrong attitudes that have spread among full-gospel preachers today. They stem from the teaching that makes God our 'servant-boy.' Since God exists for man, (as some believe) and not man for God (as it should be), the true Christian value is downplayed in the divine to meet man's temporal needs."[17] This is part of what defines the stupendous growth and expansion of Living Faith Church. The Religious Literacy Project at Harvard University captures it this way:

> Some Pentecostal leaders became wealthy themselves as they directed their services to the wealthy ones, emphasizing a prosperity gospel which holds that faith is the key to prosperity in this world. In so doing these pastors contextualized the privilege of Nigeria's Christian elite and attracted hundreds of thousands of poor and middle-class Nigerians aspiring to greater wealth. This approach provides the foundation for many of Nigeria's mega churches, including the 50,000-seat Faith Tabernacle in Lagos, run by David Oyedopo, Africa's wealthiest pastor.[18]

In a similar way, the RCCG in Nigeria is seen as one of the world's fastest growing churches:

> When Pastor E. A. Adeboye stepped into the sanctuary at Dominion chapel in Stafford, the congregation shook with loudening praise music, waving hands and applause. The 1,000 or so worshippers dropped to their knees and join the Nigerian Pentecostal leader in prayer, spoken in a calm but confident tone, promising blessings to them. They listen to

[17] Joseph Ali, "Balance of Truth" in Mayo Abaya, Peter Ozodo, Joseph Ali, eds, *Earnestly Contending for the Faith: An Agenda for Responsible Christian Leadership*, 2nd ed.(Abuja, Nigeria: Concerned Ministers' Forum, 1999), 29.

[18] Religious Literacy Project, Harvard Divinity School, "Nigeria Pentecostalism," accessed October 19, 2019, https://rlp.hds.harvard.edu/faq/pentecostalism-nigeria.

Adeboye's message, punctuated with hearty rounds of "Amen!" and "Yes, Lord!" And when he left, they lined up to sit in chair where he sat or to lie on the ground where he preached. Adeboye is the General Overseer of the Redeemed Christian Church of God, which numbers as many as 7 million followers in Africa. His church has seen rapid growth across continents, with Texas home to its highest concentration of churches in U.S.[sic][19]

The goal of the RCCG's general overseer Pastor Enoch A. Adeboye (popularly called "Daddy G.O") is to spread this church denomination virally across the entire globe. The RCCG aims at winning at least one member of every family in the world to Christ, with a plan of establishing branch churches at a five-minute walking distance from every home in developing countries and a five-minute driving distance from every home in developed countries. The fact that RCCG has grown beyond the shore of Africa is well noted.[20] For instance,

> The U.S. Census Bureau estimates that 13,000 Nigerians live in Harris County, but local leaders with the Nigerian Foundation say the area could be home to between 50,000 and 100,000 Nigerian adults. Dominion Chapel in Stafford is already one of the church's largest buildings and broke ground Sunday to double its size. The church's North America headquarters are in Greenville, an hour northeast of Dallas. Though most members are Nigerians, they reach out to all people.[21]

---

[19] Redeemed Christian Church of God Open Heavens Assembly, "Redeemed Christian Church of God Is Rapidly Planting Devout Congregations," last modified December 15, 2019, https://rccgopenhea vens.org/2018/12/15/news/redeemed-christian-church-of-god-is-rapidly-planting-devout-congregations/.

[20] Isaac Gbadebo, interview by the author, Louisville, KY, January 30, 2020. According to Gbadebo, an RCCG pastor, "Let's Go a Fishing" is a one-Saturday-a-month aggressive evangelism program that is carried out in all the branches of the RCCG. On this day, every member turns out for house-to-house and street-to-street evangelism. This evangelism day always ends with planting new churches.

[21] Redeemed Christian Church of God Open Heavens Assembly, "Redeemed Christian Church of God Is Rapidly Planting Devout Congregations," accessed December 15, 2019, https://rccgopenhea vens.org/2018/12/15/news/redeemed-christian-church-of-god-is-rapidly-planting-devout-congregations/.

However, in Nigeria, due to the excessive monetary obligations to which this denomination subjected its members, and because of the ostentatious living of many Nigerian Neo-Pentecostal pastors and leaders, this vision of expansion has been subjected to various criticisms. Nigerian lawyer and activist Femi Falana once said to Adeboye, "You are creating business centers, not Churches. This is the danger of religiosity as opposed to spirituality."[22] In agreement with Falana, the Archbishop Emeritus of the Catholic Archdiocese of Lagos, Cardinal Anthony Olubunmi Okogie, "described such branches as 'mere business centers,' insisting that there was indeed no godliness in planting churches close to each other." Osahon Ibizugbe also says, "Having churches everywhere has not resulted into godliness in Nigeria."[23]Further, talking about the pseudo-gospel missionaries in Nigeria, Daniel Sopuru writes,

> In recent times, some professionals and businessmen have established churches with some funny names spreading man-made doctrines in the name of the gospel. They establish branches not only in the width and breath of this country, but in other nations of Africa. They send "missionaries" to those places spreading what they believe is what Christianity should be, while they end up being heralds of pseudo-gospel. The founders of such movements spend huge sums of money to buy up airtime in both radio and television stations convincing people of their dire need of material things and miracles. Most of them use Eastern mysticism embellished with Jesus' Name for personal success and business performances.[24]

[22] Femi Falana, "Pastor Adeboye Creating Business Centers Not Churches," *Punch* (Nigerian newspaper), October 19, 2017.

[23] Olubunmi Okogie, *Allure Magazine*, October 9, 2017, https://allure.vanguardngr.com/2017/10/having-churches-everywhere-have-not-resulted-into-godliness-in-nigeria-cardinal-okogie/.

[24] Daniel O. Sopuru, *Modern Theology versus Biblical Theology: A Call for Biblical Christianity* (Makurdi, Nigeria: Evangelical Christian Literature and Radio Ministries, 2007), 129.

Concerning material prosperity (i.e., the wealth or prosperity gospel), J. D. Greear once wrote,

> Let me be blunt: the prosperity gospel is a lie. God does love to give gifts to his children, and he delights in our successes. But the greatest prosperity is not driving a new car; it is knowing him and having a life that bring glory to him. Preaching a message that says if you come to Jesus, he will make you rich is not only wrong, it leads people to idolatry rather than faith. It leads people to use Jesus, not love him.[25]

Hence, in presenting the gospel, it is unbiblical to bait people into Christianity with promises of wealth and health. Nigerian Neo-Pentecostal leader Emmanuel Onofurho points attention to the excessive flamboyance of his colleagues when he writes, "They are proud and flamboyant in their lifestyle. They are hardly approachable. They can hire and fire staff at will. They own a number of cars when their immediate assistants have none. Their preaching is more emotional than spiritual. When one is asked to sow seed of faith, he ends up sowing into the preacher's pocket."[26]

Sopuru once made a vivid observation on this when he said,

> Take a look at most of the Presidents and Founders of the Contemporary Churches in Nigeria and in Africa; you will notice arrogance, flamboyance, pride, pomposity etc, in their speech and way of life. They make all sorts of unattested claims that place them above any normal human being in the eyes of their Church members. Members invite people to come and meet with

---

[25] J. D. Greear, *Gospel: Recovering the Power That Made Christianity Revolutionary* (Nashville: B & H, 2011), 183.

[26] Emmanuel Onofurho, "Challenges of the End-Time Church" in Mayo Abaya and Others, eds, in *Earnestly Contending for the Faith: An Agenda for Responsible Christian Leadership, Second Edition* (Abuja, Nigeria: Concerned Ministers' Forum, 1999), 55-56.

> their pastors, not with Jesus Christ. They claim their pastors can lessen or eliminate people's burdens. They call them names that Christ alone can bear. One of these "founders" once preached that his name is synonymous with Jesus Christ and that if demons torment you, do not bother calling on the name of Jesus that his own name should be called, and the demons would flee. His members believed him. Is this not arrogance and blasphemy in the highest order?[27]

Sopuru's observation above portrays the clear situation of most Nigerian Neo-Pentecostal churches.

Victory over Enemies

The gospel of Nigerian Neo-Pentecostals promises victory over physical and spiritual enemies. In survey, 96.7 percent of the respondents agree that Nigerian Neo-Pentecostals assure people of their total victory over physical and spiritual enemies once they embrace the gospel. The concept of salvation in African Traditional Religion centers mostly on deliverance from higher human enemies (for example, the domination of a certain ethnic group over another), freedom from the oppression of evil spiritual powers, healing from droughts and epidemic outbreaks, and protection from cosmic disorders or natural disasters.[28] There is no belief in the salvation of human souls after the human fall, neither is there any idea of total depravity brought about by sin. Hence, prior to Christianity, worshippers in the African Traditional Religion sought salvation not from sin but from the evil enigma in the world around them—both physically and spiritually.[29] Moreover, in African Traditional Religion, and according to an African worldview, it is normal for people to run to local priests, herbalists, or spiritualists, who will help them by appealing

[27] Sopuru, *Modern Theology versus Biblical Theology*, 114-15.
[28] See Kato, *Theological Pitfalls in Africa,* 174-6.
[29] Samuel M. Zwemer, *The Origin of Religion*, 3rd ed. (New York: Loizeaux, 1945), 71.

to the spirits or by killing their enemies through charms, incantations, or invocations of evil powers. These sets of people are seen as religious intermediaries or functionaries.

According to J. Kwabena Asamoah-Gyadu,

> Religious functionaries or specialists are people placed in the position of honor due to their supposed closeness to the supernatural world and realities. They are the custodians of esoteric intuition, mystical power or and knowledge that reveal mysterious religious formulae and objects. They occupy central formidable states in religions as the mouthpieces of transcendent deities.[30]

Consequently, when people become Christians, due to improper discipleship, they carry this mentality into their new faith. This reality accounts for the reason that—in many parts of Nigeria—Christians always run to their pastors, prophets, or "men of God," who will help them by praying for the death of their perceived human enemies and by anointing them for victory over their spiritual enemies. Nigerian Neo-Pentecostal leaders easily attract crowds of people with promises of victory over enemies because they are religious functionaries who are seen as mediators. Furthermore, prayer and fasting programs are always scheduled in Nigerian Neo-Pentecostal churches in order to war against both physical and spiritual enemies. All forms of prayers (e.g., "my enemy must die," "die by fire," "holy ghost fire consume them," "burn to ashes") are raised against enemies.

A friend of mine was invited by another friend to his church during its special prayer meeting that was combined with fasting. During the

---

[30] See J. Kwabena Asamoah-Gyadu, "'Blowing the Cover:' Imagining Religious Functionaries in Ghanaian/Nigerian Films," in *Religion, Media and the Marketplace*, ed. Lynn Schofield Clark (London: Rutgers University Press, 2007), 224-43.

course of the prayer, the "man of God" (MOG) said, "It is now time for the business of the day." At this moment, everyone began to open his or her pocket or bag to bring out either a picture or a piece of cloth. They did so because the MOG had told the people on the first day of the prayer to come with any item or material belonging to anyone they know who is their enemy—that is, who is hindering or serving as stumbling block to their progress in life. The pews were filled to the brim as people queued before the MOG, who brought out a bottle of oil and was anointing the people's materials and shouting, "Holy Ghost fire; consume them. Die! Die! Die!" By this act, he convinced those in attendance that their enemies would die between seven and fourteen days.

Adelaja maintains that "because of religion, you could be told your parents are after you and are responsible for your failure, and you will believe it."[31] Scripture, however, maintains that victory over spiritual enemies comes through the finished work of Christ on the cross. As for human enemies, believers are to pray for them and not to curse them.[32] Like the apostles, God may allow believers to be killed by human enemies, or he may not. Hence, believers who die in the hands of their enemies through persecutions die not as a result of any lack of faith (Hebrew 11: 35-40). The danger into which most Nigerian Neo-Pentecostals have fallen is boycotting the real message of salvation and putting these ten emphases (as discussed in this chapter and the previous one) above the message of salvation and personal holiness.

Puzzling Observation

Most Neo-Pentecostal respondents agree that the gospel presented by

[31] See Adelaja, *Damaged by Religion*, 82; Afe Adogame, "Dealing with Local Satanic Technology: Deliverance Rhetoric in the Mountain of Fire and Miracles Ministries," *Journal of World Christianity* 5, no. 1 (2012): 75-101.

[32] Jesus emphasizes this truth during the Sermon on the Mount: "You have heard that it was said, 'Love your neighbor and hate your enemy.' But I tell you, love your enemies and pray for those who persecute you, that you may be children of your Father in heaven" (Matt 5:43-45; cf. Rom 12:18; 1 Pet 3:9).

some Nigerian Neo-Pentecostals fails to fall in line with the true gospel of Jesus Christ. Again, even most of the Neo-Pentecostal respondents believe that the manner in which Nigerian Neo-Pentecostals present the gospel poses a potential danger for the future of Nigerian Christianity. With responses from Neo-Pentecostal respondents themselves, it is reasonable to ask, "Why should these respondents affirm these truths and still remain in those churches?" Or better still, "How can a follower of Nigerian Neo-Pentecostal leaders concede these truths and yet keep following these leaders dogmatically?" The answers to these questions are not far-fetched. First, most of these followers have fallen into the trap of various forms of deception. For instance, Daniel Sopuru writes,

> Contemporary preachers would always crave for the love of their followers. But a closer look into that love shows a self-love, that extorts money from them. "I love you" turns out to be "I love myself and want you." The unsuspicious followers are tricked into believing that they are loved and they give all they have to maintain that seeming love. The New Generation pastors seduce them by promising them all sorts of material wealth. They obey every instruction of the pastors in order to sustain their love and in order to become materially wealthy. This is self in action in modern Christianity, especially among modern Pentecostals.[33]

Second, the ignorance of sound biblical knowledge has led to misinterpretations of several biblical passages. For instance, a former member of one Neo-Pentecostal church says,

---

[33] Daniel O. Sopuru, *Modern Theology versus Biblical Theology: A Call for Biblical Christianity* (Makurdi, Nigeria: Evangelical Christian Literature and Radio Ministries, 2007), 116-17. Sopuru adds, It is clear that the new generation theologians in Christianity are filled with self—a mark of un-regeneration. The natural man only thinks of self. This brings me to the conclusion that all who project self, no matter their influence in the Church, are un-regenerated and need to come to Christ to purge them of self. This set of believers with their flamboyance and self-oriented teachings should think about this. Christ, and Christ alone should be our focus NOT self. (117-18)

> Many Neo-Pentecostal members have been made to believe that all the spiritual leaders are God anointed ones regardless of their immoral dispositions. Hence, to them, the scriptures have fore-warned not to touch God's anointed nor do his prophets any harm (Ps 105:15). This scripture is always quoted out of context as tool for defense both by the Neo-Pentecostal leaders and their followers.[34]

Some Neo-Pentecostal members do not like talking about the errors and character flaws of their leaders due to their fear of God's judgment for "touching the anointed." Third, from a cultural-religious point of view, followers do not question the authority of the leaders. It is commonly believed that the judgment of any religious leader is in God's hands alone.[35] It must be noted that a religion whereby the followers cannot and must not ask their leaders questions is another religion of dictatorship.

Fourth, Precious Kayode maintains that many mega Neo-Pentecostal churches in Nigeria are always centers for commercial activities. As a matter of fact, several members patronizing these places do so with the aim of widening their businesses through targeting more customers.[36] This economic factor is not just limited to business opportunities. The fact remains that Nigerian Neo-Pentecostal denominations provide more job opportunities to youths than other church bodies. Apart from many schools owned by the Living Faith Church, "the church also owns and operates a bakery, bottled water processing plant, petrol station, various restaurants and shopping stores, residential houses, guesthouses, housing estate, and a community and micro-finance bank. As a major economic player, the church provides employment for over 20,000 persons."[37]

---

[34] M. Ademola Adebiyi, interview by the author, Louisville, KY, January 25, 2020.

[35] Love Adebiyi, interview by the author, Ilorin, Nigeria, April 22, 2020.

[36] Anonymous, interview by the author, Ilorin, Nigeria, February 13, 2020.

[37] Afolarin Olutunde Ojewole and Efe Monday Ehioghae, "Leadership and Power in the Pentecostal Movement: Selected Case Studies," in Afolayan, Yacob-Haliso, and Falola, *Pentecostalism and Politics in Africa*, 326. See also Enoch A. A. deboye, *As Pure as Light* (Lagos, Nigeria: CRM Book Ministry,

This reality forms part of the reason why worshippers are glued to these churches.

Fifth, a respondent who confesses that he has attended about four different Neo-Pentecostal churches in the past observes that most modern Pentecostal churches in Nigeria provide an atmosphere of freedom that allows youths to come with all forms of dress and ill-mannered attitudes that many Nigerian orthodox and evangelical churches tag as "immoral dresses and sinful immoral acts respectively." Neo-Pentecostals preach that people can come the way they are, but evangelicals say that while Jesus allows sinners to come the way they are, if sinners have genuinely received the gospel, then they cannot remain the way they were.[38] Hence, the conflict between what is seen as legalism or freedom of worship opens the door for some Nigerian Neo-Pentecostals to seduce and entice large number of followers.

To crown it all, Mike Oye, a Nigerian classical Pentecostal leader, says,

> The main reason why many of the Nigerian Neo-Pentecostal leaders are still having followers is simply because the followers are men and women with itching eyes (2 Tim 4:3) who want approval to their worldliness. The Neo-Pentecostal leaders are the sellers, and their followers are the buyers. The target of these sellers is to meet the demand of their buyers.[39]

Hence, the real problem is with these opportunistic followers; the onus is on the followers, not the preachers. However, this does not negate the fact that these false teachers and preachers will one day have to give an account before God.[40]

1999), 329.

[38] Ezra, interview.

[39] Pastor Mike Oye, interview by the author, Ibadan, Nigeria, April 22, 2020.

[40] Oye, interview.

Chapter 10
Questionable Church Growth Patterns

"Because thou sayest, I am rich, and increased with goods, and have need of nothing; and knowest not that thou art wretched, and miserable, and poor, and blind, and naked" (Rev 3: 17)

According to Luke's record, the early church grew unstoppable after the believers received the power of the Holy Spirit as promised by Christ: "They broke bread in their homes and ate together with glad and sincere hearts, praising God and enjoying the favor of all the people. And the Lord added to their number daily those who were being saved" (Acts 2:46-47 NIV); "But the Word of God continued to spread and flourish" (12:24 NIV); "In this way, the word of the Lord spread widely and grew in power" (19:20 NIV). Further, as Danie Vermeulen writes,

> If the church is a body, then it has all the necessary "DNA" to reproduce after its kind. We can conclude that both Jerusalem and Antioch were "mother" churches. The best example though is the church at Antioch. Through the church planting of Barnabas and more specifically Paul, many churches were reproduced from one local church. The essence of Paul's ministry was the church—his ministry resulted in a church but he undoubtedly expected a multiplication of churches to take place.[1]

From Vermeulen's words, one can deduce that intentionality in establishing new churches ought to precipitate all evangelism strategies. Mark J. Terry writes, "The apostles were very church-oriented in their evangelism. They did not just win persons in isolation; rather, they sought

[1] Danie Vermeulen, *The Process of Planting a Church* (Strubens Valley, South Africa: Dawn Africa, n.d.), 6.

to baptize their converts and gather them into congregations for nurture and mutual encouragement."[2] The combination of Jesus' emphasis in Matthew 28:18-20 and Mark 16:15-16 reveals that evangelistic witnessing ought to result in grooming mature disciples for Christ. Terry also states, "For Paul, faithfulness to the Great Commission meant more than preaching evangelistic messages here and there. It meant completing a sequence of activities that would result in mature churches. We could say without overstating the case that, for Paul, to 'make disciples of all nations' (Matt 28:19) required planting churches."[3] Moreover, according to Vermeulen,

> Jesus' first sermon was to announce the new Kingdom (Matthew 3:2). He said He would build His church and that the gates of Hades would not stand against it. We can therefore conclude that this new Kingdom is made up of churches, that He will subdue the Kingdom of darkness, penetrate it and rescue those in bondage through His church (Colossians 1:18, Ephesians 3:10-11, Romans 5:17). Where the light shines, darkness disappears. When a church is planted within a community, the Kingdom of God arrives in that community—a force directly opposed to the kingdom of darkness, with a vision to fulfill the last Adam's mission, ". . . The reason the Son of God appeared was to destroy the devil's work." (1 John 3:8 NIV).[4]

The early believers, in their church planting endeavors, extended the domain of God's kingdom. Further, as Ellis and Mitchell Roger say, "If a church exists which never thinks about reproducing itself . . . , never expects or anticipates that this is the natural business of growing up, then it is actually sterile."[5]The Word of Jesus Christ himself attests to this

[2] J. Mark Terry, *Evangelism: A Concise History* (Nashville: B&H Academic, 1998), 26.
[3] Terry, *Evangelism*, 5.
[4] Vermeulen, *The Process of Planting a Church*, 7.
[5] Ellis Roger and Mitchell Roger, *Radical Church Planting* (Cambridge, MA: Crossway, 1992), 73.

when Jesus affirmatively expresses, "You did not choose me, but I chose you and appointed you to go and bear fruit—fruit that will last" (John 15:16 NIV).

Further, Patrick Lai writes,

> The ultimate objective of all mission work is to establish God's church where it does not already exist (Romans 15:20). The Nevius model of church planting describes a church as a body of believers who are self-instructing, self-propagating, self-supporting, and self-governing. The development of a strong movement of God in any people group involves three essential steps: evangelism, discipleship, and church planting. Evangelism and discipleship are not ends in themselves. The church is the bride of Christ. Evangelism should lead to a gathering of new believers who come together to form a fellowship, which becomes in time a church.[6]

Lai clearly portrays here that evangelism precedes church planting, and church planting precedes church growth. Still on the issue of bearing fruit through church planting, Stuart Murray says, "Perhaps it would be better to regard reproduction through church planting as normal, and the survival of ecclesiastical structures for more than a couple of generations as abnormal and problematic."[7] However, a balance must be maintained in an attempt to see church growth, or else the temptation of exchanging quality for quantity is very possible. God has a specific plan for every local church in a given location. Studying the growth and life cycle of bonsai trees, Ken Hemphill came up with a book on church growth titled *Bonsai Theory of Church Growth*. According to Hemphill, "It should be recognized from the beginning, that as there are numerous trees, there

[6] Patrick Lai, *Tent Making: Business as Missions* (Waynesboro, GA: Authentic Media, 2005), 154.
[7] Stuart Murray, *Church Planting: Laying foundations* (Milton Keynes, UK: Paternoster Press 1998), 59.

will be many sizes of churches. The giant redwood is not intrinsically better than the diminutive dogwood. Each tree is different, each having its own form, function, and beauty."[8] In Hemphill's opinion,

> Church growth does not mean all churches should or could become very large churches; but a church, as a living organism, should grow to its natural, God given size. When Jesus established the church, as recorded in Matthew 16, He promised He would build His church. Thus, we can say that church growth is at once natural and supernatural. It is *supernatural* because God gives the growth and it is *natural* because the church was created as a living body to grow. The church must grow in such a manner that it fulfills the Great Commission in its own community.[9]

As discussed in chapter 2, Nigerian Neo-Pentecostal churches are not just multiplying within a Nigerian context alone; instead, their growth is cutting across the African continent and the entire globe at large.[10] Hence, research that centers on the critical evaluation of church-planting and church-growth models among Nigerian Neo-Pentecostals is highly needed. The ideal focus of a biblical Christianity is not to fill the pews with members but to fill the world with disciples—genuine converts who will shine as light in the midst of darkness. Having mega churches, with a reliance on money and materialism, can be a great deception and a deviation from the real truth if care is not taken. One ought to know that bigness does not always mean greatness. As stated by a popular professor of missions, a dedicated minority can have a huge impact upon a whole nation.[11]

For example, according to Sunday Adelaja,

[8] Ken Hemphill, *The Bonsai Theory of Church Growth* (Nashville: Broadman Press, 1991), 14.

[9] Hemphill, *The Bonsai Theory of Church Growth*, 14-15 (emphasis original).

[10] Read more in Gary S. Maxey and Peter Ozodo, *The Seduction of the Nigerian Church* (Lagos, Nigeria: WATS, 2017),1-8.

[11] Iselaye, Google Form survey.

> a recent study done on the richest pastors in the world showed that Nigerian pastors are among the top ten richest pastors in the world. The list began with Bishop David Oyedepo of the Living Faith Church being the richest pastor in the world with a net worth of about $150 Million. The general overseer of the Christ Embassy Church, Pastor Chris Oyakilome was found to be the third richest pastor in the world with a net worth of about $50 million. The general overseer of the Redeemed Christian Church of God, pastor E. A. Adeboye was the 5th richest pastor in the world with a net worth of about $39 Million. While the pastor of the synagogue church of all nations, pastor T. B. Joshua was the 9th richest pastor in the world with a net worth of about $10 Million.[12]

According to the findings above, it is pathetic that a country like Nigeria, with thousands of its people wallowing in abject poverty, has four of the ten richest pastors in the world. According to Adelaja, "The question, therefore, is how possible is it for that to be the case. How do world's richest pastors emanate from poverty ravaged economies like Nigeria! The answer is not far-fetched. These Nigerian pastors are rich because of the miracle-centered gospel that they preach."[13] It is not an exaggeration to say that the numerous Neo-Pentecostal churches and their miracle centers have not done much good to biblical Christianity in Nigeria. The reason why Nigeria still has a daily increase in the number of mega churches and more miracle crusades, prayer centers, vigils, and conferences is not that there has been an outbreak of genuine revival but simply that some certain individuals are benefitting from all of these events as they play on the ignorance of others.[14] In regard to these

[12] Sunday Adelaja, *How the Church Creates Economic Recession* (Kiev, Ukraine: Golden Truth, 2018), 177-78.

[13] Adelaja, *How the Church Creates Economic Recession*, 178.

[14] Adelaja, *How the Church Creates Economic Recession*, 133.

individuals, Adelaja writes,

> These individuals are the pastors who have recognized that the church and miracle-gospel is a profitable business. So, let's build more churches and get more money is the mindset of these businessmen called pastors. By building more churches, they have more platforms where they spread the deceptive message of miracles and breakthrough. They know that Nigerians have been brainwashed to always depend on miracles for anything they want in life and are ready to pay any amount of money to get those miracles. Hence, these pastors and their business empires, called churches accrue millions of dollars to themselves by milking many Nigerians dry. Unfortunately, those giving their money to pastors in exchange for miracles are not aware that they are in a business, a business that enriches the pastors and leaves the miracle seekers longing for more and more miracles.[15]

These pastors seem to have made mammon (money) their god, and they seem to go to any length to deceive the masses to rake money out of them. Why are some of them building more mega churches? The reason simply is that they want more money to buy private jets and fund their luxurious lifestyles. The pastors are getting richer as they collect all kinds of monetary seeds and offerings from gullible miracle-seeking Nigerians.[16] It is looking as if the more mega churches exist and grow in Africa; the more there is corruption among church leaders and their looting of innocent but gullible people. Recently, a church denomination sacked some pastors in the denomination on the basis that these pastors failed to meet up with the denomination's "growth index" in their respective local assemblies. the pastors were told to vacate the various accommodations the church has provided for them on immediate effect. The area pastor

[15] Adelaja, *How the Church Creates Economic Recession*, 133.
[16] Adelaja, *How the Church Creates Economic Recession*, 134.

who served these junior pastors their sack letters said, "the reason you people are released is because we are running at a lost. Remember, we are paying your house rents and the halls you use for church services, so if what you are remitting as income is not good enough, it means we are running at a lost." The general overseer openly remarked on this matter saying, "these pastors are unfruitful blatant failure, and we don't have patient for failure in this ministry." To be frank, it is the secular companies that use this type of 'modus oprandi.' This is certainly not the 'growth index' of the New Testament Church. Today, many of the Nigerian Neo-Pentecostal Churches are looking more like business empires disguising as Christian worship centers. The primary target of these churches is to make financial profits.

Seven-Time Children of Hell

Growing up as a son of an evangelical pastor and having pastored with an evangelical denomination for only twelve years, I have seen so many things that baffle me among the youths of my generation. When I was young, I saw that as soon as these new generational churches began in a community, they would erode many of the youths in the evangelical churches in the surrounding area. The messages of these Neo-Pentecostal churches are always "Your church is cold", "Your church does not have the Holy Spirit", "Your church is old school" and, "Leave your church and join ours." With their ministries, they have divided churches, destroyed homes, turned children against their parents, and turned many women against their husbands and in-laws.

Unfortunately, as time has passed, the majority of the youths who fell into these rebellious ways are living in regret today. They recently discovered that they have been deceived. The fact that some church denominations are doing evangelism and planting churches does not mean that they are accepted by God. Remember the word of Jesus to the Pharisees: "Woe to you, teachers of the law and Pharisees, you hypocrites! You travel over land and sea to win a single convert, and when you have succeeded, you make them twice as much a child of hell as you are" (Matt 23:15).

The assertion of Will Metzger deserves double attention:

> Because we are committed to evangelism, we must speak in antithesis at times. If we do not make clear by word and practice our position for truth and against false doctrine, we are building a wall between the next generation and the gospel. The unity of evangelicals should be on the basis of truth and not on evangelism as such. If this is not so, "success" in evangelism can result in weakening Christianity. Any consideration of methods is secondary to this central principle.[17]

Hence, if our gospel proclamation is not based on the truth, then it is not the gospel at all.

[17] Will Metzger, *Tell the Truth: The Whole Gospel Wholly by Grace Communicated Truthfully and Lovingly* (Downers Grove, IL: InterVarsity Press, 2013), 16-17. Metzger was quoting Francis Schaefer's 1966 address to the World Congress on Evangelism in Berlin, Germany.

Chapter 11
Businessmen in the Pulpits

"... *Their destiny is destruction, their god is their stomach, and their glory is in their shame. Their mind is set on earthly things*" (Philip 3: 18-19)

The main problem that Africa is facing presently is not the issue of liberalism that is warring against Western Christianity, though a stage for liberalism is currently in the pipeline. Instead, the central challenge right now is the renaissance of pseudo-Christianity that is characterized by an inordinate pursuit of materialism and financial gain. Becoming a general overseer (G.O) or church owner in Africa has now become one of the fastest ways of amassing quick wealth. Gone are the days when people were running away from ministerial callings because of the commitment and low or sub-standard quality of economic life attached to them.

The apostle Paul mentions "constant friction between people of corrupt mind, who have been robbed of the truth and who think that **godliness is a means to financial gain**" (1 Tim 6:5). It is pathetic today that many have seen the ministerial call as a shortcut to amass wealth. Men whose businesses are not progressing well and those whose secular jobs are not turning a profit turn suddenly to become preachers, prophets, evangelists, and general overseers all because spiritual shepherding in Africa is now one of the most lucrative jobs. In the course of research for this book, there were reports of people who will go and get loans from banks, rent some halls, and then begin churches. As members join these churches, the founders intensify their emphasis on tithing, seed-sowing, and various offerings. Within a short time, they gather all of the money they have raked from innocent prey and then pay off their loans. By doing so, they claim they are "making it" or "having a breakthrough" in ministry. If you see the preaching of the gospel as an express way to obtain quick wealth, then you are a businessman or businesswoman in the ministry. God has not called you; it is your stomach that has called you into a business venture. These kinds of people are the ones in charge of church administration; they are autonomous and make sole decisions without anyone being able to question them.

These kinds of men usually have two type of accounts:

A. A church account where the following collections go:

- Offerings (on Sundays, Wednesdays, and Thursdays)
    - Kingdom offerings
    - Building/project offerings
    - Seed of faith offerings
    - Tithes
    - And more

B. The pastor's account where the following collections go:

- Prophetic offerings
- First fruit offerings
- Anointing oil services collections
- Pastor's and his wife's birthday collections
- Collections during special days (e.g., Father's/Mother's Day, Christmas, Easter)
- Sales
    - From monthly publications (e.g., books, devotionals)
    - CD messages (part 1, 2, 3, etc.)
    - Mantles (e.g., anointing oil, prayer water, prayer cloths)
    - Bands/stickers/calendars with the pastor's photo

Interestingly, the pastors are still not satisfied with the money that goes into their private account; they are still the ones who control the account of the church at will.

When I was growing up in Christ, I remembered hearing a CD message of a particular well-known Nigerian Neo-Pentecostal pastor inside a commercial bus. Upon arriving at the city to which I was headed, I located one of the church's branches in order to buy that particular CD because the pastor was giving a teaching on marriage. When I entered the church's office, the lady who attended to me said that the CD's teaching comes in two parts and that I must buy the two CDs together. Each of the CDs cost ₦500, making a total of ₦1000. Frankly speaking, both messages were less than an hour teaching total and, thus, could be compressed into one CD and sold for ₦150-200 at most (as at early 2000s). However, because of the pastor's desire for excess gain, the message was split, and the price was inflated.

These churches require every member to purchase the pastors' monthly books and publications because the pastors force each cell group to teach from those publications. The prices for these materials are inflated. On top of the sales from all of these publications, some of these pastors still demand monthly salaries. There is no way that one man can collect money by these several means without becoming a millionaire within a short time because in most of these churches, members are put under compulsion to give money. Members are threatened with curses and manipulated with all kinds of gimmicks if they fail to comply with the commandments of their "spiritual leaders."

When these independent church owners rake in all of the money, they proceed to buy land, buy investment shares, build estates, build schools, and seek other means of investing. Over the years, their income multiplies, and they begin to live flamboyantly. They brag before their members, saying that they make their own wealth by their own creativity. They come to the pulpit to say, "Look at what I have achieved; your tithes and offering money cannot buy all of these cars, my building, and my jet. I got them all by my own money". These men have turned churches into money-making factories. The Apostle Paul rightly remarks, "For, as I have often told you before and now tell you again even with tears, many live as enemies of the cross of Christ. Their destiny is destruction, their god is their stomach, and their glory is in their shame. Their mind is set on earthly things" (Phil 3:18-19). Men who see the preaching of the gospel as wealth-making ventures are not serving God but mammon. These men hardly preach about hell, they will not preach about holiness or sanctification, and they will not preach about a life of daily crucifixion. Why? Because they are greedy and want to enjoy the empires they have built. It is never an exaggeration to say that some Nigerian Neo-Pentecostal leaders run their churches like business centers—but perhaps with some biblical principles embedded. They need to repent before it becomes too late. Similarly, it is never an over statement to say that most of the 'fat-pockets' independent church founders in Africa milk the people of God by lying to their congregations on tithes and offerings that go into their personal pockets. Beware of greedy men in the pulpit these days. They aren't serving God but their stomachs. They use God's name and His word to grow rich, yet, they are never satisfied, and always asking for more.

Someone rightly observes, today, pastors function more like CEOs, members are turned into customers, and other churches are seen as competitive organizations. The family members of these pastors are the accounting officers. Evangelism is reduced to marketing and advertisement, whereas, church planting looks more like franchising, and numbers are the primary measure of success. Prayer and Word study is replaced by programs and formulas, preaching sounds more like motivational speaking, time of praises and worships are turned into a mere performance. The saints are entertained instead of equipped; disciples of Christ become papa's sons, daughters, and fans. Church, which supposed to be living body becomes a lifeless body, the pastor becomes the super man, and a human empire is built instead of advancing the kingdom of God.[1] If you are under these patterns, you are in a club not the Church of Christ. Get out before it is too late!

In the New Testament, even when the early church was practicing a common purse, the needs of believers were met on the basis of equity (Acts 4:34-35). No one was pursuing inordinate ambitions or lustful desires. Again, none of the apostles became excessively wealthy by collecting tithes, seeds, offerings, and the like from other innocent believers. Some of the church leaders of today who keep making themselves rich by exploiting gullible minds need to stop this dubious business. History reveals the detrimental ends of many in the past who walked this path. Again, let me make it known that if you are a church member reading this book, beware of the so-called spiritual leader who is after your money and not after the salvation of your soul. Stop aiding fake men and women to expand their personal empires and luxuries. I once listened to a famous Nigerian pastor's preaching and testimony sometime in year 2019. According to this pastor, he prayed for a member of his church and the member won a contract that worth billions of naira. A week after he won the contract, he came to sow a seed of N250 million to the pastor out of the first grant he received for the contract. The issue here is, a man just won a contract which he was yet to execute, yet he has come to sow a seed of N250 million to his pastor; what kind of moral-ethic is the pastor

[1] Anonymous WhatsApp Message on the platform of ECWA Mopa DCC. Received on February 17, 2021.

teaching his members?

One more thing: some white men sold all they had to come to Africa to give us mission schools, clinics, and hospitals free of charge or at reduced costs. Many of today's political bigwigs in Nigeria and rich Neo-Pentecostal leaders benefited from the free education of the white missionaries' mission schools located all over Nigeria. I know a family of white missionaries who sold their lucrative pharmaceutical business and used the proceeds to establish a hospital in Nigeria so that the poor and less privileged could have access to medical treatment. But most of these Nigerian Neo-Pentecostal leaders, after investing their members' money to buy shares for themselves and land properties, use the proceeds to build estates that the poor in their churches cannot afford to rent houses from. They build schools that are only available for the children of rich members, rich politicians, and rich Muslims. Today, we have "more churches than hospitals and schools in Nigeria because, the businessmen-pastors know that they could easily become millionaires without hard work by simply selling miracles and breakthrough to the naïve populace. That is why the easiest way to become a millionaire in Nigeria now is to start a church that is centered on the message of miracles and breakthrough."[2]

Many of the Nigerian Neo-Pentecostal leaders teach that if people sow their seed in the wrong soil, they will not receive a harvest. Hence, they added that if people want to be rich, they must not sow seed to the poor people; they have to sow their seed to people richer than themselves (that is, to a higher anointing). Sometime ago, a Nigerian Neo-Pentecostal pastor bragging about how he sowed a seed of $500,000 to an American multi-millionaire preacher. There are others who pay the tithes of their ministries to big GOs in Nigeria, just as the big GOs in Nigeria pay their tithes to rich foreign G.Os. All the while, there are thousands in their

[2] See Adelaja, *How the Church Creates Economic Recession*, 134-5.

churches from whom they rake their money who are living in hunger on daily basis. The mantra of the Nigerian Neo-Pentecostal—"We too tithe to a higher authority"—is also a manipulating tool or mechanism to enslave followers to pay tithes to them.

One of the grievous evils these men have done in African Christianity is producing followers who are also greedy for money and material things of the world. Those members go on to make money in all kinds of dubious ways. Like begets like; their followers come to church purposely with the mind of "making it" (a phrase in Africa for those who are after breakthroughs at all costs). The devotion of these members to Christ is subject to whether God blesses them with money and materialistic things. These Nigerian Neo-Pentecostal leaders produce followers with questionable lifestyles and questionable salvations. They water down Christianity and allow blasphemy of the name of Jesus Christ to occur among unbelievers. If church founders or preachers are producing followers whose lives do not resemble Christ but who are pursuing money by all means, then, there is a need to ask the question, 'what are the reasons why people are coming into the ministry today?

Other Erroneous Teachings

A popular Nigerian lady preacher is always fond of telling people to raise an altar[3] on behalf of their children by sowing a seed of $1,000. She always tells how all of her children married as virgins and are having good homes. "If you want your children to be like mine," she always remarks, "you need to connect with my anointing by sowing a seed of $1,000 to raise an altar for your children." Some time ago, she added that she will soon buy her own private jet, too. This is pure manipulation and gimmick from the pulpit. Some preachers will say, "Write a check for

[3] 'Raising an altar' in this context is like initiating people to cut a covenant with the Lord through giving huge sum of money as a means to compel God to do what one desires. Hence, it is believed that the money you sow will force or compel God to do what you wish.

$1,000, and your mortgage will be paid off." This, too, is a big lie.

When people tell others that when they give so much to God, it is a must for God to give so much to them in return, then such people only see giving to God as a business transaction. To the contrary, giving to God should be a product of our love for God, who has ever loved us so much beyond what we can ever repay. Some claim that Abraham's blessing is for us. Yes, certainly, Abraham's blessing is ours, but the truth is that the blessing of Abraham is not a mere material possession. The blessing of Abraham is justification by faith. As a matter of fact, Abraham left his home and comfort in his homeland to live in tents all the days of his life as he harkened to the call of God (Hebrew 11: 8-10). Some equally teach that Jesus was a billionaire, who was wearing expensive designer clothes. This, too, is a lie and a false doctrine. Little do they know that Jesus did not take stripes on his back, wear a crown of thorns on his head, have his side pierced, and die on the cross so that in luxury we can drive the latest bullet proof car, live in a $40million house, and fly the latest private jet all around the world. Rather, Christ died on the cross to save all of humankind from the power and guilt of sins. Jesus died to set us free from the grip of covetousness, greed, envy, pride, selfishness, and all forms of lustful desires. Godliness is not a means to financial gain but a means to becoming more and more like Jesus on daily basis. Nigerian Neo-Pentecostal pastor and leaders: stop making Christianity a means of amassing quick riches; stop making your livelihood on the sweat of fellow brothers and sisters in Christ; stop milking the innocent sheep of Christ for your own gain.

Some will surely say, "I am only helping you to move to your next level financially, so, come and sow a seed of money you have never sown before." No! Such people need to stop that fraudulent business. They are only selling Jesus Christ for money—this is scam. They should stop turning the church into a den of robbers where they rob the people of God out of their greediness, for they will give an account to the Lord one day. Souls are dying and going to hell, and you such people are here peddling the Word of God for financial gain?! Repent from this gospel of greed.

Polluted Healing Ministry

A popular healing evangelist recently came to the city where I live here in the U.S. I went to the program because I have long been thirsty to know more of God's power and ability to heal the sick. Many people came there to be healed as well. After the man's teaching, I was expectantly waiting for him to heal the sick. Unfortunately, he made people get envelopes in which to place their seed money (seed is different from a normal offering). For people who needed healings, he made them line up in a queue and told them to hold their seed in one hand before he got to them in order to lay hands on them for healing. So, the sick had to hand over their seed before the evangelist would pray for them.

This preacher ended up calling for about three to four different kinds of offerings that day, and he was not able to make it around to all of the people in the queue, yet everyone had to drop their seed. Honestly, there was no any spectacular healing taking place except that a few people fell on the ground. I knew a brother in the queue who was battling with a stroke in his right hand and leg, and after the program, he is still the same—even to this day. Ever since I came to the U.S. from Africa, I made up my mind that if I could ever see this American anointed man, I would make sure that he lays his hand upon me. But on that day, the Spirit of the Lord told me where I sat, "***If you allow him to lay his hand upon you, you will get your calling and ministry polluted.***" It was a two-day program, and I never ventured to attend the second day. The same man mentors many Nigerian Neo-Pentecostal preachers. Several healing anointing have been polluted by the spirit of mammon. What is the essence of having the power of the Holy Spirit without the character of the Holy Spirit? (You may want to read more in my book *The Baptism of Power: Engaging the Charismatic, Evangelical and Pentecostals on the Holy Spirit*).

Chapter 12
Syncretism among Nigerian Neo-Pentecostals

"Do not be yoked together with unbelievers. For what do righteousness and wickedness have in common? Or what fellowship can light have with darkness? What harmony is there between Christ and Belial . . ." (2 Corinthians 6: 14-15)

About 80 percent of survey respondents agree that the practices of the Nigerian Neo-Pentecostals are syncretistic. Syncretism entails the mixing of elements of two religious' systems to the point where at least one system loses its basic structure and identity. Dual religious systems, on the other hand, have to do with people following the religious practices of two distinct systems simultaneously.[1] In some instances, one system is followed more faithfully than the other, while in other instances, equal allegiance is paid to both. Thus, syncretism and dual religious systems are two local forces that combat contextualization, but the challenge with Nigerian Neo-Pentecostals is syncretism.

The Concept of the Spirit World in African Traditional Religion (ATR)

In the pre-Christian era of Nigeria, African Traditional Religion (ATR) of different forms[2] was the predominant religion. ATR has a fully developed polytheism as found in West Africa. The adherents of ATR do have the concept of a "supreme being," a notion of future life, and other religious concepts. However, the concept of salvation in ATR centers mostly on

[1] Robert J Schreiter, *Constructing Local Theologies* (Maryknoll, N.Y. : Orbis Books, 1985),*144-158*.
[2] Different forms in the sense that even though there are certain belief systems and worldviews that cut across ATR, the ways and modality of practices vary from one regions to another.

deliverance from higher human enemies (such as the domination of one ethnic group over another), freedom from the oppression of evil spiritual powers, healing from drought and epidemics, deliverance from ancestral and generational curses, deliverance from poverty, protection from cosmic disorders or natural disasters, and the like. There is no belief in the salvation of human souls after the human fall; neither is there any idea of total depravity brought about by sin. Hence, people of ATR are not seeking salvation from sin but from the evil enigma in the world around them, both physically and spiritually. The gods are expected to promote fertility and bountiful harvests from farms. The observation of a Catholic priest cited by Samuel Zwemer is an accurate description of the religious and cultural situation of West Africa and befitting of Yoruba religious practices. The priest sums up five elements found among all the tribes of West Africa, which are: an organized family life, a name for a supreme unseen Power, sovereign and benevolent; a moral sense, namely of truth, justice, shame, and a knowledge that there is good and evil; the idea of soul in every African language and the universal belief that this soul does not die with the death of the body; and finally, communion with the unseen Supreme Power by prayer and sacrificial rites.[3]

Only the light of the gospel can remove this religious veil so that idolaters can see their spiritual poverty.

The Search for Powers in ATRs

Generally, in ATR, idol priests serve as intermediaries (spiritual functionaries) between people and the gods. The ability to see the future, provide solutions over bad occurrences, remove a spell, and ensure victory over the visible and invisible enemies of their followers are what characterize good priests or priestesses in ATR. The most powerful priest in any environment will have more followers. This paves the way for

[3] Samuel M. Zwemer, *The Origin of Religion* 3rd ed. (New York: Loizeaux Brothers, 1945),71.

competitions for power among the priests of various gods and idols. Priests can go to any length in search of power. On regular occasion, fasting, secluded living, abstinence from certain foods or habits, fetishism, blood sacrifices, and covenant making are some of the prices to be paid. However, the greatest power available in the religious practices of ATR is magical and diabolical power.

Followers must also be consistent in providing materials for rituals and sacrifices, pay the necessary dues and vows, and idolize the priest or priestess without any argument or questioning, for a priest or priestess is a representative of god(s), and his or her words must be obeyed and followed to letter. In the same way, Neo-Pentecostal leaders claim to have power (that is, the anointing of the Holy Spirit) to set people free from their various menaces of life. Any form of a gospel that offers freedom from poverty, curses, and spells; deliverance from enemies; healings; fertility; prosperity; and the like will sell fast and wide in Nigeria (and in Africa as a whole).

Again, the worship of gods, divinities and ancestral spirits in African Traditional Religion is partly due to the dreadfulness of the spirits who can incur spells and curses for the slightest violations.[4] For instance, phenomena such as births, deaths, illnesses, infertility, drought, road accidents, thunderstorms, and harvests are explained as purposive acts of spiritual forces, evil or benevolent. Underlying this view is the belief that humans are vulnerable and open to spiritual forces for ill or for good. No wonder, then, that salvation is perceived as freedom from spiritual powers that limit or hinder people from attaining their own well-being. Thus, in African religion, salvation has to do with physical and immediate dangers that threaten individual or community survival, good health, and general prosperity or safety.[5] Nigerian Neo-Pentecostal leaders inflict the same

[4] Geoffrey Parrinder, *Witchcraft: European and African* (New York: Barnes and Noble. 1963), 9-15.

[5] See John S. Mbiti, "Some Reflections on African Experience of Salvation Today," in *Living Faiths*

fear into their followers, who believe that they will be under a spell and curse if they fail to pray in certain ways as directed by their pastors, ignore the clergy's instructions, fail to come for deliverance prayers, refuse to pay their dues in the church, and the like. These dues include regular tithes, prophetic offerings (for the pastors), seed sowing offerings, first fruit offerings, and the likes.[6]

For instance, in Nigeria, it is a must for every member of some Neo-Pentecostal churches to give their first monthly salary of the year (i.e., January's salary) to the church as a "first-fruit offering." The leaders of these churches teach that the Bible commands us to honor God with our first fruits. Hence, some people gather their harvests and put them into bags with holes. The problem of leaking bags emanates from a failure to honor God by giving him the first fruits of one's harvest. If people do not give to God, they may end up wasting away the proceeds of their harvest. Those who harvest into bags with holes are those who refuse to put God first.[7] This kind of threat puts people in bondage. Of course, I am not against giving at all, but God does not want us to serve Him or give anything to Him out of fear but out of love for Him.

What does God want from me again? According to Zac Poonen, the attitude of the self-centered life to God and to His service is characterized by a spirit of legalism. The self can try to serve God. It can be very active in such service, too, but it is always legalistic service. It seeks a reward for the service it offers to God. "I have served you all these years," the elder son—in the prodigal story—tells his father, "But you never gave me even a young goat" (Luke 15:29). He had served his father for a reward all along, but it had not been evident until now. This moment of pressure brought out the fact. That is how the self serves God—not freely, joyfully,

and Ultimate Goals: A Continuing Dialogue, ed. S. J. Samantha (Geneva: World Council of Churches, 1974), 112.

[6] See Adelaja, *How the Church Creates Economic Recession*, 178.

[7] Adeboye, *Leaves Form Daddy G.O.'s Table*, 3:44-45.

and spontaneously but hoping for a return. The return expected may even be some spiritual blessing or reward from God, but service done with even such a motive is legalistic and unacceptable to God.

The elder son in Luke 15 considered his father hard and cruel for not having rewarded him for his service during all those years. He was like the man who was given one talent, who came up to his master at the reckoning time and said, "I've kept your talent safe (without trading it for profit), because I was afraid (you would demand my profits) for you are a hard man to deal with" (Luke 19:21 NLT). The self considers God to be so demanding and so difficult to please that it strives and strives in God's service and still condemns itself for not having satisfied the demands of such an austere God. That is not the type of service that God expects from any of us. The Bible says, "God loves a cheerful giver" (2 Corinthians 9:7). In the matter of service, too, God delights in one who serves cheerfully, neither grudgingly nor of compulsion. He would rather have no service at all than reluctant service. When people serve for reward, it is but a short while before they start complaining to God that they are not being blessed sufficiently. The matter becomes worse when others are more blessed than them.[8]

Do we ever compare our work and the blessing we receive with that of others? This can only be the result of legalistic service. Jesus once told a parable about some laborers who were employed at different hours of the day by a certain man. At the end of the day, the master gave them each a penny. Those who had worked longest came up to the master and complained, saying, "How can you give us the same wages as these other people? We deserve more." They served for wages, and when they received what they had previously agreed upon, they complained that others should not be given as much as them (Matt 20:1-16). This is exactly what

[8] Zac Poonen, "God Delights in One who serves Cheerfully," Weekly Devotion 13 December 2020

we see in the older son: "How can you give all this to my youngest brother? I am the one who has served you faithfully, not he." Self-centered Christians often serve God in order to keep up an impression of spirituality in the eyes of others. It is not pure and fervent love for Christ that keeps them active in Christian work but the fear that others will consider them unspiritual if they do nothing.[9]

What joy and what liberty there is in service that springs out of love for Christ! Love is the oil that lubricates the machinery of our lives so that it does not creak or groan! Jacob labored for seven years in order to obtain Rachel, and the Bible says that those seven years seemed to him just as a few days because of his love for her (Gen 29:20). So, will it be with us when our service for God springs out of love. There will be no strain, no drudgery, and no compulsion.

Sometime ago, a young lady called me from Nigeria to narrate her ordeal concerning how God had treated her so badly. She told me about her marital challenges. For her to get a good man to marry and to have a successful marriage, she had sown a seed of faith offering, a prophetic offering, and a project offering, and she never defaulted in her yearly Shiloh offering. Unfortunately, her marriage only lasted three months. "What does God want from me again?" was her question. She used to be a very committed member of my former church in Nigeria until she was lured away to join one of the new generational churches. I really do not know about her relationship with Christ presently. This is the common practice of Nigerian Neo-Pentecostals—that people can claim something from God when they have sacrificially given money or material things to God.

---

[9] Poonen, "God Delights in One who serves Cheerfully,"

ATR and the Neo-Pentecostals' Concepts of Spirit World

Adherents of ATR (African Traditional Religion) believe in the spiritual world governed by a myriad of demonic spirits. Hence, there is a mindset in Africa that everyone needs to wrestle with these spirit beings everyday with all of their strength and by any means. Most Nigerian Neo-Pentecostal leaders do not emphasize in detail the victory we already have in Jesus Christ. At our conversion, God has translated us out of the domain of darkness, where curses and death reign. He has rescued us from the dominion (i.e., domain or kingdom) of darkness and brought us into the kingdom of the Son He loves (Col 1:13). In *Christ the Eternal Son*, A. W. Tozer defines "accepting Christ" as having "an attachment to the person of Christ that is revolutionary, complete, and exclusive." He explains that this "attachment" is "revolutionary in that it reverses the life and transforms it completely. It is an attachment to the person of Christ. It is complete in that it leaves no part of the life unaffected. It exempts no area of the life of the total man."[10]

As earlier discussed, when people come from the background of ATR into Christianity, they come over with the same mentality or belief system. For example, when you pray for a typical Nigerian Christian, he or she will ask you, "What did you see when you were praying for me?" Similarly, when you pray for a typical Nigerian man, he will not quickly believe that the prayer has been answered unless you give him something physical, such as anointing oil, a prayer cloth, or prayer water. This is the main reason why many Nigerian Christians fall into the deceptions of deceptive Nigerian Neo-Pentecostal pastors and prophets today. Nigerians are looking for pastors and prophets who can see the future for them, who will promise them healings, who can stand between them and God as mediators, and the likes.

[10] See Jim Denison, 'Denison Forum' October 13, 2020.

According to Babatomiwa M. Owojaiye,

> In order to be free from evil attacks, one must be intentional in seeking protection from religious functionaries who have access to supernatural forces of good. This belief puts religious functionaries in a strategic position as special mediators between the realms of sacred and secular, as well as the worlds of good and evil. Africans see religious functionaries as people who possess supernatural abilities to intervene in the uncertainties of life caused by the activities of spiritual forces in the invisible world. From an African perspective, this is what explains the prevalence of the prophetic ministry, both in its genuine charismatic expression, but now, in the perverted form that is discrediting the entire church.[11]

Most of these followers do not believe that they can approach God by themselves without a need for an intermediary except Christ himself. The Apostle Paul says, "*For there is one God and one mediator between God and mankind, the man Christ Jesus, who gave himself as a ransom for all people*" (1 Tim 2:5-6). In the same way, the Apostle Peter, speaking on the priesthood of every believer, states, "*But you are a chosen people, a royal priesthood, a holy nation, God's special possession, that you may declare the praises of him who called you out of darkness into his wonderful light*" (1 Pet 2:9).

The kingdom of Christ is the kingdom of kings. Christ is the King of Kings because all of his children are kings. Do not make yourself a slave to other fellow kings besides the King of Kings! There is nothing that anyone has that you do not potentially have, too. It is right inside you. Yours may be unique! Yes, believers can pray for fellow believers, and believers can pray with fellow believers. But when you start ***idolizing***

[11] Owojaiye, "The Problem of False Prophets in Africa," 3.

the prayer of any "man of God" over your personal prayers and personal relationship with God, that is not Christianity—you are falling back into idolatry again. If you fall into the hands of such so-called men of God, they will abuse you. In many parts of Africa, many people have been damaged by religion.[12] Hence, there are a lot of idolatrous practices among some Nigerian Neo-Pentecostal churches today, including hero worship, idolizing prayer objects, depending upon religious functionaries as a means of connecting with God, fearing demonic spirits instead of focusing on victory in Christ, paying for or giving something in exchange for prayers, and more. Again, with my keen observation, the practices in Nigeria Neo-Pentecostalism look like an amalgamation of elements from Judaism, ATR and Christianity!

The mentality that God is only at certain locations

In ATRs, the priests and worshippers believe that the "gods" are only present at certain geographical locations. The gods cannot be approached except the worshippers are at those special locations. Similarly, Neo-Pentecostal leaders make their followers believe that their problems cannot be solved nor can they be touched by God unless they come to the locations where the leaders operate. For instance, many Neo-Pentecostals in Nigeria believe that they must go to places like "Prayer City," "Shiloh Ground," Holy Ghost Camp," "Apostle Babalola Prayer Mountain," etc., before they can properly approach God through men of God, prophets and prophetesses. This is one of the reasons why those places are always filled with multitudes awaiting their turns to be attended to by these special ministers. Jesus disbanded this ideology in his interaction with the Samaritan woman at Jacob's Well, saying, "*Woman, believe me, a time is coming when you will worship the Father neither on this mountain nor in Jerusalem. You Samaritans worship what you do not know; we worship what*

[12] Sunday Adelaja, Damaged by Religion, 32.

we do know, for salvation is from the Jews. Yet a time is coming and has now come when the true worshipers will worship the Father in the Spirit and in truth, for they are the kind of worshipers the Father seeks. God is spirit, and his worshipers must worship in the Spirit and in truth" (John 4:21-24). Hence, as believers of Christ Jesus, we carry God in us (Col 1: 27; 1 John 4:4).

Chapter 13
The Cultural Christianity of Nigerian Neo-Pentecostals

"Jesus replied, "And why do you break the command of God for the sake of your [man-made] tradition?" (Matt 15: 3)

Again, the personalities of some of the men mentioned in this book are esteemed high. However, some of the misleading teachings they have projected worth spotlighting and need to be brought under the scrutiny of God's undiluted Word. When someone points attention to the doctrinal error of any man of God in Nigeria, chances are high that the followers of the man will rain curses down upon that person. To these followers, that person is committing the sin of 'touching God's anointed one' (Ps 105:15). And in most cases, the man in question too goes ahead in casting such spells. I stand here expecting nothing less. However, Scripture clearly expresses, "***Like a fluttering sparrow or a darting swallow, an undeserved curse does not come to rest***" (Prov. 26: 2). Looking into Scripture, the Apostle Peter had his theological degree under the teaching of Jesus. He was in Christ's inner circle and a believer in Jesus prior to Paul. Since he was older in faith than Paul, he confirmed the genuineness of Paul's conversion and was part of the team that commissioned Paul for a missionary work. Yet, when Peter was misleading the brethren in a hypocritical way (as a manifestation of human imperfection), the Apostle Paul rebuked him sharply (Gal 2).

No matter the age or the rank of anyone, if his teaching contains errors that can lead the people listening to him toward dire eternal consequences, then one is not going against the Scriptures if in the Spirit of Christ one dares to put the person straight by confronting his error and not attacking his personality. Even though you try to speak the truth in love, such confrontations may be harsh a times. Interestingly, we never read in the Bible that the Apostle Peter ever pronounced curses upon the Apostle Paul. Rather, some years later, Peter remarked about Paul, saying, "***His letters contain some things that are hard to understand, which ignorant and unstable people distort, as they do the other Scriptures, to their own destruction***" (2 Pet 3: 16).

Culturally, in many places in Africa, it is seen as an attitude of uncultured audacity for a young person to correct an elderly person. This very practice has been carried over into Christianity. It is however, better to be offensive to an elder rather than to allow an elder to continue to perpetuate errors that may lead people to the wrong side of eternity—and then you become guilty before God. The gospel truth must be prioritized above any man's opinion or personality. The cultural "Christianity" of Nigerian Neo-Pentecostals is another defensive and protective mechanism to silence people from confronting their errors with the truth.

In the Nigerian Neo-Pentecostal religious system, people are mandated to listen and submit. They cannot express their opinions, question doctrinal stances, or challenge any decision made by the leaders all because these leaders are viewed as above reproach and as instituted authorities and principalities. According to Ademola Adebiyi, "In most Neo-Pentecostal churches, members are not permitted to stand up and look directly into the eyes of their leaders during conversations. As a sign of respect and honor, members have to bow down or kneel when talking to their leaders."[1]This is but pure religious abuse!

The practice of a religious caste system in Nigerian Neo-Pentecostal Christianity, whereby the leaders wield an unquestionable power and

[1] Ademola Adebiyi, interview by the author, Louisville, KY, January 25, 2020.

authority is wrong. It is true that honor is to be given to those who deserve it, but it must not be abused or else it will raise the ego and pride of men. Leaders who deserve this honor must be the ones that fight and stand by the truth of God's word, and with lifestyle that is in conformity with the gospel. In one of my interactions with Rev. Joseph Ezeigbo, he remarked that "the first Pentecostal leader that elevated himself to the position of an 'Archbishop' in Nigeria did so to distinguish himself from all other lower positions of bishop. He gave this title to himself by self-imposition and declared himself superior to all others." By the way, there is no such position of 'Archbishop' in the Bible. According to Danny McCain, one of the greatest dangers that leaders face is pride. People admire, respect, and followers bow down to leaders. People treat their leaders as special. Leaders get called to the high table; they do not have to wait in the queue. After leaders have been treated this way for a while, they begin to think that they *really are* important. It does not matter how big or little a person is; there is always a tendency toward pride. Africans are probably no prouder than any other group of people. However, since Africa is my home, these are the people I see daily, and I see a lot of proud people. The Bible, however, says that God hates pride (Prov. 8:13; 16:5; Jas 4:6; 1 Pet 5:5).[2]

Cultural Prayers

Neo-Pentecostals leaders have some culturally based prayer languages that are not biblically relevant but full of syncretistic ideologies. But since they wield unquestionable authority, the only thing their followers must do is to obey without complaining or asking questions. A lot could be written on the cultural prayer patterns of Nigerian Neo-Pentecostals but let make reference to a few points here. I have been to prayer places where the men of God will say, "Hold your head with your two hands, now

[2] See Danny McCain, *Tough Tests for Top Leaders: God's Strategy for Preparing Africans to Lead Global Christianity* (Jos, Nigeria: Capro Media, 2000),37.

shout at the top of your voice as you pray and say, 'My head must take me out of poverty and pilot me to the land of prosperity.'" After praying the prayers for some minutes, the people are told to shout "Amen!" seven times and to shout "FIRE!" Recently, people gathered in the hundreds of thousands at a particular prayer camp to pray. The prophet told them to bend and hold their legs tight and begin to pray in a loud voice, saying, "By fire, by force, my leg must take me to America, Europe, Asia. . . ."

According to Abimbola Adelakun,

Dr. Daniel Olukoya, is currently the General Overseer of MFM. The church features spectacular and aggressive styles of prayer and the members are encouraged to develop "violent faith" and engage in "violent prayers" to defeat their enemy. Unsurprisingly, their prayer rituals feature repeated chants of "Die! Die! Die! Fall down and die! Die by fire!" Their ritual language includes such expressions as "spiritual bullets," "Holy Ghost machine gun," and other colorful phrases that appropriate the language of modern warfare. According to the church website, "aggressive prayer is considered as an aid to spiritual focus and a check against being overwhelmed by the flesh."[3]

Of course, I am not against prayer. As matter of fact, prayer is the life-wire for spirituality, and a prayerless Christian is powerless. But some of the practices that go with the ways some Nigerian Neo-Pentecostal leaders force their followers to pray still go in line with the practices in the old African Religion.

[3] Adelakun, "Pentecostal Panopticism and the Phantasm of the Ultimate Power," 101.

Chapter 14
The Emptiness of Competing for Mega Buildings

"*We do not dare to classify or compare ourselves with some who commend themselves. When they measure themselves by themselves and compare themselves with themselves, they are not wise*" (2 Corinthians 10: 12)

During the early church era, one of the methods that led to the sporadic expansion of Christianity was the multiplication of home churches. In the writings of Paul, we see him referring again and again to churches in the homes of different believers (see, e.g., Rom 16). In the same way, Apostle John refers to a church in the home of a certain individual believer (2 John 1:1). After the encounter of Pentecost, the early believers congregated in Jerusalem instead of going out to Judea, Samaria, and other parts of the Roman world. As a matter of fact, God seems to have intentionally scattered the Jerusalem church through persecution. It is hard to find many mega churches in the early church.

Competitions for the Largest Church's Capacity Building

Let me again point attention to the danger of Christian leaders today who are competing for the biggest church buildings. A lot of pastors are competing to have church buildings with capacity for 50,000, 100,000, 150,000, 200,000, and so on. This is simply because we forget history so soon. Many centuries ago, the Roman Catholic papacy wanted to build St. Peter's Basilica in Rome, but they ran out of money to execute this huge project. A prominent priest named Tetzel came up with the idea that the papacy and the priests could convince people that if they paid money, they would obtain indulgences that would forgive their sins. People were coming to the priests, paying money, and receiving certificates of forgiveness. People were told that they could also pay money to the priests on behalf of their dead relatives; once they paid the money, the souls of their dead loved ones would leave purgatory and ascend to heaven. These two ideas became widely accepted by the Roman Catholic leadership. People came en masse, paid money for their sins, and then received certificates of forgiveness.

Within a short time, enough money was raised to build the historic St. Peter's Basilica. Of course, on October 31, 1517, Martin Luther nailed his ninety-five theses on the door of **Castle Church in Wittenberg**, Germany, condemning the wrong practices of the Roman Catholic. This is the beginning of the Protestant Reformation, which led to what we know as Protestantism today. Genny Justice puts it this way:

> The main funding for the early stages of building New St. Peter's came from the sale of indulgences. Indulgences did more than help pay for the basilica, however. The abusive means of selling indulgences, including lies from priests and the papacy about their efficacy, resulted in an uprising, led by Martin Luther of Germany, and the result was the Reformation and split in the Church.[1]

Unfortunately, history is repeating itself today in a similar way—the same formula is still in operation today among Nigerian Neo-Pentecostals churches. Among such churches, people are told to pay for healing, pay for prayers, sow monthly mandatory seeds for church buildings, sow seeds to connect to prosperity, higher anointing, breakthroughs, successes and the likes. Some Neo-Pentecostal leaders invest the money

[1] Genny Justice, "The Role of Indulgences in the Building of New Saint Peter 's Basilica," Rollins College: Rollins Scholarship Online, Spring 2011. Accessed on October 12, 2020 at: https://scholarship.rollins.edu/cgi/viewcontent.cgi?article=1006&context=mls

they gathered through these gimmicks to buy shares, estates, or schools or to establish businesses. Hence, by these gimmicks of raking money from their vulnerable followers, many Neo-Pentecostal preachers have become excessively wealthy and have built gigantic auditoriums in the name of the Lord. Today, Neo-Pentecostal leaders are almost operating 100 percent like the old papacy of the Roman Catholic Church, whose system led Christianity into centuries of darkness.

There are many church campgrounds in Nigeria that can hold hundreds of thousands to millions of people at a time. Unfortunately, during the global COVID-19 pandemic, many of these places have been rendered empty, and many mega churches in the U.S. have broken into smaller congregations. This is nothing but a parable from God that the real beauty of Christ's church is not the multiplication of mega buildings on earth but the multiplication of true disciples of Christ in all corners of the world. If we fail to take our Christianity out of our mega buildings and into the streets, homes, offices, etc., then Christianity in Nigeria—as we have seen in the Western world—may fade away in a matter of time.

For instance, Turkey is in the present-day Europe and partly in Asia. Apostle Paul was a citizen of Turkey because Tarsus exists in Turkey. Christianity existed in Turkey for over a millennium before it began to experience a downward trend as it is today. The seven churches Jesus spoke to in Revelations 2 and 3 (Ephesus, Smyrna, Pergamum, Thyatira, Sardis, Philadelphia and Laodicea) existed in the old Turkey. Turkey once had the largest Christian auditorium in Europe called Hagia Sophia in Constantinople. Some traditions maintain that Mary, the mother of Jesus was taken to Turkey by Apostle John[2] and till date, her room has become a tourist center. But the present-day Turkey now has 96% Muslims and 0.02% Christians. The Hagia Sophia (once the largest church in Europe)

[2] https://turkisharchaeonews.net/object/house-virgin-mary-ephesus

was taken over by Muslims and converted to a mosque for over 400 years and later used as an Islamic Museum. Just this month of August 2020, the country's president signed a new order converting it into a mosque and to be handed over to the Islamic leaders. The Pew Research maintains that, on September 30, 2020, the Greek Orthodox Church of the United States said it is petitioning United Nations experts to coerce Turkey into protecting Orthodox Christianity's cultural heritage following the Turkish government's conversion of Istanbul's landmark Hagia Sophia (once a historic Christian church building) from a museum to a mosque.[3] Who would have believed in some centuries back that this will happen to Christianity in Turkey?

During the COVID-19 pandemic, in the months of June and July 2020, we baptized about five people in our church (1stECWA in Louisville, Kentucky) to God's glory. The first thought that came to my mind then was that even though the walls and doors of churches are closed, the door of salvation is still open wide. Jesus Christ will not reward anybody for gigantic church building when he appears, but he will reward us based on the quality of the souls we win to his kingdom. Remember the Scripture that says, "*He that must boast, must boast in this that he knows the Lord. Boasting on having gigantic buildings is an empty boast*" (Jer 9:24). All this boasting about gigantic church structures are meaningless. Research reveals that four out of the ten richest pastors in the world are from Nigeria (some Nigerian Neo-Pentecostal pastors are richer than a whole state in Nigeria). The many private jets, many estates, and huge amounts of money in these men's banks all reveal how greedy these men are. Sadly, in Africa, these men can flaunt and flex their monetary muscles in an endless accumulation without anyone questioning or challenging them.

Moreover, the Lord has not saddled us with the task of the Great

[3] See Hagia Sophia (Pew Research September 30, 2020.

Commission so as to fill our pews (or church buildings) with members. Rather, the Lord commissioned us to fill the world with disciples. Similarly, as gospel messengers, we are called not primarily to fill the nook and cranny of the cities with church buildings. We are called to fill the cities with genuine disciples who will turn the cities around for Christ. With all the mega churches of various capacities in Nigeria, our cities are still full of poverty, immoralities, lawlessness, corruption and the likes. We need to build disciples not just walls.

Real Church can exist without wall or Building

An Afghan pastor and evangelist named David Paiman was recently interviewed by Christianity Today. His father was a Muslim imam; Paiman went to Mecca six times before coming to faith in Jesus. He first heard the gospel from a former Muslim who had a vision of Christ during a pilgrimage to Mecca. Paiman came to Christ after Christians prayed for a friend with epilepsy who was healed. Despite the severe persecution and brutal killings of Christians, the real church is still going on in Afghan; this church never depends on great walls or giant buildings. As the Talibans took over government by August 2021 in Kabul, the hope of Afghans in American government and her military collapsed. With this collapse of hope, an interviewer asked, "With the hope that you experienced, what did you think might happen?" Paiman replied, "The real hope is Jesus Christ. Afghanistan has been trying many ways to get hope, to get peace inside Afghanistan, but they did not try Jesus Christ. They did not try God. They did not try his love and his mercy. My prayer and zeal are to share Christ with them. "They can receive Christ and they can get the real hope, the living hope that never ends." Then the pastor noted: "In Afghanistan, people know they are the church, and they understand that. But here, in most of America, they say the building is a church. There is a building with a cross on it. That's what they call church but, in Afghanistan, the real church is going on.[4]

[4] "My Heart Is Broken': An Afghan Pastor Grapples with the US Withdrawal." https://www.christianitytoday.com/ct/podcasts/quick-to-listen/afghanistan-christian-pastor-us-withdrawal-taliban accessed August 25, 2021.

Chapter 15
Not an Impact but an Exploitation

"Be shepherds of God's flock that is under your care, watching over them . . . as God wants you to be; not pursuing dishonest gain, but eager to serve; not lording it over those entrusted to you, but being examples to the flock" (1 Pet 5: 2-3)

In history, the continent of Africa has not suffered repeated natural disasters (e.g., floods, earthquakes, hurricanes, tsunamis) at the magnitude seen in other parts of the world. However, one of the worst evils perpetrated on earth was the human-to-human oppression seen in the slave trade, through which hundreds of thousands[1] of blacks died on the roads and seas on their way to foreign lands. But another horrible internal disaster was the self-inflicted ***leadership disaster (which equally triggers followership disaster as well)*** brought about by the selfishness of African leaders in both the past and the present. This issue has rendered many parts of African nations impoverished. Unfortunately, many preachers of the gospel in Africa today are unduly exploiting others to make themselves rich. There are various ways by which these men exploit their followers. There are stories upon stories of sexual molestation (I have personally intervened in several cases), and there are countless numbers of brainwashing mechanisms used to interpret the Scriptures to their own personal advantage.

Personalized Spiritual Authority

Religious functionaries serve as personalized spiritual authorities in ATR. In the same way, Nigerian Neo-Pentecostal leaders wield power

[1] Byang Kato, *African Cultural Revolution and the Christian Faith* (Jos, Nigeria: Challenge Publication), 4.

that cannot be questioned. Jesus Christ told his disciples,

> You know that the rulers of the Gentiles lord it over them, and those who are great exercise authority over them. Yet it shall not be so among you; but whoever desires to become great among you, let him be your servant. And whoever desires to be first among you, let him be your slave—just as the Son of Man did not come to be served, but to serve, and to give His life a ransom for many. (Matt 20:25-28)

I have seen Neo-Pentecostal members fearing their pastors more than they have reverence for God. I heard a story about something that recently happened in Nigeria. A young medical doctor was in a theater room with other team members as they were about to perform a surgery on a patient. Suddenly, the doctor's phone rang, and it was his papa (pastor) who was calling and saying with a threatening voice, "I want you to be in the meeting that is going to come up in the church in about 25 minutes. You need to drop whatsoever you are doing and anywhere you may be to be in that meeting." To everyone's amazement, the doctor left his colleagues and headed straight to the meeting at the church. The Apostle Peter clearly pointed out that church leaders should not pursue dishonest gain but should be eager to serve; they should not lord their authority over those entrusted to them but be examples to the flock (1 Pet 5:2-3).

Once you allow anyone to convince you that God loves him more than you and that he is more special in the eyes of God than you, then you have set the stage for abuse. Such a man will likely abuse you because you have made yourself his slave. Once you are in Christ, however, you are just as anointed as anybody else. Christ is the Anointed One, and he resides in you without measure. You only need to grow in your fellowship and relationship with the Anointed One who is in you. You can reach God by yourself without any man standing as intermediary between you and God. Pastors should set people free. Pastors should let people know that the best prayers are the prayers that the people can pray for themselves. Pastors should encourage people to grow in their personal relationship with God and not try to serve as intermediaries between people and God. This is not the Christianity that the apostles practiced. This is not the kingdom that Christ brought.[2]

It is so painful to see that men and women who are supposed to be in their offices working during business hours are—instead—congregating on mountains tops, at prayers camps, retreats, and weekly conferences for church programs. Some spent 30 percent of their time at their jobs or offices but spent over 60 percent of their time at churches and church programs. In Nigeria, the first three months of the year are being spent at prayer camps and other related church programs. It is so pathetic to see Nigerians being deluded with the grip of religiosity and living under the manipulations of their G.Os, pastors, prophets, and the likes. From the meager work that people do, they must pay tithes, first fruits, offerings, seed, and more in their churches. All of these things have contributed to wrecking and paralyzing the economy of the nation.[3] It is very common to hear Neo-Pentecostal church members say things such as "My Papa says, ...", "My GO says, . . . ," and "I believe the words of my Papa." There are members who fear the words of their so-called men of God more than the Word of God. I call such an attitude among Neo-Pentecostals and charismatics "papal infallibility," a doctrine of the Roman Catholic Church that says that the Pope cannot err doctrinally. For Nigerian Neo-Pentecostals, papal infallibility would mean that the word of a G.O., pastor, or prophet is as authoritative as the Bible. This attitude is highly misleading.

---

[2] Sunday Adelaja Damage by Religion

[3] See more in Sunday Adelaja, *How Churches Contribute to Economic Recession.*

One-Man-Show Style of Nigerian Neo-Pentecostal Leaders

There are several one-man-show kinds of ministries among today's modern preachers. I know a pastor in Nigeria who used to run more than six services each Sunday. In all of these services, he would not allow any of the pastors under him to preach or teach. Only he, his wife, his spiritual father(s) who visited by invitation, and some foreign preachers during special church programs are qualified to preach. Many Nigerian Neo-Pentecostal pastors do not trust the people around them. As a result of a lack of rest, a G.O once collapsed and was rushed to a foreign country for treatment while the congregation was told that the man was enjoying his vacation. They will not say their pastor is sick because "it is a taboo to say a man of such anointing is sick." It is not only that many of the Neo-Pentecostals leaders in Nigeria do not trust the people around them, most of them also do not trust their fellow Neo-Pentecostal pastors. They are so insecure among themselves. For instance, I know a handful number of some Neo-Pentecostal GOs who gives command to their followers never to read any book written by any other man of God. Their followers must stick to reading their books alone under the disguise that they do not want their followers to swallow wrong teachings. But the truth is, some of these men do not want their followers to discover the truth they are hiding away from them.

Another thing is that in these kinds of 'one-man-show' churches, the wife is the second in command after the G.O. After the wife comes the eldest son as the next in authority while the other children and relations follows in that order. Gone are the days when the children of the pastors in Africa never wanted to become pastors. But today, as children see their fathers riding in the latest cars, flying in private jets, and living in the most expensive houses in the country, they, too, begin to train to become mighty orators so as to inherit their parents' church businesses. The G.Os post their sons to the best churches in their denominations. Hence, the inheritance of the church's wealth is passed down through the family lineage. It baffles me to see how church business has graduated to become a family business affair.

In most instances, the man is the general overseer, the wife is the assistant, and the children manage church finances according to the directives received from the G.O. The in-laws, too, handle some other sensitive ministry positions. As the father ages in the ministry, he prepares to hand it over to his son. We have seen cases of mother and her son fighting over who should be the leader after the demise of the father. The mother wants to be the general overseer; the son wants to be as well. These types of denominations are purely private family business affairs. Innocent members are exploited to make the family extremely rich with flamboyant lifestyles. These pastors cannot handover their ministries to committed followers who do not belong to their family circles. We read of Moses, who handed over the mantle of leadership to Joshua, who had no family ties to Moses. These men are afraid to lose their empires; hence, they cannot withstand handing over their ministries to anyone else except their own wives or children. In addition, the Nigerian church leaders must stop the habit of using their congregations to build future riches for their children, and children-children, through playing on the gullibility of their followers.

Promotions Based on Financial Remissions

Many of today's Nigerian Neo-Pentecostal pastors are being promoted by their G.Os based on the amount of money they remit to the headquarter office. Thus, many junior pastors are using all kinds of means to rake money out of church members' pockets so as to please the top leaders. I recently heard a story of pastors and their wives who were remitting the salary they received from their secular jobs to the church's head office all because they wanted recognition and promotion from their GO. In the same way, cell group or unit leaders in the church are promoted and honored yearly based on the money their various departments remit to the main office. Sometime in May of this year, 2021, a popular Nigerian general overseer (GO) gave an award, and a hug to a member of his, who donated money that worth billions of naira to his church. Sooner after the honorary award, the same man was reported to have defrauded his business partners (and investors) of several billons of naira. The investors to his company marched to the church head quarter demanding that the GO should speak to his spiritual son to refund their money.

Ordination of the Wrong People into the Pastorate

Neo-Pentecostal leaders are quick to ordain members who are well to do as pastors/lady pastors, assistant pastors, prophets/prophetess, apostles, or evangelists. Some ordain men and women after four to six weeks or a couple of months' trainings. This is why there are too many half-baked church leaders among modern African churches as a whole. There are several politicians or their wives who exhibit questionable lifestyles. But because such people donate huge sums of money to church projects, Neo-Pentecostal leaders have ordained them as ministers of the gospel. I know of two young men who were recently ordained as pastors in a particular denomination in Nigeria. These two young men are no longer in the church today, and worst still, they are on Facebook and YouTube, telling people that Christianity is another brainwashed religion. They both are claiming that people do not need Jesus to get to heaven—if there is even such a thing as heaven. This is one of the dangers of saddling immature people with shepherding responsibilities. Nigerian Neo-Pentecostals have given careers or ministries to many half-baked men and women who are anti-Christ-like in all of their dispositions.

The Demoralization of Young Women

In the Western world, unmarried women give themselves to developing their talents, giftings, or professions. But in Africa, women twenty-five years old and above congregate on mountain tops, at prayer camps, or at prayer centers, lifting up deliverance prayers so that their husbands will appear miraculously. They are subjected to sequential days, weeks, and months of prayer and fasting. Their so-called men of God have convinced them that generational curses are hindering them from finding a spouse. Several young ladies who should have developed themselves and become noble people in life have instead wasted their precious years under many prophets, and some of them have ended up being sexually abused by the very men who are praying for them.

Cutting Short the Futures of Young People

The bright futures of many young men are equally being cut short as they are being "grounded" with church positions. Young graduates from universities are being given positions in churches in efforts to hold them down rather than allowing them to advance in their careers and professions. Recently, I was speaking to a young graduate about the need for him to apply for admission to a school in Canada so that he could further his education, but the young man refused, giving the excuse that he was in a mentoring program with his G.O, so he could not leave the country. But today, with the modern technology, mentoring can be done in any part of the world. The main issue is that these church leaders know how to send their own children abroad but confiscate and surround themselves with other's people children so that the children can continue to serve them while being enticed with peanuts as stipends. In fact, these men will even make the people they have grounded around them serve their own children once they have returned from foreign countries. These men are living exactly like the worldly politicians.

Idolization of men of God

During a birthday celebration, in honor of his G.O, a member of a particular Neo-Pentecostal denomination wrote this on his Facebook page; "Happy Birthday to the Spirit in Motion, the number one God of riches in the whole world, the King of kings, the Lord of lords, the Jesus of this generation and the generation to come. I bow to you sir, and I love you immeasurably." Another Neo-Pentecostal pastor was once preaching in another branch of his church-denomination, located in a big city. Making a comment about his GO, he told his congregation, "Dare to believe the man of God, my pastor (GO). Dare to believe his word. You know, when we share things like these—when we share fundamental truth of this nature, there are some skeptics and some critics who think we are worshipping a man. The truth is, I wish I could worship him, because he is worship-able."[4] This is a practical and pathetic situation of most of the African Neo-Pentecostal churches.

The last epistle written by John the Beloved is the Book of Revelation. Let me point your attention to one important and hidden truth about John. At the age of above 90 as the tradition (history) revealed, see what John wrote, "I John your brother . . ." (Rev 1: 9). At the end of his entire ministry, the title John gave himself was 'brother.' He did not call himself 'Pope', 'Reverend', 'Bishop', 'Snr Apostle', 'Prophet', etc. It is high time for all those who exalt themselves to the 'seat of Moses' (Matt 23: 2) in Christendom to know that we are all brothers in Christ. In a similar way, when the Apostle John himself wanted to make a mistake of bowing down to worship the angels who revealed the mysteries of the things to come to him, the angel exclaimed; "Don't do that! I am a fellow servant with you and with your brothers and sisters who hold to the testimony

[4] Unfortunately, after this pastor said this, the whole congregation shouted the praise of this GO and applauded him in standing ovation.

of Jesus." Worship God! . . . (Rev 19:10). Man of God, stop accepting or taking the worship of your follow brothers and sisters in Christ. It is a dangerous thing to do!

Chapter 16
Nigerian Neo-Pentecostals and Gospel Pluses

"For it is by grace you have been saved through faith, and this not from yourselves; it is the gift of God, not by works, so that no one can boast" (Ephesians2: 8-9).

The Death of Jesus Plus Money

There are two versions of Nigerian Neo-Pentecostalism; those who follow hyper-grace doctrine, and those who think that works are needed in addition to faith in order to obtain salvation and reach heaven. It is this latter version that I want to discuss further in this chapter (the former comes later in chapter 20). For instance, arguments for tithing were hot in Nigeria for about two years (2018-2020). Some pastors came up with various shocking visions and revelations in which they saw people burning in hellfire because they refused to pay their tithes when they were on earth.

Many pastors, GOs, founders, and the like place curses on members who will fail to pay tithes. They also pronounce curses on bloggers who teach that tithing is no longer a compulsion for those under the New Covenant. Well, the argument here is not on tithing. Even though throughout the New Testament, there is no income tax system or any compulsory giving (2 Corinthians9:7), my conclusion is that Christians should follow the biblical financial contribution system adopted by their churches. If you are genuinely converted, you will feel compelled to open your pocket for the advancement of the gospel, not for the extension of the empires of those using gimmicks and manipulations to exploit people. Do not rebel within a local church against the doctrinal stance to which you have consented. Nevertheless, the biblical understanding and interpretations of many GOs in Nigeria and Africa at large baffle a lot. An influential GO once said, "The reason why Job was attacked by the devil was because Job never paid his tithes. So, his belongings were not secured." In the heat of the argument on tithes, a famous church leader in Nigeria said, "People have used Matthew 23:23 as excuse not to pay their tithes. But I am going to give you pastors [in this denomination] the opportunity to repent tonight. And immediately after this convention, go and restitute yourselves with your respective congregation. Make it clear to them; ***anyone who does not pay his tithes is not going to Heaven***. Full Stop!" The whole place was in dead silence as he spoke, and you could perceive tension and the spirit of fear all over the faces of the people.

There is no doubt that this is another labor theology. In my inductive study of the Scriptures, I cannot find any passage to back up the claim that "***anyone who does not pay his tithes is not going to Heaven***." This is simply saying that the atoning death of Jesus Christ on the cross is not enough for salvation. To say that man's effort is needed to achieve salvation is nothing but pure heresy. Nigerian Neo-Pentecostal leaders are fond of saying, "If you don't listen to my words as the spiritual father over you, you cannot make heaven." Followers see the words of their leaders as powerful and anointed as the Word of God. It is on the subject of a similar kind of brainwashing that the Apostle Paul challenged the Galatian church, saying, "*Oh, foolish Galatians! Who has cast an evil spell on you? For the meaning of Jesus Christ's death was made as clear to you as if you had seen a picture of his death on the cross*" (Gal 3:1).

The Name of Jesus Plus Objects

When Neo-Pentecostal pastors pray over objects such as oil, handkerchiefs, water, wristbands and the likes, those objects are then referred to as "mantles," which are made available for members to purchase. The mantles are seen as carriers of miracles, and they can be used for various miraculous activities as deemed fit. At this juncture, permit me to use a story from my book *The Baptism of Power*. As soon as you add something to the name of Jesus, your gospel will sell quickly because it has become very similar to the practices of African Traditional Religion, which most Africans came out of. A well-known pastor some time ago said he was under the leading of the Holy Spirit when he brought a rod to the pulpit and commanded the audience to keep their gaze on the rod as they make their prayers to God. The truth, however, is that Jesus Christ has been lifted up on the cross. We can no longer go to the time of Moses again in the wilderness.

At the beginning of a new year, an African preacher once told his members to buy hair combs and to bring them to the church for special prayer. Some came with bags and loads of combs. After the man of God finished praying upon the combs, he told the members to use one comb each to comb their hair backward several times with a repetitive word of prayer: "I comb away all the evil in this new year." To this man of God, the comb served as a symbol with which members could ward off and avert all evils for the year. This is part of modern-day syncretistic practices. Unfortunately, many of those who came with bags of combs began to ship them out to foreign countries where there are Nigerians; they began to sell them as the "anointed combs" that a respectable man of God (a GO) in Nigeria had blessed. This became a source of income or business for them.

One time, I was in a commercial bus with a particular lady. Just when our bus was about to depart, the woman got off the bus and flagged down a commercial motorcyclist to take her back home so that she could pick up the bottle of oil that she had forgotten. She attached much importance to the oil because her GO had prayed over it—thus, the oil served as another Holy Spirit in a bottle. The woman believed that this anointing oil would serve many purposes, including protection, favor, blessing, healing and more. My argument on mantles is that most members of Nigerian Neo-Pentecostal churches see those things as small "gods"; hence, another form of modernized idolatry has crept into the churches. We must be careful not to replace Jesus Christ with objects in our lives, homes, and churches.

Chapter 17
Fraudulent Activities among African Neo-Pentecostals

"Beware of false prophets, which come to you in sheep's clothing, but inwardly they are ravening wolves. You shall know them by their fruits. . ."
(Matt 7:15-16)

A Malawian prophet who once lived in South Africa has named himself the "Number one prophet in Africa, Major Prophet 1". He was charged with fraudulent activities and money laundering in 2019, and, again, he is being charged with fraud, theft, and money laundering in 2020 to the tune of $6.3 million—together with his wife. There have also been sexual allegations leveled against him. News has it that in November 2020, the so-called prophet secretly fled South Africa in order to escape a court trial. This man recently bought an expensive car worth millions of dollars for his daughter's eighth birthday celebration. The flamboyance of many African prophets does not reflect the lifestyle of Jesus and the early apostles in any way.

There is another prophet who has made himself laudable in Africa. For some years, several news media have been reporting some of his fake miracles and prophecies, but he has been maneuvering his way out of trouble until recently, when he was caught red-handed. In 2019, he paid a man to lie down in a coffin as a corpse because he wanted to perform a miracle of raising the dead. The man seemed to stay too long in the coffin such that when the prophet was praying for him to raise from dead, the man's lips were shaking, and cameras picked it all up. It became evident that the man feigned death. The prophet was forced to apologize, which he did, but many opined that his apology was only a defensive measure. There are several fake miracles of this kind that many African men of God have paraded around.

Fake Marital Life

In 2018, a popular prophet in Nigeria came out to stand in front of his congregation, saying, "Some years back, my wife went out of our marriage to commit adultery and had a baby, and I covered her. It is my turn now as I had a baby out of wedlock, but she failed to cover me, therefore, I am divorcing her". However, the man's wife came out publicly to dispute the allegations, calling them false accusations and demanding that DNA tests be carried out on all her children so that the truth could be established. The woman claimed that her husband wanted to elope with another lover, a prophetess based in South Africa—that was why he wanted to blackmail her (i.e., his wife). Yet today, this same prophet has a pool he calls "a miraculous pool," where people go to dip themselves for healing or to solve their problems—as this prophet claimed. A single dip in this pool cost ₦50,000. Recently, the same prophet just bought a private jet, with thousands of people still following him gullibly and treating him like a savior.

A well-known Neo-Pentecostal pastor has been accused of rape several times. In one of the cases, before he forcefully had sex with a particular young girl, he convinced her that because he is a man of anointing, the Lord would not charge the girl for committing fornication with him. He convinced the girl that it is a great privilege for her to have sex with such a respected man of God like him. He added, "My anointing covers the sin." I have intervened in many cases of this nature. My wife, Peace, and I, before we left Nigeria for further studies, were able to help several young girls who were sexually molested by this modern generation of pastors so that they could recover from their trauma.

In 2015, a cousin of mine was preparing for his wedding with his fiancée—let us call her "Tammy." His fiancée was an office assistant to a particular pastor in a city, while he was serving as a short-term missionary in a remote village. Knowing that Tammy was a virgin, the city pastor started making advances toward her. After work one day, Tammy narrated some of her ordeals with this pastor to my wife. Knowing some of the signs of these kinds of men, my wife warned Tammy and told her to be vigilant and never be careless in the office. On one fateful day, the pastor told Tammy that she would run some errands for him after closing hours. Tammy tried to ask why the errands needed to be after closing hours, but the pastor threatened her with termination of her work appointment. After he allowed all of the other staff to leave entire building, the man sent Tammy to go and wash his bathroom. Tammy already knew at this point that something was fishy, and she was ready to do whatever it would take to protect herself. He entered the bathroom and tried to approach her in a low-key manner with some kind of brainwashing, but it did not work. Tammy refused to yield. When the man noticed that she would not comply, he engaged force to try to rape her. The young lady kneed him right on his erect manhood. The man fell backward on the floor and Tammy ran out of the building. I could keep on telling scores of stories like this one.

There are several cases of Nigerian Neo-Pentecostal pastors being caught in sexual scandals featured on the pages of several Nigerian newspapers and on the internet. Some members are ashamed to be identified with such pastors and their churches, but other members continue following their leaders blindly and dogmatically saying, "Touch not the anointed of the Lord."[1] Sometime ago, a couple lost a son by a protracted sickness. A

[1] See Jon Batiste, "Mega Churches Pastor Stays on despite Multiple Affairs," *Christianity Today* 60, no. 6 (July/August 2016): 18-19

friend directed the woman who lost her son to go to a well-known man of God in the city for prayer. Driving the new SUV that she and her husband recently purchased, the woman headed to meet the "man of God." After several minutes of prayer, the man of God told the woman that he saw a horrible revelation concerning the family again. He told her that the "Spirit" of God said to him that if this couple did not want to lose their only last child (a girl), then they needed to 'sow' the SUV to him as a seed of faith in order to wade off the looming danger. In fear of not wanting to lose the only child she had left, the woman dropped the car key and returned home by a commercial bike (popularly called Okada). When one of my senior evangelical pastors heard about this incident, he became furious and headed straight to a police station with two other pastors. In short, they went to this so-called man of God and returned the vehicle to the family. Countless numbers of people have found themselves being duped by these kinds of notorious men masquerading as clergymen—but they are actually wolves in sheep's clothing.

The high rate of divorce among these fake men of God is becoming alarming. Unfortunately, they will always find some Scriptures to justify their questionable ways of living. Not too long ago, a Neo-Pentecostal bishop in Africa divorced his wife after twenty-five years of marriage, claiming, "I was not mature enough when I married my first wife." Now he has remarried another young lady after he has finished with his first wife. I know some of these men who are in their second and third marriages, yet all of them are still leading crowds of people who idolize them as small "gods."

Nigerian Neo-Pentecostals Turn Churches into Comedy Centers

Some survey respondents pointed attention to Nigerian Neo-Pentecostals' use of comedians in their churches as a means of gathering crowds. To Nigerian Neo-Pentecostals, the ends justify the means, and the results silence the critics. The negative effect of this slogan (that is, "the ends justify the means") is a clear deviation from the biblical approach to evangelism. Wale Aerogun, a very reputable Nigerian preacher and teacher, once lamented in his sermon, "It is so pathetic how these comedians will climb the church pulpits and crack all form of ungodly jokes that appeal to the emotions of their audience."[2] He adds,

> We allow comedians to come into churches and be playing with the Holy things of God. One of the most terrible assaults of hell against the Church of God in Nigeria in these last days is invasion of comedians on the pulpits. The devil is making the things of God look stupid to us and the things of the world to look wise, thereby weakening our power for spiritual warfare. Where have we gotten these pastors that do not understand the terms and the consecration of the calling of God?[3]

Most times, when one looks at the ways some of these comedians perform in churches these days, one is tempted to ask, are churches turning to mere congregations or clubs? Someone rightly said, "When ministry becomes performance, then the sanctuary becomes a theater, the congregation become an audience, worship becomes entertainment, and man's applause and approval become the measure of success."

Fake Predictions and Prophecies

Deuteronomy 18:21-22 reads, "*You may say to yourselves, 'How can we know when a message has not been spoken by the Lord? 'If what a prophet proclaims in the name of the Lord does not take place or come true, that is a message the Lord has not spoken. That prophet has spoken presumptuously, so do not be alarmed.*"

---

[2] Sola Areogun, "Declination of Ministerial Ethic" (sermon preached at Lagos Region Apostolic Ministration, Nigeria, December 2018).

[3] Areogun, "Declination of Ministerial Ethic"

From 2008 onward, there have been several prophecies and predictions from several Nigerian Neo-Pentecostal leaders about the year, month, and day that Islamic Jihadists—Boko Haram—will be completely wiped off the face of the earth. Many a prophet has come up to speak like this: "If I be a man of God, by the end of October 2014, Boko Haram will become history in Nigeria." I have heard this kind of prophecy thousands of times, but Boko Haram is still actively carrying out its heinous activities in disastrous ways. Where are the Nigerian prophets and their prophecies when the COVID-19 global pandemic began? A renowned Nigerian prophet came out to say publicly that God told him that by March 27, 2020, COVID-19 would cease to exist on earth. But, of course, that has not been the case.

Some Nigerian prophets are good in following up the projections of CNN, the World Health Organization (WHO) and others. So, during the crossing over night service of every December 31/January 1, they normally come up with prophecies for the New Year. Some of their prophecies are pure repetitions of the projections of CNN and others news media. Again, in a crowd of over 100,000, the men of God will give prophecies such as "God just told me now that before the end of this year, someone here will buy a car or build a house or get an American Visa." Then, the whole congregation will shout at the top of their lungs, "AMEN!!!"

A few years ago (around 2014), a well-known Nigerian Neo-Pentecostal preacher prophesied to one of his members, who was a former senior cashier with Sheraton Hotels and Towers, Ikeja, Lagos, that God was set to do a mighty thing in his life. This prophecy prompted the man to become rich by instant gratification. Not long after this, the man was in the Nigerian police force's list of wanted suspects for theft. He had donated stolen money and gifts worth ₦39million to the Neo-Pentecostal preachers' church. Another member of the same church-denomination was caught in similar act, when he defrauded a bank of ₦40 million, out of which he donated ₦10 million to the church. Another member of this same church was arrested by the Economic and Financial Crimes Commission (EFCC) for defrauding foreigners to the tune of $96,607 through the internet, of which more than 80 percent of the proceeds were given to the church as tithes and offerings.[4]

The survey work of this book reveal that there are many people who have stopped going to church all because prophets have prophesied over them but those prophecies never came to pass. There are too many fake prophecies among the so-called men of God. It is so unfortunate that many people think that the prophetic ministry in the church is all about predicting the future. The prophetic voices that expose sins in the innermost places are lacking in Christendom today. The biblical prophetic ministry should be exposing and rebuking hidden sins through the anointing of the Holy Spirit and the undiluted truth of God's Word. This is what always leads people to genuine repentance from the sins that are destroying them (1 Corinthians 14).

According to Babatomiwa M. Owojaiye,

> I do not know of any other ministry that has damaged the image of the church in the African public square today more than that of the self-proclaimed prophets who have perverted what charismatics believe is a genuinely biblical prophetic ministry. While this phenomenon is not peculiar to Africa, this kind of public abuse of the pastoral and prophetic ministry seems to be more obvious here than elsewhere. For this growing breed of avaricious pastors, the greater their material accoutrements, the more apparent is the stamp of God's approval on their ministry.

[4] See more in Adelaja, *How the Church Creates Economic Recession*,50.

> The Bible does warn that in the last days there will be many false prophets, and false prophets have come and gone throughout the history of church. Yet this is now too prevalent in the church in Africa.[5]

In some churches, the leaders will say, "If you worship with us for three months and do not receive a miracle, then stop coming." Saying like this make people keep going all of the time, yet they will not receive anything. Eventually, when three months lapsed and they have not received anything, their leaders will tell them to keep the faith and that after one year, they will receive their miracles. At the end of the year, however, the people are already entangled in the web of the church, so they cannot get out anymore.[6] One more thing: most of the promises of Neo-Pentecostal preachers come with a price tag attached to them. The price tag is always a seed of money required to connect with the blessing or promise. Nothing goes for nothing; they must pay something in addition with their faith, and what they pay is always money. Many Nigerian Neo-Pentecostal leaders teach that for people to receive healings, miracles, breakthroughs, successes and the likes; certain principles, such as tithing, sowing seeds, sacrificial offerings, and positive confessions, have to be followed. However, only these leaders become richer and richer by these principles of extortion and exploitation, while the followers continue to struggle with poverty.

A lot of African preachers have divided peaceful homes and families by fake prophecies. A man called me sometimes ago after he lost his job and again fell into the hands of a fraudster. His complaint was that a prophet told him that his wife was a witch and that he needed to send her away before he can make it in life. Well, I prayed with him and told him the opposite. I told him, "Carry your wife along with you in all you do, be

[5] Owojaiye, "The Problem of False Prophets in Africa," 3.

[6] Sunday Adelaja, *Damaged by Religion: Path to Healing* (Kiev, Ukraine: Golden Truth, 2019),100.

open to her, love her as the Scripture says, take advice together, and pray together." I know the family very well, so I added, "Your wife is a brilliant and a submissive woman; love her as Christ loves his bride—the church." I am glad to report that the man and his wife have both recovered all of their losses. They are living happily together and prospering.

In addition, today, regardless of the sinful lives people may be living, these modern preachers keep giving people prophecies to their followers that they claim are from the Lord. Some followers are living with other people's wives or husbands, some are cohabiting sexually without legal marriages, some are in the business of online frauds; yet, these preachers keep giving them juicy prophecies, saying God is set to bless them! Remember the words of prophet Jeremiah:

> Concerning the prophets: My heart is broken within me; all my bones tremble. I am like a drunken man, like a strong man overcome by wine, because of the LORD and his holy words. The land is full of adulterers; because of the curse the land lies parched and the pastures in the wilderness are withered. The prophets follow an evil course and use their power unjustly. "Both prophet and priest are godless; even in my temple I find their wickedness," declares the LORD. . . . And among the prophets of Jerusalem, I have seen something horrible: They commit adultery and live a lie. They strengthen the hands of evildoers, so that not one of them turns from their wickedness. They are all like Sodom to me; the people of Jerusalem are like Gomorrah" ". . .because from the prophets of Jerusalem ungodliness has spread throughout the land." This is what the LORD Almighty says: "Do not listen to what the prophets are prophesying to you; they fill you with false hopes. They speak visions from their own minds, not from the mouth of the LORD. They keep saying to those who despise me,

> 'The LORD says: You will have peace.' And to all who follow the stubbornness of their hearts they say, 'No harm will come to you.' . . . "I have heard what the prophets say who prophesy lies in my name. They say, 'I had a dream! I had a dream.' (Jer 23:9-11, 14-17, 25)

There is certainly no doubt that in Nigeria today, the more the number of these modern-day prophets, the more the corruption in the land.

Gucci Pastors

There are pastors who wear the most expensive clothes and brag about their clothing on the pulpits as they preach. Knowing that I am an African pastor from Nigeria, a brother called me sometime in 2019. He hosted a Nigerian pastor and wanted him to come and preach in the little congregation that I pastor on a voluntary basis. I was about to consent until this brother raised the issue of an honorarium. At this point, I discovered that whenever these types of pastors come to the Western world to preach, their aim is to rake honorariums from one place to another. As they gather currency, they will travel through Italy and Dubai to shop for the latest shoes, phones, gold, and other wares. Anyway, I turned down the brother's offer for the pastor to preach because we do not have the kind of money he wanted and his motive to preach was not godly. There are many of these kinds of men going around the world, building connections to preach.

One of the respondents told me an incident that happened recently. The leaders of the youths in his church organized a one-day spiritual program for all the youths. A guest speaker, whom they respected to be a spiritual man, was invited. At the end of the day, an envelope containing money (as honorarium) was handed over to him. In a rush, he opened the envelope to count the money. Upon counting the money, he handed it back in annoyance saying; "*this money is small to my worth. I know how much I make if I'm invited to a program like this.*" There are several men of God in Nigeria that will tell you up-front how much they will charge you if you invite them to teach or preach in your church. More shameless to say, some of them will tell you to pay 70% of the amount into their bank account before they honor your invitation. Then, after their ministration, you will pay the remaining 30% balance. There are pastors who are known to be experts in fund raising. But some of them will tell you that 20% of the money they raise on your fund-raising day in your church belongs to them as their own commission. No matter how sweet their messages may look like, they have been polluted because they are being driven by the spirit of mammon.

The Selling of Churches and Members

I remember a particular incident in a city where I once lived. A particular church founder seemed to lose control over his church members, and his church business was no longer yielding money as he had planned. The next thing he did was to sell the church and all of its members to another pastor. There are several Neo-Pentecostal leaders who have chosen this pattern of raising churches and then selling them. This is a highly ridiculous practice. You cannot find this kind of pattern among the apostles of Jesus Christ. All of these types of men are in the pulpits for money—they are not true shepherds.

Chapter 18
Ministry of Curses

"*You have heard that it was said, 'You shall love your neighbor and hate your enemy.' But I say to you, love your enemies, bless those who curse you, do good to those who hate you, and pray for those who spitefully use you and persecute you, that you may be sons of your Father in heaven; for He makes His sun rise on the evil and on the good, and sends rain on the just and on the unjust*" (Matthew 5:44-45).

Some Nigerian Neo-Pentecostal leaders are experts in placing curses on people. It is like they have inherited the ministry of Balaam, who loved the rewards of wickedness (Numbers 22-25; 2 Peter 2:15). Several Nigerian Neo-Pentecostal pastors have been seen cursing public figures and bloggers who do not agree with them on doctrinal and lifestyle issues, people who talk ill of them or of their "spiritual fathers" and the likes. The issue of spiritual fatherhood is becoming a cultic association in Nigeria. One man will say, "This GO is my spiritual mentor, and I can fight for him to death." Another will say, "If you touch or insult my spiritual father, 'I will kill you.'"

Recently, a blogger insulted a man of God in Nigeria.[1] The spiritual son of the man insulted went after the blogger, saying,

> If you insult me, I may not talk, but if you insult my spiritual father. . . , I won't take it easy. Go and tell that bastard . . . does he has a father? Who knows his father? He is a bastard. . . ; the day he insults my father again, I will deal with him. I can't be alive

[1] As a disclaimer, it is wrong to insult people in the name of correcting error. It is sinful to go after someone's personality instead of addressing the issue at hand. This blogger was addressing what he saw as a heresy, but he went too far in insulting the man's personality. This is wrong. However, two wrongs will never make a right.

> and you insult my father. I curse the day he was born. . . . I will tear you into pieces . . ., you bastard. . . . I will fight him till he crashes.

In another incident, a well-known man of God recently built a mega church with a seating capacity of 100,000. A blogger remarked that he wished the man of God could have built factories for the jobless youths in Nigeria instead of another mega church building. In response, the man of God became angry and spouted out ravenously, saying,

> I heard that some very highly irrelevant, insignificant, infinitesimal, microscopic, statistical piece of material that are only relevant for census purposes, who only hang on internet to talk against people, they have not achieved anything, and will never achieve anything in life; who will never be remembered for nothing. They said why do you build a big church and not build factories? . . . but I have bad news for that devil. You have seen nothing yet? Get ready for heart attack.

Placing curses on people who disagree with us on issues or actions is really not of Christ. We need to stop people from placing curses on others by preaching the message of salvation to them.

A well-known man of God in Nigeria was recently bragging to his followers, saying, "When I pray, God hears me; when I curse a man, he remains cursed. When I pray that you should die, you will die." Frankly speaking, this is not the mind of Christ (Phil 2:5-8); it is an attitude of a manipulator and an oppressor. People cannot listen to such words every week and not be ridiculed or damaged.[2]This is how many Neo-Pentecostal pastors have enslaved their followers with the threat of curses. There is so much madness going on in African churches today. What

---

[2] Sunday Adelaja, Damaged by *Religion: Path to Healing*, 100-101.

many churches are practicing is another form of slavery, not Christianity. Beware of the religious slave camps. A man once said, "No one can make you feel inferior without your consent!"

The Old Testament tells the story of people who were judged instantly because they rebelled against Moses (Numbers 16). The contest between the prophet Elijah and the prophets of Baal ended up with the destruction of Baal's prophets (1 Kgs 18). Elijah called down fire to consume some military troops of a rebellious king of Israel (2 Kgs 1). Similarly, the prophet Elisha called down curses in the name of the Lord on forty-two young men who were making fun of him, calling him a bald-headed man. Two wild bears came out and killed them all (2 Kgs 2:23-25). The list continues.

But in the New Testament, the reverse is the case. Jesus was once accused of casting out demons with the spirit of Beelzebub, but he never cursed people for calling him the prince of demons. Rather, he said, "*Whoever speaks a word against the Son of Man [i.e., Jesus] will be forgiven, but whoever speaks against the Holy Spirit [i.e., to die in unbelief] will not be forgiven*" (Matt 12:32). Even when Jesus was crucified, he prayed to God for the forgiveness of his killers (Luke 23:34). This does not mean that God no longer rises to defend His children, but He told us to forgive others, pray for our enemies, and leave revenge to Him alone. (I have written extensively on this in my book "*Forgiveness: A Divine Key for Brokenness*").[3]

When we are genuinely empowered by the Spirit, we will come to a point where we will no longer be afraid of dying for the sake of the gospel. Consider the example of Stephen in the book of Acts:

[3] Tunde A. Samuel, *Forgiveness: A Divine Key for Brokenness* (Las Vegas: WorkBook Press, 2021).

> But he [Stephen], full of the Holy Spirit, gazed into heaven and saw the glory of God, and Jesus standing pat the right hand of God. And he said, "Behold, I see the heavens opened, and the Son of Man standing pat the right hand of God." . . . And as they were stoning Stephen, he called out, "Lord Jesus, receive my spirit." And falling to his knees he cried out with a loud voice, "Lord, do not hold this sin against them." And when he had said this, he fell asleep. (Acts 7:55, 59-60)

No doubt, this scenario of Stephen's death communicated a unique message to Saul (a.k.a. Paul) because he witnessed it.

From the passage above, first, it is a genuine mark of the fullness of the Spirit to die in the hand of persecutors without denying Christ. Second, it the highest mark of the baptism of power to pray for the forgiveness of one's killer while drawing one's last breath. Stephen took after Jesus, whose last petition to God was to forgive his persecutors. Hence, it is a clear mark of immaturity when Christians engage in raining down curses upon their persecutors. When one of the killers of Jesus saw Jesus' reaction to his crucifixion by praying for those who crucified him, he said, "Definitely, this is the Son of God." In the same way, Saul (who later became known as Paul) was there when Stephen was being stoned to death: "*But they* [the Jewish leaders] *cried out with a loud voice and stopped their ears and rushed together at him. Then they cast him out of the city and stoned him. And the witnesses laid down their garments at the feet of a young man named Saul*" (Acts 7:57-58). Definitely, Saul was touched when he saw the way Stephen died without cursing his persecutors. He heard Stephen saying, "Lord forgive them." So, when he saw the great light on the road to Damascus and heard the voice calling his name, he said, "Who are you, Lord?" (Acts 9:5). Our reactions to insults, oppositions, and persecutions define the level of our immersion in the Holy Spirit.

Many of the early martyrs faced death with joy because of their faith on Christ.

Unfortunately, just as Neo-Pentecostal leaders are too quick to curse people, the followers of Nigerian Neo-Pentecostal leaders also go as far as using speaking in tongues as a weapon to curse their neighbors or their enemies. They engage in prayers and fasting solely to place curses on the people they tag as enemies. This practice is aberrant from biblical Christianity (Matt 5:44; Rom 12:14; 1 Pet 3:9). Many Nigerian Neo-Pentecostal leaders always go to Old Testament passages whenever they want to pronounce their curses. However, the principles of life in the old covenant are different from those of the New Covenant. Jesus has raised the bar. In his teachings on the beatitudes, Jesus established the New Covenant way of life. For instance, Jesus said, "*You have heard that it was said, 'You shall love your neighbor and hate your enemy.' But I say to you, love your enemies, bless those who curse you, do good to those who hate you, and pray for those who spitefully use you and persecute you, that you may be sons of your Father in heaven . . .*" (Matt 5:44-45). Hence, we are to bless and not to curse.

A pastor friend here in the States invited a preacher he once met (through another friend) to come for a weekend revival program here in the States. Being a foreign guest speaker, members praised and hailed him as he preached with some arranged oratories, and he convinced my friend and his members of the need for him to return in the following years. For each of the three days he preached, this Nigerian preacher raised money for himself. The following year, he came again during the church's anniversary. Eventually, he imposed himself as the spiritual father or mentor over my friend. Interestingly, during the COVID-19 Lockdown in Nigeria (we also had a longer period of Lockdown here in the States), this Nigerian Neo-Pentecostal preacher called my friend several times and demanded money. When the money was not forthcoming, the preacher told my friend, "I am your spiritual father; do you know that if you fail to remit your due [i.e., tithe] to me, I can place a curse upon you and your ministry." Nigerian preachers of this kind are real armed robbers in the pulpit.

Sunday Adelaja writes, "A General Overseer recently proclaimed to his followers that anyone who misses coming to church more than five times will die prematurely. He warns that any of his members who leave his 'fatherly coverage' over them will die instantly."[4] These types of Neo-Pentecostal leaders threaten those who oppose their commands, and plant seeds of fear in their followers' hearts. They protect themselves with Scripture like Ps 105:15 ("Touch not my anointed and do my prophet no harm"). Hence, people obey such leaders to the letter not because of the love they have for God but because of the fear they have of their pastors' curses.

---

[4] Sunday Adelaja, *Damaged by Religion: Path to Healing* (Kiev, Ukraine: Golden Truth, 2019), 51-52.

Chapter 19
Occultism in the Modern African Christianity

"For such men are false apostles, deceitful workers, masquerading as apostles of Christ. And no wonder, for Satan himself masquerades as an angel of light It is not surprising, then, if his servants masquerade as servants of righteousness . . ." (2 Corinthians 11: 13-15)

Occultism has to do with getting involved with the magical powers of Satan. There are several occultic or demonic people today who are parading themselves as ministers of the gospel. A Spirit-filled Christian does not need to wander too far to discover that some new churches in Nigeria and Africa are in the danger of making occultism the measure of recognized Christianity. Though the word "occultism' may seem to be too negative or biased, as Daniel Sopuru explains, the practices of some modern preachers fit such nomenclature.[1] Sopuru tells a story of how fetish practices are penetrating Nigerian Christianity through some Neo-Pentecostal leaders. According to him, one man from Nigeria went to study in India. After failing all of his courses, he decided to get involved in the practice of mysticism. He spent more years in India and came back to Nigeria with mysterious powers. Upon his return, he convinced many people of the call of God upon his life. He established a "church" and became its president and founder. Today, there are several branches of his church in villages and cities, where he goes around, seducing and hypnotizing unsuspecting victims.[2] There are scores of such fake pastors

[1] Daniel O. Sopuru, *Modern Theology versus Biblical Theology: A Call for Biblical Christianity* (Makurdi, Nigeria: Evangelical Christian Literature and Radio Ministries, 2007), 2. The equivalent of "occultism" in the Western world today is the "New Age Movement."

[2] Sopuru, *Modern Theology Versus Biblical Theology*, 129.

all over Nigeria.[3] Some experience failure in their careers or businesses and all of a sudden turn to ministry as way out. As Sopuru avers, "It is a pity that these management-professional-turned-preachers have saturated Nigeria and indeed Africa with their pseudo-gospel to the detriment of the spiritual life of millions on this continent."[4] For some decades now, Manly P. Hall has highlighted how occultism has crept into modern-day Christianity: "There is abundant evidence that in many forms of modern thought—especially the so-called 'prosperity' psychology, 'will-power building' metaphysics and systems of 'high-pressure' salesmanship—black magic has been passed through metamorphosis, and although its name may be changed, its nature remains the same."[5]

There are myriads of stories of fake Nigerian pastors who are caught with human body parts. Recently in Ondo State, a couple came to a church for vigil prayer with their less than ten-year-old son. When the prayer night was over, they discovered their son was missing. It was discovered that the pastor had orchestrated the kidnapping of the boy. Sadly, he ordered the boy to be killed, and he used parts of his body for a ritual to fill himself with spiritual power so that he could demonically attract more crowds to his church. This pastor is already serving his term in jail, but this couple has lost their son. You can read more of occultic practices among modern African modern pastors by reading Makhado Sinthumule Ramabulana's book *Church Mafia Captured by Secret Powers: An Untold African Narrative*. (You can also listen to his confession on YouTube). Pastor Makhado narrated how he backslid from the right path and started seeking voodoo power to attract crowds to his church until

[3] After spending fourteen years of her life in what she described as a "demonic cage" at the Synagogue Church of All Nations (SCOAN), Bishola Johnson sees her liberation as the miraculous act of God's mercy. According to her testimony, she and others young ladies were abused by the famous Nigerian prophet T. B. Joshua for over a decade. For more details, see Bisola H. Johnson, *The T. B. Joshua I Know: Deception of the Age Unmasked* (Lagos, Nigeria: n.p., 2018).

[4] Sopuru, *Modern Theology versus Biblical Theology*, 129.

[5] Manly P. Hall, *Masonic, Hermetic, Dabbalistic and Rosicrucian Symbolical Philosophy* (Los Angeles: n.p., 1969), 101-2.

the hand of God reached down to him in mercy to draw him back to right way. There are hundreds or thousands of acclaimed men of God in Africa who are combining fetishism with Christianity. It is so pathetic that millions of people in Africa patronize these fake pastors just because they are looking for instant miracles.

Chapter 20
The Danger of the Gospel of Nigerian Neo-Pentecostals

"*No wonder the Scriptures say, "The Gentiles blaspheme the name of God because of you*" (Rom 2: 24 NLT)

From the information gathered from the survey, the Nigerian Neo-Pentecostalism seems to be derailing from the biblical gospel presentation. The Nigerian Neo-Pentecostals seem to be completely off the true course of biblical Christianity right from the start. Reacting to the issue of immorality among some Nigerian Neo-Pentecostal leaders, one survey respondent writes,

> Many of the Nigerian Neo-Pentecostal leaders have discouraged many people from going to church, especially the young people, due to their act of atrocities and exploitation of all forms. They ordain people (men and women) who have not really known the Lord as ministers because of money. They are fond of abusing young ladies and girls. They make doubt the reality of the supernatural. They are also mainly interested in money not in saving lost souls. They brainwashed people with their eloquent words and many more. But worst still, they make the unbelievers to speak blaspheming words about the name of Jesus, and many unbelievers think that Christians are bunch of fake people.[1]

Gary Maxey and Peter Ozodo admit, "We are struggling as a Church . . . . The Prince of Persia is blocking our prayers and the prayers of the saints in Nigeria for Nigeria. [We have] never seen a nation awash with

[1] Peace B. Samuel, Google Form survey, December 11, 2019.

so many Churches and aglow with so much unrighteousness, corruption and rank hypocrisy."[2] Unlike its reputable integrity of the past, today, "the Nigerian Church has lost the credibility it once had within the society. The reputation of the Church leadership has declined; we have seen the erosion of our Christian heritage."[3] Maxey and Ozodo go on to say, "Unfortunately, it is now noticeable that a significant segment of the Christian Church in this country is gradually but steadily departing from the basic goals of Christianity . . . The entire Church is in the danger of losing its basic direction."[4]

Daniel E. Sopuru notes that the effects of the Neo-Pentecostal gospel are spreading like cancerous cells to every nook and cranny of Nigeria:

> Neo-Pentecostalism has really watered-down Christianity. Secondly, Pentecostal pastors have thrown the dignity of the Clergy to the pigs. They tell a lot of lies to win people to themselves, and they make their followers see them as next to Jesus Christ, if not like Jesus Christ Himself. The fact is that if the Lord himself does not intervene, many people would go to hell from Pentecostal Churches. It seems this fits the description the Lord gave about the road that leads to destruction (wide and smooth, and many people find it), against the narrow and thorny and few people find it. I tend to believe that the Neo-Pentecostal Movement was from the Devil to counter what the Church stands for. It is a pity that many "evangelicals" run to those Churches thinking that they are models.[5]

The gospel of Nigerian Neo-Pentecostals is so contagious that many evangelicals are cheaply falling for it. Regardless of the international

---

[2] Maxey and Ozodo, *The Seduction of the Nigerian Church*, 16.
[3] Maxey and Ozodo, *The Seduction of the Nigerian Church*, 16.
[4] Maxey and Ozodo, *The Seduction of the Nigerian Church*, 16.
[5] Daniel E. Sopuru, Google Interview, October 18, 2019.

recognition of the global shift of Christianity toward the global South, the nation of Nigeria seems to be at a crossroads presently concerning the quality of her Christianity.

Ironically, the gospel of Nigerian Neo-Pentecostals seems to be gaining wider recognition and attention:

> Many well-known Church leaders around the world are seriously proclaiming that we are in the midst of the greatest revival the Church has ever known. Yet nobody who reads the New Testament with an open and sincere mind will agree with those who believe that the Church is experiencing a revival at present. The result is that increasingly, many Christians are living in ways not in keeping with the standards of the Scriptures. Materialism is enthroned and sin is tolerated, while holiness is largely ignored.[6]

The attention seems to have been largely placed on the popularity of Neo-Pentecostal preachers; hence, the biblical lifestyle of godliness and contentment has been eroded by a quest for popularity. Consequently, churches are multiplying all throughout Nigeria today, but there is no marked change in the way people live. It is sad to say that "the Nigeria revival is losing its cutting edge. One obvious reason for this is that there are doctrinal errors in the camp of those pushing the Church forward. A result of this is that the Church is in serious danger of losing sight of the very reason for its existence."[7] Hence, there is convincing evidence that Nigerian Neo-Pentecostals are pursuing trajectories that do not bode well for the future of Christianity in Nigeria.

---

[6] Maxey and Ozodo, *The Seduction of the Nigerian Church*, 16.
[7] Maxey and Ozodo, *The Seduction of the Nigerian Church*, 15.

Practical Implications

When the gospel is presented with a promise that the recipients will be free from any form of suffering, pain, sickness, and poverty; it is a "gospel" that falls short of the biblical gospel. In most parts of Africa, Nigeria most especially, as soon as you convince people that there are positive earthly incentives that come with the gospel you are presenting to them, you are likely igniting the fire of warm reception. But the danger is that you make people focus on the incentives rather than on Christ. This phenomenon is best described in the words of J. C. Ryle: "There is a common, worldly kind of Christianity in this day, which many have—a cheap Christianity which offends nobody, and requires no sacrifice—which costs nothing, and is worth nothing."[8]Nigerian Christian researcher and writer Austen Chimdi Ukachi, in his effort to identify some of the reasons why the early revival in Nigeria has dwindled, writes,

> The responses of over 70 percent of the interviewees in areas where revival had previously taken place point to the fact that the tempo of the revival began to decline when the Church [Neo-Pentecostal] shifted emphasis from a Christ-centered gospel to a self-seeking and self-gratifying gospel. Pastors who were interviewed, some of whom have retired after several years of service in the ministry, lamented about the serious harm and damage that unbalanced gospel messages have caused the church. They testified that sacrificial living, prayer, and total commitment to the gospel were factors that contributed to the revival they experienced in the past years.[9]

The challenge with Neo-Pentecostals preachers today is not that Jesus

[8] Quoted in Omar C. Garcia, "A Cheap Christianity," Go Beyond (blog), January 10, 2020, https://gobeyond.blog/2020/01/10/a-cheap-christianity/.

[9] Austen C. Ukachi, *The Best Is Yet to Come: Pentecostal and Charismatic Renewals in Nigeria 1914-1990s* (n.p.: Xulon Press, 2013), 367. Ukachi is a Neo-Pentecostals man who is calling the attention of the fellow Neo-Pentecostals men back to the point where he thought they have missed the real gospel.

is not being mentioned as the savior but the fact that Nigerian Neo-Pentecostals lift healing, miracles, material prosperity, and other supposed remunerations—which they claim are waiting for anyone who accepts the gospel—above the real gospel message. Observers have pointed attention to the fact that in their preaching, Nigerian new wave prosperity preachers exalt the preaching of miracles and material prosperity at the expense of the message of salvation, and godliness. Hence, Jesus Christ is being projected as the medicine or pill needed for anyone who wants to live a complete stress-free, sorrow-free, and suffering-free life here on earth because Jesus will give health, riches, miracles, and more to everyone who follows him.[10]

The gospel that centers on sudden breakthroughs and miracles does not do harm to the biblical gospel alone but remains a threat to the economic well-being of the nation. Sunday Adelaja maintains that miracle and breakthrough messages convince gullible minds (i.e., the masses) to think that the process of labor and production is not necessary for prosperity and that all that is needed is to "name it [i.e., confess it] and claim it." If Nigerian Neo-Pentecostal churches do not cease this kind of preaching, then the nation will continually breed Christians who will be the masterminds of corrupt practices in society. Such a gospel can only produce followers who will eventually become hackers, scammers, and thieves. Frankly speaking, "if we don't want to be a nation known for fraud and corruption, we must urgently begin to teach people that it is better to work hard than to pray for financial breakthrough."[11]

When the gospel presentation focuses on deliverance from both physical and spiritual enemies, the recipients of such a gospel live perpetually in fear and primarily conscious of enemies rather than of Christ their redeemer. This is the situation of many Nigerian Neo-Pentecostal Christians who

[10] Ukachi, *The Best Is Yet to Come: Pentecostal and Charismatic Renewals in Nigeria 1914-1990s*, 368.
[11] Adelaja, *How the Church Creates Economic Recession,* 24.

see or blame one enemy or more for every bad occurrence of life. Again, when the gospel presented compels every convert to experience the sign gifts of the Holy Spirit, there will be a possibility of winning people into "signs" but not unto Christ. As earlier mentioned, many Neo-Pentecostals maintain that the ability of a convert to be able to speak in tongues authenticates his or her genuine conversion and baptism in the Holy Spirit.[12] All of these open doors for the possibility of counterfeit conversions and the downplay of the quality of members among Nigerian Neo-Pentecostal denominations.

Another important point that survey participants draw attention to is the church-to-church conversion tactics of Nigerian Neo-Pentecostals' evangelistic practices. Akila Adamu points out that "evangelical Christians reach out to non-Christians while the Nigerian Neo-Pentecostals reach out to members from other churches. As soon as they convince members from the evangelical church to join them, they quickly position such members as pastors or elders with the aim of retaining them as permanent members."[13] This approach of winning members from existing churches to Neo-Pentecostal churches has generated a lot of rancor in Nigeria. The wide margin between the doctrinal positions of the evangelical and Pentecostal denominations in Nigeria paves the way for crises and divisions among Christians throughout the whole country. As noted above, many Nigerian evangelicals do not emphasize the signs gifts,[14] and they never focus on the "health and wealth gospel" like Nigerian Neo-Pentecostals do. In lieu of these points, and coupled with the impoverished situation of Nigeria, Pentecostal pastors—in most places—find it easy to persuade evangelicals to leave their

[12] See more in Chris Oyakhilome, *How to Pray Effectively: Volume One* (Lagos, Nigeria: LoveWorld Publishing Ministry, 2001), 36-42.

[13] Akila Adamu, Google Forms survey, November 17, 2019.

[14] For instance, according to the article of faith of my home church denomination, Evangelical Church Winning All (ECWA), "Some of the Spiritual gifts listed in Scripture, for example tongues, healing, etc., were sign gifts. However, an undue emphasis on possession of any of those sign gifts as a means or prerequisite for salvation is unscriptural and is rejected (Jn. 6:3-16; Jn. 16:13-14; Acts 1:8; 1 Cor. 14:1-40)." See Evangelical Church Winning All, *ECWA Articles of Faith and Practices* (Jos, Nigeria: Challenge Press, 2018), 6.

churches.

Beginning in the late 1990s, there has been a mass drift of members from evangelical denominations to Pentecostal denominations. Some evangelical preachers have titled this movement "sheep stealing," calling Pentecostals wolves and hyenas.[15] However, as a means of a counterattack, vibrant Pentecostal leaders—such as David Oyedepo, Chris Oyakhilome, and Paul Eneche—have refuted evangelicals on this point. For example, Eneche, whose church and ministry are flooded with vibrant members from mainline denominations, has eloquently preached, "There is nothing like sheep stealing. If you feed your sheep very well, your sheep will stay back at home in the pen."[16] On this point, Eneche may not be totally correct because the ultimate objective of all evangelistic strategies should center on how to win unbelievers to Christ, not believers of another church to one's own church. In the presentation of the gospel, it is more appropriate to turn to places where there are many unbelievers in order to convert them to Christ rather than stealing members from other existing churches. The Apostle Paul was clearly against the attitude of sheep stealing when he said, "*It has always been my ambition to preach the gospel where Christ was not known, so that I would not be building on someone else's foundation*" (Rom 15:20).

The survey responses revealed that in Nigeria today, the waning of respect for Neo-Pentecostal churches and their leaders among the unbelievers is unprecedented. There is little regard and honor for the clergy and their churches due to their substandard Christian practices. Most Neo-Pentecostal churches in Nigeria have become very earthly minded and have vastly lost their spiritual power and authority. The aim of Nigerian Neo-Pentecostals is how they can make Christianity more marketable. They place more emphasis

[15] From the middle of the 1990s to 2010, the battle between Nigeria evangelicals and Pentecostals was so hostile that it resulted in a conflict over church-to-church conversion. See more in Maxey and Ozodo, *The Seduction of the Nigerian Church*, 46-57.

[16] Paul Eneche, "Hour of Healing and Deliverance" (Sermon, Dunamis Gospel Centre, Abuja, Nigeria, July 2010).

on packaging the gospel in a more attractive way.[17] Jared C. Wilson has a good description for this when he writes on attractional churches. According to Wilson, the term "attractional" refers to "a way of doing church ministry whose primary purpose is to make Christianity appealing."[18]In fact, the attractional model is not just a matter of mere style; rather, it has become a paradigm. Nigerian Neo-Pentecostals have adopted the *modus operandi* of pragmatism and consumerism. "Pragmatism" has to do with "If it works, then work it." In this ideology, the ends always justify the means. Pragmatism is one of the plagues ravaging the modern Christianity. What is right is being defined by whatever works. The assumption always is, long as it works, then it must be right. In January 2020, I interviewed a member of a Neo-Pentecostal assembly concerning the renaissance of a materialistic gospel among Neo-Pentecostals. In part of his response, the man said, "My Papa use to say, 'only a fool will deny the proof."[19] Statements like this are highly misleading. It sometimes simply the end justifies the means. On the other hand, "consumerism" is a business term with an ideology of trying to satisfy the desire of consumers (or customers) at all costs. The ideologies behind these terms seem to fit into Wilson's description:

> "We will do whatever it takes to get people in the door," I often hear pastors say. "We just want them to be able to hear the message of Jesus." That latter motivation is wonderful, but the problem is that "doing whatever it takes to get people in the door" can replace or undercut what we want them to be attracted to. Whatever you win people with is what you win them to. The best motives in the world cannot sanctify unbiblical methods.[20]

[17] As part of the ways of achieving this goal, many NNPs always invite worldly singers, comedians, and motivational speakers to their churches in order to attract large crowds of people.
[18] Jared C. Wilson, *The Gospel-Driven Church: Uniting Church-Growth with the Metrics of Grace* (Grand Rapids: Zondervan, 2019), 24.
[19] Anonymous, interview by the author, January 15, 2020.
[20] Wilson, *The Gospel-Driven Church*, 24.

Hence, to keep their converts in their churches, Nigerian Neo-Pentecostals must continue to focus members' attention on the ten emphases discussed above (e.g., financial prosperity, miracles, healings, breakthroughs, success). Nevertheless, if a method does not depend on the genuine leading of the Holy Spirit, then adopting pragmatism in order to win souls remains awkward. Whatever one's approach to evangelism, redirecting people to anything (or anyone) other than Jesus jeopardizes the real gospel.

Nigerian Neo-Pentecostals boast about not being legalistic like orthodox and evangelical churches. However, in an attempt to avoid the error of legalism (into which some of the older Nigerian Pentecostal churches fell with their mantra for holiness), Nigerian Neo-Pentecostals have equally fallen into an even greater error: the modern error of the hyper-grace doctrine. According to Lola Charles,

> The hyper-grace doctrine concerns those who are of the opinion that a Christian can live anyway he or she deems fit because the sacrifice of Jesus has covered every sin—past, present, and future. However, part of what really qualifies someone to be a Christian is that sin no longer rules over the person (Rom 6:14). To be a Christian is to continue to live a Christ-like life, to be a true disciple of Jesus.[21]

Further, Francis Chan and Mark Beuving clearly write, "Yet somehow many have come to believe that a person can be a 'Christian' without being like Christ. A 'follower' who doesn't follow. How does that make any sense? Many people in the church have decided to take on the name of Christ and nothing else."[22]

---

[21] Lola Charles, interview by the author, Ilorin, Nigeria, January 10, 2020.

[22] Francis Chan and Mark Beuving, *Multiply: Disciples Making Disciples* (Colorado Springs: David C. Cook, 2012), 16-17.

One survey respondent reports, "In most of his teachings and preaching, Chris Oyakhilome, the founder and General Overseer of the Christ Embassy (a.k.a. Believers' LoveWorld) maintains that believers in Christ Jesus cannot sin; they may make a mistake, but they cannot sin again because in this world, believers are exactly like Christ himself."[23] Oyakhilome also teaches that believers in Christ Jesus cannot be sick:

> Let this be dawn on your spirit for all time—you were not re-created for sickness, but for divine health. The moment you were born again; the life you came with from your mother's womb ceased to reign in your being; a new life from God took over. The day a man is born again **the law of physical death is reversed**. . . . The fallen nature of the first Adam came with sickness and could be influence by it, but the nature of God, which you have now received came with life. It came with health. The power of sickness is destroyed. It cannot have a home in your body. Sickness has become a thing of the past. Health became yours the day you received Jesus into your life. It became your present tense possession.[24]

In his references to the prayer of the Apostle Paul in Ephesians 1:17-18 and Colossians 1:9, Oyakhilome writes, "I believe we need to pray these prayers for the Church in these days. It's not God's will for you to be sick or to suffer, but ignorance of the word of God can keep you under the hold of sickness. It can make you think God wants things that way,

[23] Adebiyi, interview. Adebiyi adds that even with the failure of Oyakhilome's first marriage, which ended in divorce and concerning which his wife accused him of marital infidelity, Oyakhilome still maintains that believers cannot sin again. At Christ Embassy, "sin" is not called sin but a "mistake." To this day, Oyakhilome, who is a close follower of Benny Hinn, has millions of people following him as members both in Nigeria and abroad.

[24] Chris Oyakhilome, *None of These Diseases* (Lagos, Nigeria: LoveWorld Publication, 2001), 59-60. Later, Oyakhilome adds, "When you are born again it was the seed of God that came to you and produced life in you. You are full of God as Jesus is. He told his disciples, "I am the vine, ye are the branches" (John 15:5). The same life that flows through the vine flows through the branches. That means there is a new blood type, blood type-D for Divine. And the life you now have is the indestructible life! This is the reason no sickness can destroy you"(85-86).

particularly when you think about the fact that some ministers actually teach this."[25] These kinds of teachings are customary for many Nigerian Neo-Pentecostals; they form part of their evangelistic messages. By the way, it must be made clear here that being born again in Christ Jesus is not a matter of biological rebirth, but a spiritual rebirth of soul through the Holy Spirit and the finished work of Christ. Based on these kinds of Oyakhilome's teachings, some Neo-Pentecostals do not believe that believers should die at young age or even die (physically) at all. Hence, they do not announce the death of any member that dies in their churches.

According to Joseph Ali, "The record must be set straight; it is not that the Nigeria Neo-Pentecostals are not preaching the gospel at all. The problem lies in putting other things in place or above the cross of Jesus; and if the cross is not the central focus, then, it is not the gospel. For decades, myself and few other Pentecostal friends have been raising alarms about this deviation."[26]Ali further adds,

> There is a need to return to the balanced or total gospel. We need to emphasize the gospel without de-emphasizing the blessings (i.e., prosperity, healing, deliverance, sign and wonders etc.) that accompany the gospel. Nevertheless, our fellow Nigerian Neo-Pentecostals preachers have lowered the standard of the gospel, and the ultimate priority have been misplaced. Someone like me left an evangelical church in the late of 80s because the holistic gospel was not preached then. The failure of the Nigerian Evangelicals in preaching the total gospel gives room for many of the Nigerian Neo-Pentecostals to adulterate the gospel.[27]

---

[25] Oyakhilome, *None of These Diseases*, 129.

[26] Joseph Ali, interview by the author, Ilorin, Nigeria, April 22, 2020. Joseph Ali is the leader of a Pentecostal denomination known as Christ Assembly Church, Nigeria. For many years, Ali, Mike Oye, Onofurho, and few others (all of them Pentecostal leaders) formed a forum known as "Contending for the Faith" with the aim of correcting the heretical teachings of Nigerian Neo-Pentecostals.

[27] Ali, interview.

Nevertheless, Ali maintains that there are a few Pentecostal churches that are still striving to strike the balance; some are still contending for the truth at all cost even though we may still have some imperfections.[28]

In a point of view similar to Ali's, Mike Oye says,

> All hope of restoring the true gospel back in Nigeria is not completely lost, because, having seen the fake life and false gospel of some of the Neo-Pentecostal churches, many of the orthodox and evangelical members who once migrated (through church-to-church conversion) to these churches are beginning to return back to their former churches which they initially tagged as 'cold churches.' Some remnants are leaving these fake churches and are seeking for orthodox, evangelical and classical Pentecostal churches who still retain the truth. Much so, today, there is an insurgent of revival among many orthodox and evangelical denominations with a balance teaching on the gospel and the Holy Spirit.[29]

Some who are disappointed with the Neo-Pentecostal aberration are finding their way back to the orthodox and evangelical denominations. This return is a continuous trend today in Nigerian Christendom. Nevertheless, many will still remain in these Neo-Pentecostal churches with the adulterated gospel because that is what they want. Jesus forewarned his disciples about this issue—that the road to eternal life is narrow, and few are those that find it (Matthew 7:14). The rise of fake prophets with fake miracles to deceive even the elect is part of the end-time signs that Jesus spoke about (Matthew 24:2).[30]

Another discovery from the survey revealed that due to heavy financial

[28] Ali, interview.
[29] Mike Oye, interview by the author, Ibadan, Nigeria, April 22, 2020.
[30] Oye, interview.

tasks, unfulfilled prophecies and promises, and the immoral lives of their leaders, some youths are already boycotting churches. They prefer to sit down at home and watch online worship programs of their choice. Some of these youths buy internet data to watch some Christian programs they like online instead of going to church on Sundays.[31] Finally, in the quest for quick riches, some Nigerian Neo-Pentecostal pastors are embracing Islam. There are a handful of young Neo-Pentecostal pastors that have converted to Islam and turned into Islamic clerics.[32]

[31] Responses from Google Form survey.

[32] Muslims in Nigeria reward any Christians who intentionally and openly convert to Islam with monetary and material gifts. Hence, because of these instances and due to fake Christians' conversions or lack of discipleship, many young Christians in Nigeria are heading that way. This is part of a major concern today in Nigerian Christendom.

Chapter 21
The Way Forward

"*. . . I will build my church; and the gates of hell shall not prevail against it*" (Matthew 16: 18)

Based on personal observations from the trend of responses from my interviews and survey, coupled with the argument of this book, below are a few of my recommendations. First, my argument in this book recognizes that although there are clear-cut signs of deviation seen among some Nigerian Neo-Pentecostals, there are still a few Neo-Pentecostal leaders who are striving to retain sound biblical teachings. Hence, it is advisedly recommended that Neo-Pentecostal leaders who are still standing on the true teaching of God's Word need to separate themselves from, and point out the truth to, those on the other side. Second, though Pentecostalism has impacted Nigeria's religious space, it is necessary to curtail the excesses that today's Nigerian Neo-Pentecostals are perpetrating. Hence, this there is an urgent call to Nigerian Neo-Pentecostal leaders to harness their energy toward producing mature Christians who can, in turn, help in building up the nation as they labor with an ecumenical spirit to synergize with evangelicals and other religious bodies.

Third, the Christian Association of Nigeria (CAN) needs to develop and encourages solid pastoral training for all church leaders. The growth of mushroom churches throughout the geographical regions of Nigeria without having a commensurate moral and spiritual impact on the people involved makes no sense. Pastoral ministry is more than an employment opportunity; it is a calling that ought to be backed up with sound formal training. Neo-Pentecostal denominations in Nigeria need to go back to standard Bible schools. Some of the leaders are highly sincere in their erroneous convictions, but this reality is never a justifiable ground for aberrant versions of the gospel. For instance, the error of placing personal revelations, personal experiences, and the words of general overseers (GOs) above the Scriptures—as most Nigerian Neo-Pentecostal leaders and members do—is due to biblical illiteracy. But no amount of sincerity can justify the damage of propagating a pseudo-gospel. Hence, the Nigerian Christian body needs to advocate for the formal training of a would-be church leader.

Fourth, there is an urgent need for disciple-making. As a way of concluding this book, attention is hereby drawn to an urgent and inevitable task of discipleship making so that the Nigerian church's missiological enterprise will produce a fruitful and lasting result. But the question now is "Who is to disciple whom?" There is frankly no simple answer to this question. Considering the current state of Christianity in Nigeria, the subject of discipleship cannot be over emphasized. Disciple-making is really a part of the inevitable process of turning new converts into mature believers in Christ. To this point, Patrick Lai writes, "A man may be consecrated, dedicated and devoted but of little use if undisciplined. Discipleship is disciplining (or training) the new believers in the basics of the faith. Once the basics are mastered, discipleship continues into all other aspects of faith."[1] Therefore, it is very important to know that evangelism, discipleship, and church planting are inseparable processes. Again, as Lai points out,

> The goal of discipleship is to teach new believers to identify with Christ and be obedient to God's word, so that fruit may be harvested both in and through their lives for Jesus. As believers mature, leaders should be appointed in culturally acceptable ways. These leaders must be trained to shepherd the fellowship, evangelize the unbelievers, disciple believers and plant other churches in nearby communities. In all church planting efforts,

[1] Lai, *Tent Making: Business as Missions*, 155.

> there should be a plan for raising up national leaders and as quickly as possible, giving the leadership of the fellowship into their hands.[2]

Well-discipled members are always good tools for evangelism, serve well for the growth of any given local church, and portray a life of unquestionable integrity for the world. Hence, contextual research on discipleship will go far in providing good grounding for Nigerian converts to Christianity.

Speaking on the expansion of Christianity inside and outside of Nigeria by Nigerians, the fact that mass conversion is characterized by syncretism in most parts of Nigeria is undeniable. To make matters worse, the delusion of Neo-Pentecostalism concerning a health-and-wealth gospel has really posed a big challenge. In some areas, the spread of Christianity among some Nigerian Neo-Pentecostals can be likened to those old and ever-relevant words of the Apostle Paul to the Philippians: "*For, as I have often told you before and now tell you again even with tears, many live as enemies of the cross of Christ. Their destiny is destruction, their god is their stomach, and their glory is in their shame. Their mind is set on earthly things*" (Philippians 1:18-19). In a similar way, the same Apostle Paul described the followers of false preachers of the gospel as those with itching ears: "*For the time will come when people will not put up with sound doctrine. Instead, to suit their own desires, they will gather around them a great number of teachers to say what their itching ears want to hear*" (2 Timothy 4:3). There are thousands out there preaching other gospels different from the gospel of our Lord Jesus Christ. This reality supports the need for an urgent call for Nigerian evangelicals to rise to this challenge.

Hence, run away from those who use the name of Christ only for their personal gain (Philip 3:18). Stay away from those who are picking your pocket in the name of Jesus. Be far away from gospels that only focus on self-improvement without total loyalty to Christ. Stay away from churches where

[2] Lai, *Tent Making: Business as Missions*, 155.

Christ is not glorified but where men are deified. Run away from churches where "men of God" preach about themselves—with their preaching filled with stories upon stories of their trips to different foreign lands—but who will not open the Scriptures to expound the Word of God. Be far away from gospels where the cross—repentance from sins and a life of daily crucifixion—has been replaced with love for materialism. Run away from churches where you are comfortable in your sins. If you go to a church with sin in your life and you are not convicted of it, you are probably at citadel of Babylon and not on Mount Zion, where holiness and deliverance from sins reign. Many of today's modern preachers and prophets know nothing of God. Hence, beware of several deceptions going on in the name of Christ. If you have a genuine love for the truth, then you will not fall prey (2 Thessalonians 2:10-11).

This Is Not a Condemnation

When you confront the falsehood of some Nigerian Neo-Pentecostals with the truth of the Scriptures, their immediate response is "Who are you to condemn?" People who are going astray have weaponized themselves with phrases like "You are homophobic," "You are judgmental," "You are a hater," and "You are condemning." All such responses are to keep people from exposing their lies. In the New Testament, there are three Greek words used for the word "judge" that are worthy of clarification. The first word is *krino*, which is normal word for judge—to judge cases as in the law court. Paul used this word in 1 Corinthians 5. The second word is *diakrino*, which is always used in the context of "discernment." It means to discern between what is right and what is wrong. Believers are encouraged to discern between right and wrong spirits, between real and fake brothers and sisters in Christ, and between right and wrong apostles, prophets, and the like. The Berean Christians are good examples of this. They didn't swallow all that Paul told them at first until they searched the scriptures themselves (Acts 17). The last

Greek word is *katakrino*, which is always used for "condemnation." This last one is what we must not do as believers. To condemn is like banishing someone to hell without giving any room for repentance. In addition, when biblical truth is used to expose erroneous practices, as done in this book, some are tempted to respond with the accusation of Christians persecuting fellow Christians. No, what is being done here is by no means persecution.[3] Error must be confronted and corrected with love among the people of God (Galatians 5: 6; Ephesians 5:11; 2Timothy 2: 14-18; 4: 1-5).

Throughout this book, effort has been made not to condemn but to point out the truth and the need for repentance. Much so, some of these men began on a good footage and with good motives before they started derailing. In conclusion, "*Even if I caused you sorrow by my letter, I do not regret it. Although I did regret it, I now see that my letter caused you sorrow, but only for a short time. And now I rejoice, not because you were made sorrowful, but because your sorrow led you to repentance. For you felt the sorrow that God had intended, and so were not harmed in any way by us*" (2 Corinthians 7: 8-9). This is my earnest desire—that this book will produce godly sorrow that will lead to genuine repentance. If the Christianity in Africa is to be the hope for the global Christianity as many have projected, then we need to get it right and nip this upsurge of pseudo-Christianity in the bud. What we tag as revival in Africa today, especially among the new generational churches, is far away from biblical Christianity.

[3] I have written more on these in my next Book tittle, "Church or Human Empire." (The book is on the queue waiting for publication any moment from now).

Other Books by the Author

Bibliography

Books

Abaya, Mayo, Peter Ozodo, and Joseph Ali, eds. *Earnestly Contending for the Faith: An Agenda for Responsible Christian Leadership*. 2nd ed. Abuja, Nigeria: Concerned Ministers' Forum, 1999.

Achunike, H. C. *Catholic Charismatic Movement in Igboland 1970-1995*. Enugu, Nigeria: Fourth Dimension, 2009.

Adams, J. E. *Shepherding the God's Flock*. Grand Rapids: Zondervan, 1975.

Adeboye, Enoch A. *As Pure as Light*. Lagos, Nigeria: CRM Book Ministry, 1999.

________. *How to Turn Your Austerity to Prosperity*. Lagos, Nigeria: CRM Book Ministry.

________. *Leaves from Daddy G.O.'s Table*. Vol. 3, *Prosperity*. Lagos, Nigeria: Printme Communication, 2017.

________. *Open Heaven*. Vol. 13, *A Daily Guide to Close Fellowship with God*. Lagos, Nigeria: Open Heavens International Center, 2013.

Adelaja, Sunday. *Damaged by Religion: Path to Healing*. Kiev, Ukraine: Golden Truth, 2019.

________. *How the Church Creates Economic Recession*. Kiev, Ukraine: Golden Truth, 2018.

Afolayan, Adeshina, Olajumoke Yacob-Haliso, and Toyin Falola. *Pentecostalism and Politics in Africa*. Ibadan, Nigeria: Springer International, 2018.

Agang, Sunday Bobai. *No More Cheek to Turn.* Nairobi, Kenya: WorldAlive Publishers, 2017.

Agbenson, Victorson. *Moment of Truth: The Compelling Story of Pastor Tunde Bakare.* Ibadan, Nigeria: Safari Books, 2014.

Aina, John O. *How to Cub Youths Exodus from the Church.* Jos, Nigeria: ECWA Challenge Book, 2015.

Alexander, Paul. *Signs and Wonders: Why Pentecostalism Is the World's Fastest Growing Faith* San Francisco: Jossey-Bass, 2009.

Alexander, T. Desmond, Brian S. Rosner, D. A. Carson, and Graeme Goldsworthy, eds. *New Dictionary of Biblical Theology: Exploring the Unity and Diversity of Scripture.* IVP Reference Collection. Downers Grove, IL: InterVarsity Press, 2001.

Allen, Rolland. *Missionary Methods of St. Paul: A Study of the Church in the Four Provinces.* Mansfield, CT: Martino, 2011.

________. *Missionary Methods: St. Paul's or Ours?* Grand Rapids: Eerdmans, 1962.

________. *Pentecost and the World.* London: Oxford University Press, 1917.

________. *The Spontaneous Expansion of the Church: And the Causes Which Hinder It.* Eugene, OR: Wipf & Stock, 1997.

Anderson, Allan H. *An Introduction to Pentecostalism: Global Charismatic Christianity.* New York: Cambridge University Press, 2004.

________. *Spread the Fires: The Missionary Nature of Early Pentecostalism.* Maryknoll, NY: Orbis Books, 2007.

Aremu, Tunde, and Emmanuel O. Malomo. *Christian Theology in Africa Context*. Ilorin, Nigeria: Amazing Grace Print-Media, 2016.

Arment, Ben. *Church in the Making*. Nashville: B & H, 2010.

Arnett, Randy Ray. "Pentecostalization: The Changing Face of Baptists in West Africa." PhD diss., The Southern Baptist Theological Seminary, 2012.

Ashford, Bruce Riley, ed. *Theology and Practice of Mission*. Nashville: B & H, 2011.

Azurdia, Arturo G., III. *Spirit Empowered Mission: Aligning the Church's Mission with the Mission of Jesus*. Ross-shire, UK: Christian Focus, 2016.

Babatunde, Roland S. *The Faith of Our Fathers: Feared Not Sword and Fire*. Ilorin, Nigeria: Tanimola Press, 2014.

Bach, Eugene, and Brother Zhu. *Crimson Cross: Uncovering the Mysteries of the Chinese House Church*. Edited by Minna. Blountsville, AL: Back to Jerusalem, 2012.

Balia, Daryl, and Kristeen Kim, eds. *Edinburgh 2010: Witnessing to Christ Today*. Vol. 2 Eugene, OR: Regnum Books International, 2010.

Barnes, Albert. *Notes on the New Testament Explanatory and Practical: Acts of the Apostles*. Grand Rapids: Baker Book House, 1949.

Beougher, Timothy. *Overcoming Walls to Witnessing*. Charlotte, NC: Billy Graham Association, 1993.

Bock, Darrell L. *A Theology of Luke and Acts: Biblical Theology of the New Testament*. Grand Rapids: Zondervan, 2012.

Bonnke, Reinhard. *Evangelism by Fire: Igniting Your Passion for the Lost*. Frankfort, Germany: Full Flame, 2003.

Bosch, David. *Transforming Mission: Paradigm Shifts in Theology of Mission.* Maryknoll, NY: Orbis Books 1991.

Bounds, E. M. *Power through Prayer*. Grand Rapids: Baker Book House, 2000.

Brown, Michael L. *Hyper Grace: Exposing the Danger of the Modern Grace Message*. Lake Mary, FL: Charismas House, 2014.

Carson, D. A. New Testament Commentary Survey. Grand Rapids: Baker Academics, 2013.

Cecil, Douglas M. *The 7 Principles of an Evangelistic Life*. Chicago: Moody, 2003.

Chafer, Lewis Sperry. *Systematic Theology*. Vol. 7. Dallas: Dallas Seminary, 1948.

Chan, Francis, and Mark Beuving. *Multiply: Disciples Making Disciples*. Colorado Springs: David C. Cook, 2012.

Clark, Lynn Schofield. *Religion, Media and the Marketplace.* London: Rutgers University Press, 2007.

Coleman, Robert E. *The Master Plan of Evangelism*. Old Tappan, NJ: Fleming H. Revell, 1963.

Collins, Travis M., and S. Ademola Ishola, *Baptists and the Charismatic Movement*. Ibadan, Nigeria: Nigeria Baptist Convention, 1995.

Cook, Harold R. *An Introduction to Christian Missions.* Chicago: Moody Press, 1971.

Cox, Harvey. *Fire from Heaven: The Rise of Pentecostal Spirituality and the Reshaping of Religion in the Twenty-First Century.* Cambridge, MA: Da Capo Press, 2001.

Dallimore, Arnold A. *George Whitefield.* Carlisle, PA: Banner of Truth Trust, 1970.

Dayton, Edward R., and David A. Fraser. *Planning Strategies for World Evangelization.* Grand Rapids: Eerdmans, 1990.

Deere, Jack. *Surprised by the Power of the Spirit.* Grand Rapids: Zondervan, 1993.

Dever, Mark. *The Gospel and Personal Evangelism.* Wheaton, IL: Crossway, 2007.

Douglas, J. D. *Let the Earth Hear His Voice: WorldWide Missions.* Minneapolis: WorldWide, 1975.

DuBose, Francis M. *Classics of Christian Missions.* Nashville: Broadman Press, 1979.

Eboda, Gbeminiyi. *Accelerate Your Success Rate.* Lagos, Nigeria: Move Your World International, 2013.

Edman, V. Raymond. *Finney Lives On.* Minneapolis: Bethany Fellowship, 1971.

Engen, Charles Van. *Mission on the Way.* Grand Rapids: Baker Books, 1996.

Erickson, Millard J. *Christian Theology.* Grand Rapids: Baker Book House, 1983.

Escobar, Samuel. *The New Global Mission: The Gospel from Everywhere to Everyone*. Downers Grove, IL: InterVarsity Press, 2003.

Evangelical Church Winning All. *ECWA Articles of Faith and Practices*. Jos, Nigeria: Challenge Press, 2018.

Evangelical Church Winning All (South West Forum). *2019 Sunday Manual for Adults*. Vol. 28. Ilorin, Nigeria: Victory Signs International, 2019.

Ferguson, Sinclair B. *The Holy Spirit.* Contour of Christian Theology. Downers Grove, IL: InterVarsity Press, 1996.

Fielding, Charles. *Preach and Heal: A Biblical Model for Missions.* Richmond, Virginia: International Mission Board, 2008.

Finney, Charles G. *Memoirs of Rev. Charles G. Finney: Written by Himself.* New York: Fleming H. Revell, 1903.

Forum, Zacharias T. *You Can Receive the Baptism into the Holy Spirit Now.* Lagos, Nigeria: Conquest Communication, 2007.

Gaffin, Richard B. *Perspectives on Pentecost: New Teaching on the Gift of the Holy Spirit*. Phillipsburg, NJ: Presbyterian and Reformed, 1979.

Garrison, David. *Church Planting Movements: How God Is Redeeming a Lost World.* Richmond, VA: WIGTake Resources, 2004.

Gehman, Richard J. *African Traditional Religion in Biblical Perspective.* Kaduna, Nigeria: Baraka Press, 2000.

Gill, John. *An Exposition of the New Testament; In Which Sense of the Sacred Is Taken*. Waterford, Ireland: Bonmahon Industrial Printing School, 1954.

Glover, Robert H. *The Bible Basis of Missions.* Chicago: Moody Press, 1964.

Goheen, Michael W. *Introducing Christian Mission Today: Scripture, History and Issues*. Downers Grove, IL: IVP Academic, 2014.

Gordon, A. J. *The Holy Spirit in Missions.* Harrisburg, PA: Christian, 1968.

Graham, Billy. *The Holy Spirit: Activating God's Power in Your Life.* Waco, TX: Word Books, 1978.

Greear, J. D. *Gospel: Recovering the Power That Made Christianity Revolutionary.*

Nashville: B & H, 2011.

Green, Michael. *Thirty Years That Changed the World: A Fresh Look at the Book of Acts*. Downers Grove, IL: InterVarsity Press, 2002.

Grudem, Wayne, ed. *Are Miraculous Gifts for Today? Four Views.* Grand Rapids: Zondervan, 1996.

________. *Systematic Theology: An Introduction to Biblical Doctrine.* Grand Rapids: Zondervan, 2000.

Guder, Darrell L. *Be My Witness: The Church's Mission, Message, and Messengers.* Grand Rapids: Eerdmans, 1985.

Guthrie, Stan. *Missions in the Third Millennium: 21 Key Trends for the 21st Century*. Cumbria, UK: Paternoster Press, 2000.

Hall, Manly P. *Masonic, Hermetic, Dabbalistic and Rosicrucian Symbolical Philosophy.* Los Angeles: n.p., 1969.

Hanegraaff, Hank. *Christianity in Crisis: The 21st Century.* Nashville: Thomas Nelson, 2009.

Haykin, Michael A. G., and Jeffrey Robinson, Sr. *To the End of The Earth.* Wheaton, IL: Crossway, 2014.

Hemphill, Ken. *The Bonsai Theory of Church Growth.* Nashville: Broadman Press, 1991.

Henard, William. *Can These Bones Live? A Practical Guide to Church Revitalization.* Nashville: B & H, 2015.

Hesselgrave, David J. *Planting Churches Cross-Culturally: A Guide for Home and Foreign Missions.* Grand Rapids: Baker Book House, 1995.

________. *Planting Churches Cross-Culturally: North America and Beyond.* 2nd ed. Grand Rapids: Baker, 2000.

________. *Theology and Mission.* Grand Rapids: Baker Book House, 1976.

Hesselgrave, David J., and Ed Stetzer, eds. *Mission Shift: Global Mission Issues in the Third Millennium.* Nashville: B & H, 2010.

Hiebert, Paul G. *Anthropological Insights for Missions.* Translated by Eun-Soo Chae. Seoul: Presbyterian General Assembly Theological Seminary Press, 1987.

________. *Anthropological Reflections on Missiological Issues.* Grand Rapids: Baker Books, 1994.

________. *The Gospel in Human Contexts: Anthropological Exploration for Contemporary Missions.* Grand Rapids: Baker Academic, 2009.

________. *Transforming Worldviews: An Anthropological Understanding of How People Change.* Grand Rapids: Baker Academic, 2008.

Hornby, A. S. *Oxford Advanced Learner's Dictionary.* 9th ed. Oxford: Oxford University Press, 2015.

Hughes, Kent R. *Preaching the Word Acts: The Church Afire.* Wheaton, IL: Crossway, 1996.

Idahosa, Benson. *Stranger to Failure: Developing Faith and Power in an Awesome God.* Tulsa, OK: Harrison House, 1993.

Jenkins, Philip. *The New Faces of Christianity: Believing the Bible in the Global South.* Oxford: Oxford University Press, 2006.

________. *The Next Christendom: The Coming of Global Christianity.* Oxford: Oxford University Press, 2011.

Jewell, Elizabeth J., ed. *The Pocket Oxford Dictionary and Thesaurus.* 2nd ed. Oxford: Oxford University Press, 2002.

Johnson, Bisola H. *The T. B. Joshua I Know: Deception of the Age Unmasked.* Lagos, Nigeria: n.p., 2018.

Johnson, Dennis E. *The Message of Acts in the History of Redemption.* Phillipsburg, NJ: P & R, 1997.

Johnstone, Patrick. *The Church Is Bigger Than You Think.* Ross-Shire, UK: Christian Focus, 1998.

Jones, David W., and Russell S. Woodbridge. *Health, Wealth, and Happiness: Has the Prosperity Gospel Overshadowed the Gospel of Christ?* Grand Rapids: Kregel, 2011.

Kaiser, Walter C., Jr. *Revive Us Again: A Biblical Principles for Revival Today.* Ross-shire, UK: Christian Focus, 2001.

Kalu, Ogbu. *African Pentecostalism: An Introduction.* Oxford: Oxford University Press, 2008.

Kane, J. Herbert. *Christian Missions in Biblical Perspective.* Grand Rapids: Baker Book House, 1976.

________. *A Concise History of the Christian World Mission: A Panoramic View of Missions from Pentecost to the Present.* Grand Rapids: Baker Book House, 1998.

________. *Understanding of Christian Missions.* Grand Rapids: Baker Book House, 1978.

Marshall, Howard I., A. R. Millard, J. I. Packer, D. J. Wiseman, eds., 3rd Edition, New Bible Dictionary. Leicester, England: Inter-Varsity Press, 1996.

Menzies, William W. "The Holy Spirit in Christian Theology." In *Perspectives on Evangelical Theology*, edited by Kenneth Kantzer and Stanley Gundry, 61-72. Grand Rapids: Baker, 1979.

Kato, Byang H. "A Critique of Incipient Universalism in Tropical Africa." PhD diss., Dallas Theological Seminary, 1974.

________. *Theological Pitfalls in Africa*. Nairobi: Evangel, 1975.

Kennedy, D. James. *Evangelism Explosion.* Wheaton, IL: Tyndale, 1970.

Kraft, Charles H. *Christianity in Culture: A Study in Biblical Theologizing in Cross-Cultural Perspective*. Maryknoll, NY: Orbis Books, 2005.

________. *Christianity with Power: Your Worldview and Your Experience of the Supernatural*. Eugene, OR: Wipf & Stock, 1989.

Kumuyi, Williams F. *Adultery Forbidden*. Lagos, Nigeria: Life Press, 1984.

________. *Believers in the Last Days*. Lagos, Nigeria: Life Press, 1995.

________. *Deeper Life Bible Church Article of Faith*. Lagos, Nigeria: DLBC Gbagada Press, 2005.

________. *Sanctification: A Christian Experience*. Lagos, Nigeria: Life Press, 2008.

Lai, Patrick. *Tent Making: Business as Missions*. Waynesboro, GA: Authentic Media, 2005.

Lake, Kirsopp. *Eusebius: Ecclesiastical History in Two Volumes I*. Cambridge, MA: Harvard University Press, 1949.

Larkin, Williams J., Jr. *Acts*. IVP New Testament Commentary. Downers Grove, IL: InterVarsity Press, 1995.

Larry, R. *Free and Clear*. Grand Rapids: Kregel, 1997.

Livingstone, E. A., ed. *The Concise Oxford Dictionary of the Christian Church*. Oxford: Oxford University Press, 1977.

Maigadi, Barje S. *Divisive Ethnicity in the Church in Africa*. Kaduna, Nigeria: Baraka Press, 2006.

Malomo, Emmanuel O. *Evangelism and Church Growth*. Ilorin, Nigeria: Amazing Grace, 2010.

Marshall, Howard I., ed. *The Book of Acts of the Apostles*. Tyndale New Testament Commentaries. Grand Rapids: Eerdmans, 1988.

________. *New Bible Dictionary*. 3rd ed. Downers Grove, IL: InterVarsity Press, 1996.

Maxey, Gary S. *Capturing the Lost Vision: Can Nigeria's Greatest Revival Live Again?* Lagos, Nigeria: WATS Publication, 2016.

________. *The WATS Journey: A Personal Narrative*. Lagos, Nigeria: WATS, 2014.

Maxey, Gary S., and Peter Ozodo. *The Seduction of the Nigerian Church.* Lagos, Nigeria: WATS, 2017.

Mbewe, Conrad. *19 Pastoral Thoughts on COVID-19.* Luzaka, Zambia: Ever Green, 2020.

Mbiti, John S. *African Religions and Philosophy.* New York: Fredrick A. Praeger, 1969.

McCain, Danny. *Tough Tests for Top Leaders: God's Strategy for Preparing Africans to Lead Global Christianity.* Jos, Nigeria: Moore Books, 2005.

McConnel, D. R. *A Different Gospel.* Peabody, MA: Hendrickson, 1995.

McDow, Malcolm, and Alvin L. Reid. *FireFall 2.0: How God Has Shaped History through Revivals.* Wake Forest, NC: Gospel Advance Books, 2014.

McGrath, Alister. *Christian Theology: An Introduction.* 1st ed. Oxford: Blackwell, 1994.

McKinney, Carol V. *Globe-Trotting in Sandals: A Field Guide to Cultural Research.* Dallas: SIL International, 2000.

McLoughlin, William G. *Revival, Awakening, and Reform.* Chicago: University of Chicago Press, 1978.

Metzger, Will. *Tell the Truth: The Whole Gospel Wholly by Grace Communicated Truthfully and Lovingly.* Downers Grove, IL: InterVarsity Press, 2013.

Miles, Delos. *Introduction to Evangelism.* Nashville: Broadman, 1983.

Miller, Darrow L., and Scott Allen, *Against All Hope: Hope for Africa.* Phoenix: Disciple Nations Alliance, 2005.

Mohler, R. Albert, Jr. *Acts 1-12 for You.* n.p.: Good Book, 2019.

Moreau, A. Scott, Harold Netland, and Charles Van Engen, eds. *Evangelical Dictionary of World Missions.* Grand Rapids: Baker Books, 2000.

Munroe, Myles. *Rediscovering the Kingdom: Ancient Hope for Our 21st-Century World*. Shippensburg, PA: Destiny Image, 2004.

Murray, Stuart. *Church Planting: Laying foundations*. Milton Keynes, UK: Paternoster Press, 1998.

Neill, Stephen. *Call to Mission*. Philadelphia: Fortress Press, 1970.

________. *A History of Christians Missions*. New York: Penguin, 1964.

Nevius, John L. *The Planting and Development of Missionary Churches*. Hancock, NH: Monadnock Press, 2003.

Newman, Barclay M., and Eugene A. Nida. *A Handbook on the Acts of the Apostles*. New York: United Bible Society, 1972.

Noll, Mark. *The New Shape of World Christianity*. Downers Grove, IL: IVP Academic, 2009.

Noll, Mark A., and Carolyn Nystrom. *Clouds of Witnesses: Christian Voices from Africa and Asia*. Downers Grove, IL: InterVarsity Press, 2011.

Ojo, Matthews. *The End-Time Army: Charismatic Movements in Modern Nigeria*. Trenton, NJ: Africa World Press, 2007.

Oludiran, Victor. *The 7 Levels of Prayer: A Tested Formula for Approaching the Throne of Grace*. Smyrna, GA: LICAIM, 2015.

Olukoya, Daniel K. *The Hour of Freedom*. Lagos, Nigeria: Battle Cry Christian Ministries, 2014.

________. *Mountain Top Life: Daily Devotional*. Lagos, Nigeria: MFM Press, 2019.

________. *Power for Explosive Success*. Lagos, Nigeria: MFM Press, 2005.

________. *The Prayer and Deliverance Bible*. Lagos, Nigeria: MFM Ministry, 2007.

________. *Prolong Your Life*. Lagos, Nigeria: MFM Press, 2013.

________. *Strange Enemies, Strange Prayers*. Lagos, Nigeria: MFM Press, 2019.

________. *When the Deliverer Needs Deliverance: Deliverance Manual for Ministers and Church Workers*. Lagos, Nigeria: MFM Press, 2007.

Oyakhilome, Chris. *How to Pray Effectively*. Vol. 1. Lagos, Nigeria: LoveWorld, 2001.

________. *None of These Diseases*. Lagos, Nigeria: LoveWorld, 2001.

________. *The Oil and the Mantle*. Lagos, Nigeria: LoveWorld, 1997.

Oyedepo, David O. *Anointing for Breakthrough*. Lagos, Nigeria: Dominion Press, 2014.

________. *Breaking Financial Hardship*. Lagos, Nigeria: Dominion Press, 1995.

________. *Breaking the Curses of Life*. Lagos, Nigeria: Dominion Press, 1997.

________. *Exploits of Faith*. Lagos, Nigeria: Dominion Press, 2005.

________. *Exploits in Ministry*. Lagos, Nigeria: Dominion Press, 2006.

________. *Signs and Wonders Today: A Catalogue of the Amazing Acts of God among Men*. Lagos, Nigeria: Dominion Press, 2006.

________. *Success Strategies*. Lagos, Nigeria: Dominion Press, 2003.

________. *Understanding Your Covenant Rights: A Scriptural Guide to Supernatural Breakthroughs*. Lagos, Nigeria: Dominion Press, 2003.

________. *Understanding Your Covenant Rights*. Canaan Land, Lagos: Dominion Press, 2003.

________. *Walking in Dominion*. Lagos, Nigeria: Dominion Press, 2006.

________. *Winning the Invisible Battles*. Lagos, Nigeria: Dominion Press, 2006.

Packer, J. I. *Evangelism and the Sovereignty of God.* Downers Grove, IL: InterVarsity Press, 2012.

Parrinder, Geoffrey. *Witchcraft: European and African.*

New York: Barnes and Noble, 1963.

Payne, J. D. *Apostolic Church Planting: Birthing New Churches from New Believers*. Downers Grove, IL: IVP books, 2015.

Peters, George W. *A Biblical Theology of Missions.* Chicago: Moody Press, 1972.

Pierson, Paul E. *Themes from Acts*. Ventura, CA: Regal Books, 1982.

Piper, John. *Let the Nations Be Glad: The Supremacy of God in Missions.* Grand Rapids: Baker Books, 1993.

Platt, David. *Follow Me: A Call to Die, a Call to Live*. Carol Stream, IL: Tyndale House, 2013.

Pobee, John S. *West Africa: Christ Would Be an African Too.* Geneva: World Council of Churches, 1996.

Poonen, Zac. *Through the Bible: A Message for Today from Every Book of the Bible*. Bangalore, India: CFC Production, 2016.

Popoola, Moses R. *Freedom from Generational Curses*. Ilorin, Nigeria: Modern Impressions, 2011.

Pratt, Zane, M. David Sills, and Jeff K. Walters. *Introduction to Global Missions*. Nashville: B & H, 2014.

Purves, George T. *Christianity in the Apostolic Age.* Grand Rapids: Baker, 1975.

Reisinger, Ernest C. *Today's Evangelism: Its Message and Methods*. Phillipsburg, NJ: Craig Press, 1982.

Roger, Ellis, and Mitchell Roger. *Radical Church Planting*. Cambridge: Crossway, 1992.

Rudnick, Milton L. *Speaking the Gospel through the Ages*. St. Louis, MO: Concordia, 1984.

Samantha, S. J. *Living Faiths and Ultimate Goals: A Continuing Dialogue*. Geneva: World Council of Churches, 1974.

Sanders, Oswald J. *Spiritual Leadership*. Chicago, IL: Moody Press, 1967.

Sanneh, Lamin O. *Disciples of All Nations: Pillars of World Christianity*. Oxford: Oxford University Press, 2008.

Schnabel, Eckhard J. *Acts*. Zondervan Exegetical Commentary of the New Testament. Grand Rapids: Zondervan, 2012.

Schreiner, Thomas. *Spiritual Gifts: What They Are and Why They Matter*. Nashville: B & H, 2018.

Schreiter, Robert J. *Constructing Local Theologies*. Maryknoll, NY: Orbis Books, 1985.

Shaw, Mark. *Global Awakening: How 21st-Century Revivals Triggered a Christian Revolution*. Downers Grove, IL: IVP Academic, 2010.

Shaw, Ryan. *Spiritual Equipment for Mission*. Downers Grove, IL: IVP Books, 2014.

Sopuru, Daniel O. *Modern Theology versus Biblical Theology: A Call for Biblical Christianity*. Makurdi,

Nigeria: Evangelical Christian Literature and Radio Ministries, 2007.

Speer, Robert E. *Missionary Principles and Practice: A Discussion of Christian Missions and of Some Criticisms upon Them*. New York: Fleming H. Revell, 1902.

Sproul, R. C. *Acts*. St. Andrew's Expositional Commentary. Wheaton, IL: Crossway, 2010.

Stalker, James. *The Life of St. Paul.* New York: Fleming H. Revell, 1912.

Stott, John R. W. *Christian Mission in the Modern World.* Downers Grove, IL: IVP Books, 2008.

________. *Christian Mission in the Modern World.* Translated by Myung-Hyuk Kim. Seoul: Sungkwang, 1981.

________. *The Cross of Christ: Study Guide Edition.* Downers Grove, IL: IVP Books, 2006.

Studebaker, John A., Jr. *The Lord Is the Spirit: The Authority of the Holy Spirit in Contemporary Theology and Church Practice.* Eugene, OR: Pickwick, 2008.

Taylor, John V. *The Go-Between God: The Holy Spirit and Christian Mission.* Minneapolis: Fortress Press, 1973.

Tennent, Timothy C. *Invitation to World Missions: A Trinitarian Missiology for the Twenty-First Century*. Grand Rapids: Kregel, 2010.

________. *Theology in the Context of World Christianity.* Grand Rapids: Zondervan, 2007.

Terry, J. Mark. *Evangelism: A Concise History.* Nashville: B & H Academic, 1998.

Thomas, Geoffrey. *The Holy Spirit.* Grand Rapids: Reformation Heritage Books, 2011.

Thomas, Norman E., ed. *Classic Texts in Mission and World Christianity.* Maryknoll, NY: Orbis Books, 2001.

Thompson, Alan J. *The Acts of the Risen Lord Jesus: Luke's Account of God's Unfolding Plan*. Downers Grove, IL: InterVarsity Press, 2011.

Tinling, Christine I. *Heroes of the Cross*. Salem, OH: Schmul, 1984.

Towns, Elmer, and Douglas Porter. *From Pentecost to the Present: The Ten Greatest Revivals Ever*. Nashville: Thomas Nelson, 2000.

Tucker, Ruth. *From Jerusalem to Irian Jaya: A Biographical History of Christian Missions*. Grand Rapids: Zondervan, 1983.

Ukachi, Austen. *The Best Is Yet to Come: Pentecostal and Charismatic Revivals in Nigeria 1913-1990s*. Lagos, Nigeria: Summit Press, 2013.

Verkuyl, Johannes. *Contemporary Missiology: An Introduction*. Grand Rapids: Eerdmans, 1978.

Vermeulen, Danie. *The Process of Planting a Church*. Strubens Valley, South Africa: Dawn Africa, n.d.

Wagner, C. Peter. *Acts of the Holy Spirit*. Ventura, CA: Gospel Light, 1982.

________. *Frontiers in Missionary Strategy*. Chicago: Moody Bible Institute, 1978.

Wagner, C. Peter, and Joseph Thompson. *Out of Africa: How the Spiritual Explosion among Nigerians Is Impacting the World*. Ventura, CA: Regal, 2004.

Walls, Andrew F. *The Missionary Movement in Christian History: Studies in the Transmission of Faith*. Maryknoll, NY: Orbis Books, 2000.

Ware, Bruce A. *Father, Son, and Holy Spirit: Relationships, Roles, and Relevance*. Wheaton, IL: Crossway, 2005.

Werner, Roland William Anderson, and Andrew C. Wheeler, *Day of Devastation Day of Contentment: The History of the Sudanese Church across 2000 Years*. Nairobi, Kenya: Pauline's Publications of Africa, 2000.

Wilson, Jared C. *The Gospel-Driven Church: Uniting Church-Growth with the Metrics of Grace*. Grand Rapids: Zondervan, 2019.

Wimber, John, and Kevin Springer. *Power Evangelism.* Bloomington, MN: Chosen Books, 2009.

Wright, Christopher J. H. *The Mission of God: Unlocking the Biblical Narrative.* Downers Grove, IL: IVP Academic, 2006.

Zwemer, Samuel M. *The Origin of Religion.* 3rd ed. New York: Loizeaux, 1945.

Journal/Articles

Achunike, H. C. "The Challenges of Pentecostalism to the Mainline Churches in Nigeria." *Koinonia* 2, no. 2 (December 2004): 17-25.

Adogame, Afe. "Dealing with Local Satanic Technology: Deliverance Rhetoric in the Mountain of Fire and Miracles Ministries." *Journal of World Christianity* 5, no. 1 (2012): 75-101.

Allison, Gregg R. "Baptism with and Filling of the Holy Spirit." *Southern Baptist Journal of Theology* 16, no. 4 (2012): 6-10.

Ausaji, A. A. "The Pentecostal Transformation of Nigerian Church Life." *Asian Journal of Pentecostal Studies* 5, no. 2 (2002): 189-204.

Ayegboyin, Deji, and F. K. Asonzeh Ukah. "Taxonomy of Churches in Africa: The Case in Nigeria." *Ogbomoso Journal of Theology* 13, no. 1 (2008): 1-15.

Bakare, Tunde. "Pastors Are Turning to Traders." *Sunday Sun* (Lagos, Nigeria). September 25, 2005.

Bamidele, Oluwaseun. "Boko Haram Catastrophic Terrorism: An Albatross to National Peace, Security and Sustainable Development in Nigeria." *Journal of Sustainable Development in Africa* 14, no. 1 (2012): 1-5.

Bamigboye, Ezekiel A. "Pentecostalism and Cross-Cultural Mission in the 21st Century Nigeria." *Ogbomoso Journal of Theology* 8, no. 1 (2008): 167-170.

Batiste, Jon. "Mega Churches Pastor Stays on despite Multiple Affairs." *Christianity Today* 60, no. 6 (July/August 2016): 18-19.

Burgess, Richard. "Nigerian Pentecostal Theology in Global Perspective." *PentecoStudies* 7, no. 2 (2008): 27-34.

Diara, B. C. D., and N. G. Onah. "The Phenomenal Growth of Pentecostalism in the Contemporary Nigerian Society: A Challenge to Mainline Churches." *Mediterranean Journal of Social Sciences* 5, no. 6 (April 2014): 394-397.

Effa, Allan L. "Releasing the Trigger: The Nigerian Factor in Global Christianity." *International Bulletin of Missionary Research* 37, no. 4 (October 2013): 214-17.

Ehioghae, Efe, and Joseph Olarewaju. "A Theological Evaluation of the Utopian Image of Prosperity Gospel and the African Dilemma." *IOSR Journal of Humanities and Social Science* 20, no. 8 (2015): 66-75.

Enyinnaya, John O. "Pentecostal Hermeneutic and Preaching: An Appraisal." *Ogbomoso Journal of Theology* 8, no. 1 (2008): 147-152.

Escobar, Samuel. "A Missiological Approach to Latin America Protestantism." *International Review of Mission* 87, no. 345 (April 1998): 170-174.

Fatokun, Samson A. "Women and Leadership in Nigerian Pentecostal Churches." *Studia Historiae Ecclesiasticae* 32, no. 3 (2006): 193-205.

Haar, Gerrie Ter. "A Wondrous God: Miracles in Contemporary Africa." *African Affairs* 102, no. 408 (2003): 409-28.

Harman, A. M. "Mission in the Thought of Jesus." *Evangelical Quarterly* (July-September 1965): 138-43.

Kitause, R. H., and H. C. Achunike. "Religion in Nigeria from 1900-2013." *Research on Humanities and Social Sciences* 3, no. 18 (2013): 45-55.

Owojaiye, Babatomiwa M. "The Problem of False Prophets in Africa: Strengthening the Church in the Face of a Troublesome Trend." *Lausanne Global Analysis* 8, no. 6 (November 2019):1-5.

Online Materials

Adeboye, Enoch Adejare. "Anyone Not Paying His Tithes Will Not Get to Heaven." YouTube (video), 6:04. April 13, 2018. https://www.youtube.com/watch?v=PX4T9teq97o.

Agang, Sunday Bobai. "The Greatest Threat to the Church Isn't Islam—It's Us." *Christianity Today*. April 21, 2017. https://www.christianitytoday.com/ct/2017/may/radical-islam-not-nigerian-churchs-greatest-threat.html.

Asake, Mussa. Quoted by Bayo Akinloye. "There Is a Grand Plan to Wipe out Christians – CAN General Secretary." *Punch*. July 17, 2016. https://punchng.com/grand-plan-wipe-christians-can-general-secretary/.

Baba, Stephen Panya. Quoted by Isaac Shobayo. "Insecurity: Nigerian Existence Is at Stake – ECWA President." *Nigeria Tribune*. February, 2, 2020.https://tribuneonlineng.com/insecurity-nigeria-existence-is-at-stake-%e2%80%95-ecwa-president/.

Falana, Femi. "[Pastor Enoch Adeboye] 'You Are Creating Business Centers, Not Churches.'" *Pulse* (Nigeria). October 20, 2017. https://www.pulse.ng/news/metro/pastor-enoch-adeboye-you-are-creating-business centers-not-churches-femi-falana-bombs/vxh101f.

Garcia, Omar C. "A Cheap Christianity," Go Beyond (blog). January 10, 2020. https://gobeyond.blog/2020/01/10/a-cheap-christianity/.

Gramlich, John. "Fast Facts about Nigeria and Its Immigrants as U.S. Travel Ban Expands." Pew Research. February 3, 2020. https://www.pewresearch.org/fact-tank/2020/02/03/fast-facts-about-nigeria-and-its-immigrants-as-u-s-travel-ban-expands/.

Ibizugbe, Osahon. "Having Churches Everywhere Has Not Resulted into Godliness in Nigeria – Cardinal Okogie." *Allure Magazine*. October 9, 2017.

https://allure.vanguardngr.com/2017/10/having-churches-everywhere-have-not-resulted-into-godliness-in-nigeria-cardinal-okogie/.

Odunsin, Wale. "I Tore Oyedepo's Book Because He Said Anointing Oil Is God's Life in a Bottle – Tunde Bakare." *Daily Post* (Nigeria). September 7, 2014. https://dailypost.ng/2014/09/07/tore-oyedepos-book-said-anointing-oil-gods-life-bottle-tunde-bakare/.

Oladimeji, Babatunde. "A History of Charismatic Influence on the Anglican Church in Nigeria," *Asian American Theological Forum* 6, no. 2 (May 29, 2017), https://aatfweb.org/2017/05/29/a-history-of-charismatic-influence-on-the-anglican-church-in-nigeria.

Ososanya, Tunde. "Biodun Fatoyinbo: CAN Reacts to Sexual Allegations against COZA Pastor." Accessed April 29, 2020. https://www.legit.ng/1246454-biodun-fatoyinbo-can-reacts-sexual-allegations-coza-pastor.html.

Oyakhilome, Chris. "The Benefits of Speaking in Spiritual Tongues." YouTube (video), 3:34. April 29, 2017. https://www.youtube.com/watch?v=MhhXazexrM8.

Center for Online Judaic Studies. "250 B.C.E. The Septuagint and the Library of Alexandria." October 10, 2016. http://cojs.org/250-b-c-e-septuagint-library-alexandria/.

Huffington Post. "Billy Graham Preached 'Jesus Was Not a White Man' in South Africa in 1973." Last modified December 19, 2013. Video (2:02). https://www.huffingtonpost.com/2013/12/19/billy-graham-white-jesus_n_4474404.html.

Redeemed Christian Church of God Open Heavens Assembly. "Redeemed Christian Church of God Is Rapidly Planting Devout Congregations." Last modified December 15, 2019. https://rccgopenhea vens.org/2018/12/15/

news/redeemed-christian-church-of-god-is-rapidly-planting-devout-congregations/.

Religious Literacy Project, Harvard Divinity School. "Nigeria Pentecostalism." Accessed October 19, 2019. https://rlp.hds.harvard.edu/faq/pentecostalism-nigeria.

Vanguard (Nigeria). "Pastor Begins Sales of 'Holy Oil' to Protect Members from Coronavirus." February 6, 2020. https://www.vanguardngr.com/2020/02/pastor-begins-sales-of-holy-oil-to-protect-members-from-coronavirus/.

Unpublished Materials

Adeyanju, James O. "A Critical Examination of the Emergence of Pentecostalism and the Diversity of its Practices in Nigeria." A Paper presented to the faculty of Christian Education, ECWA Theological Seminary, Igbaja, Nigeria, March/April 2018.

Alabi, Ponle S. "The Exegesis of Jude 20: Speaking in Unknown Tongues and Praying in the Spirit." Lecture delivered at Ajilete Discipleship Center, Ogbomoso, Nigeria, February 6, 2020.

Areogun, Sola. "Declination of Ministerial Ethic." Sermon preached at Lagos Region Apostolic Ministration, Nigeria, December 2018.

Blessing, Tosan. "The Holy Spirit." Lecture delivered at the Word of Faith Bible Institute, Abuja, Nigeria, June 2007.

Eneche, Paul. "Hour of Healing and Deliverance." Sermon preached at Dunamis Gospel Centre, Abuja, Nigeria, July 2010.

Eunice Abogunrin, "Understanding What the Prosperity and Wealth Gospel Is All about." Lecture delivered at ECWA USA International Conference, Chicago, IL, July 21, 2018.

Kato, Byang. "Africa under the Cross." Typescript of Voice of Kenya at Nairobi Baptist Church, Nairobi, Kenya, November 16, 1975.

________. "The Power of the Holy Spirit." Lecture Delivered at ECWA Headquarter. Jos: Nigeria, September/October 1974.

Ladipo, Francis. "Three Types of Evangelism Styles." Lecture delivered at ECWA Ilorin Mission Department, Ilorin, Nigeria, January 25, 2020.

Owojaiye, Babatomiwa M. "ECWA Yesterday, Today and Tomorrow." Speech delivered at ECWA IDCC Convention, Ilorin, Nigeria, November

14, 2015.

Tennent, Timothy. "The Translatability of the Christian Gospel." Convocation speech delivered at Asbury Theological Seminary, Wilmore, KY, 2011.

Milton Keynes UK
Ingram Content Group UK Ltd.
UKHW040754010224
437095UK00001B/66